Until 1983 Jack Pollock was the owner of the Pollock Gallery in Toronto, where he exhibited new Canadian artists. Then, abruptly, he lost both his business and his health. Twenty years of a flamboyant lifestyle had led to drug addiction, open-heart surgery and bankruptcy and to a profound spiritual and psychological malaise. A broken man, he retreated to the south of France, expecting to die.

He didn't die. Instead, he began to come to terms with himself and his life, in part by confiding his deepest feelings in a torrent of letters to M, a psychiatrist he had consulted briefly before his departure. These letters, as outrageous and courageous as the man who wrote them, together constitute an utterly honest assessment of his life, his work, his self-worth. They speak of his daily life in France, of his past – including stories of encounters with David Hockney and other painters – and of religion and the power of sexuality.

Pollock's forthright manner and his vivid, individualistic style make *Dear M* a powerful autobiography of rare frankness and insight. Through it emerges a portrait of an extraordinary, talented, gentle man.

Jack Pollock was born in Toronto in 1930. After leaving school he came to England to study at the Slade School of Fine Art in London. In 1960, in the heart of what was then known as "Greenwich Village" in Toronto, he opened the first Pollock Gallery, where he promoted new Canadian artists and introduced to Canada artists from Europe and the United States, among them David Hockney, Victor Vasarely and Richard Hamilton. In 1983 the gallery went bankrupt, and the following year Pollock moved to the village of Gordes in the south of France, where he wrote the letters in this book. He currently lives in Toronto, where he paints and teaches.

DEAR M

dear M

letters from
a gentleman
of excess

JACK POLLOCK

BLOOMSBURY

First published in Great Britain 1990
Bloomsbury Publishing Limited, 2 Soho Square, London W1V 5DE

First published in Canada by McClelland & Stewart Inc.,
481 University Avenue, Toronto, Ontario M5G 2E9

A CIP catalogue record for this book
is available from the British Library

Cased ISBN 0 7475 0739 2
Paperback ISBN 0 7475 0809 7

10   9   8   7   6   5   4   3   2   1

Front cover painting: Jack, 1989 © by Telford Fenton
Author photograph: from the author's collection

Printed by Butler and Tanner Limited, Frome and London

**To M
and to the people of Gordes**

Preface

In 1960, more by accident than design, I opened the first Pollock Gallery on Elizabeth Street in Toronto's old Greenwich Village. In 1983, after eight different locations and hundreds of exhibitions of young, talented Canadian artists and of such international artists as David Hockney, Claude Yvel, and George Grosz, the Pollock Gallery collapsed.

I was mentally, physically, and financially bankrupt. My property was placed in the hands of the receiver – including my share of a house, Lou Paradou, in the south of France, which I co-owned with Eva Quan, who had been my secretary for over fifteen years. I fled there to find refuge for my ravaged mind and body, fully expecting to die. I wanted only some dignity and to be able to spare family and friends.

Before my departure, I visited just three or four times a psychiatrist, M, who had been recommended to me. We had barely begun to get to know each other when I left for France, yet, as I was leaving that last session with him, he said quite casually, "Write me and I'll answer you." I took him at his word, and over the next three years obsessively committed my thoughts, fears, and philosophies in a torrent of letters to him – as many as four or five a week.

Through the cathartic act of recalling a lifetime of excess in these letters to M, and through the simple acceptance of the villagers I lived among and the kindness of friends who visited, I not only survived but I produced a major body of paintings and drawings while I lived at Lou Paradou.

At one point M remarked on my powers of observation, my intuition, and complimented me on my turn of phrase. Never one to do anything by half-measures, I started to think of publishing a book based on my letters to M. I believed, and still believe, that within the thoughts I poured onto paper were truths that are rarely told. As well, I wanted to set the record straight and change into fact the whispered speculations about me I was hearing even as far away as the south of France. Finally, I thought that many readers would be interested in learning about the crazy world of art, as it was in Toronto in the sixties and seventies.

The book you are holding is an edited version of my letters to M. It is an autobiography – of sorts. The letters combine stories of my survival in France with vignettes of my childhood, of my years running the gallery, and of the Toronto art scene. They speak also of my experiences as a gay man, of the insights I have gained after more than fifty years of living excessively, and of the joy and pain that, I believe, is universal.

Because I have no wish to hurt anyone I mention in this book, I have taken the precaution of abbreviating some names to a single initial, others I have changed totally to protect the innocent.

There are many people I should thank for their help and for their belief, their caring, and their support. I cannot thank them all by name here, but I must mention Lesley Wyle; Paul Gardner; Jane Somerville; Rick Archbold; Frances Hanna, my agent; Lynne Reilly, my excellent typist; and Doug Gibson, Tania Craan, and the rest of the McClelland & Stewart team. I would also like to thank the Canada Council for its financial support. Last, I especially want to thank the two people who made this book possible – M, for his unfailing support, and Dinah Forbes, my wonderful editor, who brought patience, intelligence, and sensitivity to the task of making hundreds of letters into a book.

April–May 1984

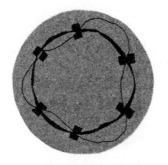

April 10, 1984

Dear M.

I hope you don't mind me using your initial, but I have trouble with Dr. and am not presumptuous enough to call you by your first name.

I am in Gordes at last, sitting in the tiny house of my friend Jean-Pierre. The logs are burning brightly in the fireplace and I am feeling quite detached. It's hard now to realize that just two weeks ago, my world in Toronto had collapsed. Tomorrow I will have been in the village a week.

The electricity will be turned on in Lou Paradou tomorrow so I will finally sleep in my house. Portable electric heaters are the only means of heat, other than the fireplace, and Jean-Pierre promises wood for it before too long. For now I will heat one bedroom in which to sleep and spend the entire day on the terrace, where the sun is almost too brilliant, and, thank God, I will be able to be alone with me.

I am feeling well, and aside from a cough and a fair amount of blood daily in my phlegm, I have no pain or discomfort. If the cough should clear up (and I am not smoking these days) then somebody up there is more forgiving than I can possibly imagine. If by any chance it does not clear up, but becomes uncomfortable, then at least it will happen here, and Barb and Ron and all the others whom I love so dearly need not know or worry about me. I confided in you before I left about the blood in my phlegm and pray you keep it confidential.

Each day I write. I'm not sure what it's all about, but most days I write about art and the constant raping of its values by pseudo-intellectual acrobats. I'm still striving for definitions of the creative process (me and a few million others through-out history). What has, for years, haunted me as a major flaw in my development, my lack of formal university education, now seems to be a distinct advantage.

"The plastic presence of diametrically opposed attitudes on the picture plane." What the fuck is that supposed to mean? I think they're trying to say that the tactile or raised surface of the paint is in contrast to the background of the canvas. So much for that, but what does that surface *really* say? Is it an act of aggression, angular and filled with a sense of assault, or is it a lyric caress, subtle and joyous? Is the contrast of colour dazzling, or a gentle fusion of light and shade?

God, I wish for so many yesterdays to have been different. I am truly grateful you have been in your steel-gridded tower for me to visit and dump on. I thought many times of asking you to share dinner and conversation with me because you are thirsty for the same kind of exchange I enjoy. I wish now you could visit my village, where pretension seems impossible, and enjoy the *paysage* of Van Gogh and Cézanne.

It seems very odd how totally different our approaches must have been when, as youths, we decided how best to cope with *them* (mass thinking, herd instinct, and Judeo-Christian limitations). I, consciously or unconsciously, decided to, as my dear grandmother urged, "Go big or go home." So I went big, and have paid ever since for every high of the roller-coaster of my life with a dip so long, low, and seemingly endless that I am constantly amazed another high is possible.

You, as I perceive it, are temperate. I know nothing except what I see and feel, but I sense in you the gentleness of a learned social behaviour; a spirit that stops, unlike mine, for society and, more important, for survival. I wish for you a small touch of my madness, and I crave so much for continuing strength from your logic.

Shit. I had better stop.

Dear M.

It is now Monday morning. I had a truly enjoyable weekend, with the grand exception of Friday night, when I was robbed. Yes, my dear sir, robbed!

Friday evening I had planned to spend alone as I had been painting for almost three days straight and was exhausted. However, a friend of Jean-Pierre's arrived and invited me to Chez Georgette in Roussillon for fish soup. I love fish soup and, of course, jumped at the chance of a good meal. We arrived back at about midnight, had a *poire* nightcap (a strong liqueur) at Chez Appy's bar on the square, and I came home. I unlocked the door, turned the lamp on, but nothing happened. I went over to it, saw it was unplugged, replugged it, and stood for a moment, wondering. No, Jack, you are not going mad. Yes, Jack, your large and expensive ghetto blaster is gone.

I yelled, but there was no answer. I took the eight-room, four-floor tour – still no clue. I went into my bedroom and found the silver bracelets I have always worn, the silver chains I wear when I'm being a little pretentious, and my expensive Canadian-made cowboy boots all gone. My chequebook, passport, and other documents were on the table in full view. A large tumbler filled with small coins (centime coins) was untouched.

I discovered the windows on the second floor, though closed, were not locked. The police, and I agree, say young *méchants* boys are responsible. They've probably passed by several times and seen my tape machine through the open doorway. It would take two to hoist each other up through a window. As the door was locked, they must have left the same way, dropping to the silent street, whose peacefulness I have so often marvelled at.

Well, so much for Friday night. I only wish there had been some pleasure involved. Being fucked without even being kissed is not at all polite!

April 18, 1984

Dear M.

Why do we have our best thoughts and original ideas the few minutes before we fall asleep? Last night I had many ideas and associations but was too tired to get my ass out of bed and write them down. So now, tonight, I sit here trying to remember how bright and original I was then. I do recall thinking about a certain shade of blue that in the world of fashion they call French Blue. Intense, but not dark – subtle, yet not easy to ignore. Then I thought of you and your eyes (I've never really had that kind of recall before), and I think it would be a welcome and fitting shade for you. I also saw orchards of cherry trees in full bloom and thought of fields of vestal virgins, complete with veils, awaiting the ultimate union with God (or whoever)!

Lou Paradou is wonderful these days, as is Provence. The sun has brought a sense of awakening that is slow and deliciously teasing, a kind of spring we never know in Canada. Today, the first iris of the season said good morning from my tiny terrace, and the lilac cannot deny pregnancy any longer.

I have finished three new canvases of Provence (still-life – flowers, chairs, etc.) that I think are pretty good. I work each day for about five or six hours, broken by a two-hour lunch, and topped with a long and usually memorable dinner. I sometimes feel guilty and not deserving of such continued pleasure. I wrote to my niece Barbara the other day and tried to explain my sense of gratitude for all the kindness and love I have been given. I said that I wish I were a *great* talent, because so many people believe in me and care that I would like to live up to their expectations. However, I am these days, if nothing else, a realist, and know that although, God knows, I am not mediocre, I am also not a giant.

So, I intend to do my best.

I just remembered another night thought. If you give to all your patients the depth and continued support I feel from you, the extension of your feelings must surely take its toll. I certainly feel privileged to be among your "problem children."

I had X-rays taken yesterday in the hospital in Cavaillon. It's a strange process–you pay your money, and they give you the X-rays in a large brown envelope (not unlike those received with naughty and explicit sexual literature. I've got a strange mind!) Anyway, I was supposed to take them to the doctor today but forgot. I painted instead. I will go tomorrow.

You know, I really know nothing of your life, and that's the way I am sure it should be, so all I can do is trust that all goes well in the orbit of your wishes and desires.

The only thing that I find irritating these days is my obsessive waiting for the mail. I really miss certain positive things my Toronto offers. I do get sentimental (a word I don't much like) and lonely for all of you, my dear friends.

I sometimes miss the raunch of *Notre-Dame des Vapeurs* (the baths)–the Oak Leaf, the Continental. (They sound like exotic dances rather than the delicious trash they really are.)

I miss Egg McMuffins and coffee in the morning with some one-night stand who actually *slept* with me.

I miss conversations on the meaning of art and life and all that heavy nonsense that sometimes results in original thinking. (It's difficult enough to talk in French, and as yet almost impossible to think in French.)

I miss my audience, because as you know all too well, I am always on stage. It gets boring here–I cannot perform as a professional because of my inadequate French and have to resort to being the clown.

But the scales are certainly not too imbalanced here, and I think it truly possible that I shall be able to get roots and, time permitting, become a Gordian. (The villagers say you must be at least third generation to count, so I guess I mean accepted as one of their own.)

I started smoking again. Damn! I put it down to the oral fixation all you shrinks have talked about for years. Did you know that a *pompier,* or fireman, is a word for a blow job? I was with a wonderful family for dinner the other night, and the candle on the table toppled and set fire to the cloth. I exclaimed, *"Vous désirez un pompier très vite!"* and Mama stared in strange silence while the father, two sons (one thirtyish, the other in his late teens), broke up. I now have a slightly larger vocabulary (but not, alas, the sons).

Goodnight. I leave you with that for your morning smile.

April 24, 1984

Dear M.

Spring is certainly here! It's seventy degrees, sunny, and every day some new flower says hello. Yesterday it was the first poppies, sprinkled like drops of shimmering blood on the acid-green carpet of the roadside grass. Blood, not in any way negative or destructive, maybe the reminder of virgin discovery. (Shit, that's heavy.)

I wonder if I will ever have sex in France? I suppose I have had just about all the variations possible (at least all I desire), and now I am thinking of ideal moments, of what would give me great pleasure. It is at times like this that the cursed word "rejection" becomes larger than life and holds me back from any attempt at active participation. The scars and marks of time are on my body as well as in my mind, so I suppose the saying "old age never comes alone" applies. I enjoy the company of many people here, young and not so young, and find them physically attractive, but the combination of small-village mentality, a true respect for the innocent, and the great fear of making a mistake in judgement leaves me with vicarious pleasures at best, and my hand as my only bed mate.

As I do not drive (I have never learned) I am also, in a sense, a prisoner to the simplicity of this village. Now, as you are well aware, that is certainly not all bad, but I do wish to be Jackie "the naughty boy" once in a while. I also miss the dictatorial aspects of my sexual role as master. I guess overriding all of this is the impossible dream that someone might care, *really* care for me, and would be able to put up with my strange, warped personality.

It's the extremes of my life I have the most problems with. All (orgies, fantasy costumes, and so on) or nothing. I overdid the "all," and now I have nothing – nothing that is, but time to see the beauty around me, moments to glimpse a wonderful young profile, and hours to spend joyously cooking and painting. That is certainly more than nothing! In fact, to most sane and sensible creatures, that would be everything. (You see how fucked up I am?)

Aggression is a word I am trying to understand. Outwardly, I appear to be the word personified; however, that tremble, that doubt, that nervous laugh, give me away to such as yourself. Glib remarks, fast retorts, catch phrases, and a truly accelerated mind, those are my secret façades, and they work well most of the time for most of the people. But, as you once said, you can fool some of the people . . . Now comes the real problem. Suppose, just suppose, someone *really cared,* how the hell could he put up with all that theatrical bullshit? How could he even find the real me?

I don't believe in miracles, and I also know the adage of old dogs and new tricks, so I hardly expect to become something other than the eccentric, larger-than-life buffoon I am. I think the answer may be not to live too long. No, my dear sir, that is not in any way a suicidal remark; it is a practical thought. I do not want to overstay my welcome.

Well enough of that. I have to find someone in the village to take me to Cavaillon – there is no bank in Gordes, and I have been spending like a drunken sailor. (There's a good idea, a drunken sailor. I don't like sex with drunks, but sailors are a different matter!)

I am getting silly, so bye for now.

April 26, 1984

Dear M.

Here I am needing to dump on you again in some seemingly vain attempt at self-enlightenment. I try very hard with you (and, through the mirror of you, with myself) to be candid, honest, and clear. I admire your intellect, compassion, and intuition. (Notice I do not say education, for although I know it's important in the so-called real world, I do not equate it with quality – not in your profession, especially.)

I cannot care for myself. I self-destruct – one way or another. I arrived with over four thousand dollars, but it's almost all gone. I have enough left only to survive a few weeks before requesting more from my Toronto reserve (which is shallow). It would be much less expensive for me to keep someone (someone who would appreciate a simple but shared existence) than to keep going out in search of company and good times.

But all the joking and fun in the world, plus all the belief of others, do not equate with any sense of self-esteem. And I realize that behavioural modification can only work if a degree of self-worth exists. Pity!

I have never, and at this moment it seems I will never be able to assume responsibility for my continued survival. And I cannot expect anyone to coddle and indulge my infant emotional mentality. I am also in constant battle with my intellect, which is far more advanced than my personality and behaviour.

Can you – can anyone – toilet train an aging semi-creative emotional retardee? No, I do not believe it possible. This is why, perhaps, in the past I have tried so hard to make sure those who truly care for me become disillusioned. If I break their faith in me, they can go on to others who can and, I trust, do measure up. I don't know how to handle anyone who cares, most of all people who love me. Please remain remote enough to see all this shit. I don't want you to sit in judgement, but your eyes should be open to the real me.

Facing death is for most people the biggest and most difficult challenge of life. For me, although I do not choose death, I feel nothing could be more work or pain than life itself.

I will be in Toronto in June. I hope, by then, to have a small sense of who I am, but I certainly am not betting on it.

Shit, shit –

April 28, 1984

Notes to myself:

I feel quite depleted of emotional currency these days. The constant and almost obsessive questioning of both myself and others seems a riddle without an answer. My major problem seems to be understanding my facility, ease, and sincere consideration for others, and my inner unrest and relentless lack of comfort with myself.

Although, once when I was asked to write a list of plus and minus aspects of my personality I retorted, "Lead is far heavier than feathers," I suppose I should try. Here goes –

Plus +

• I care for people (I think).

• I enjoy giving pleasure (I know).

Natural talents and gifts:

• Painting (not Picasso, but not merely decoration).

• Communication (probably my strongest asset).

• Cooking (*le bon chef – je pense*).

• A highly active sense of intuition which is usually proven right.

• An ability to draw from others candid, natural, and often quite intense responses. (Like strong spices, this must be used with caution.)

- Also, although not usually listed in your average curriculum vitae, a certain amount of sexual expertise.

Minus –

- Although I try to hide it, a sense of superiority in most situations and with most people.
- An ability to justify most of my actions to my own satisfaction and that of others.
- A creeping, constant belief that I am a giant, total fake, a fabrication of my own making living in a world filled with facades and fallacies.
- An imposed personal morality so strongly upheld that I fear and question the other side of its coin.
- A seemingly insatiable desire for self-abuse.
- An urge I continually try to bury for total destruction, my own, and that of those around me.
- Facility – that fucking word again, which I use and abuse – *raison d'être*, scapegoat, you name it.

Okay, enough's enough.

Many traits I admire in others seem intolerable when applied to myself. Routine. Pattern. Repetition. My life has been, and I am certain will continue to be, a roller-coaster, a high dive, a theatre of the absurd. If I can only prevent the ultimate catastrophe of total self-indulgence, I might be capable of true contribution and, who knows, may even acquire a certain sense of self-worth.

I enjoy painting, the battleground of the picture plane, but where the hell am I going? Back, then forward, but, it seems, always within the confines of technical excellence and acceptable form. Paul Klee once wrote, "I continue to go in circles, I only trust it's a spiral upwards." I think I am caught in some strange Rubic cube which, when solved, spells taste.

In the midst of working on three canvases today, I had the insatiable urge to defile, defecate, totally destroy their pleasantness, their good form and colour, their safety. But did I? No. Instead I completed them as art objects to be liked and perhaps even desired by others. Dada seems to have taken away the possibility of desecration. After urinals, moustaches on the sacred cow (apologies to da Vinci), what is left? Perhaps the ultimate is performance art, but damn it, those bloody Buddhist monks beat me to it with their human torches.

The destructive impulse I just felt for those canvases is typical of feelings I have had for most of my life. But, in the bright light of the "real world," I behave, I please. No wonder my nocturnal visits to hell and back have been frequent! They are not only desired, but demanded. Some balancing of the scales is essential!

I am stimulated and receive a natural (please note that word) high from intelligent verbal argument. But too often I find myself acting the part of guru (a self-imposed role or otherwise), and although I admit it does feed the sagging ego, verbal discourse without challenge and wit is much like a good Chinese dinner – filling for the moment, but with very little retainable substance.

My ability to engage people in conversation that leads to self-revelation (usually for them, not me) has been, over the years, a scapegoat of immense proportions. It allows me to feel needed, caring, and bright, and my usually intelligent offering of advice is safe and easy. No need to apply that same thoughtful yardstick to my own tattered existence. Bullshit!

Pleasing others again, while ignoring my own pleas. Pleas for help, understanding, and above all, lessons on the ability to love.

I believe I learned long ago, but just recently am attempting to face the fact, that the conundrum is that giving, caring, desiring are not the mirror images of love.

Giving: possibly one of the most used, abused, misrepresented, and bastardized words in our society. It suggests Judeo-Christian charity (read love) but is rarely separated from the concrete, specific, and often devious goals of man: power and domination.

My life seems to have been one of not only giving, but *giving*. Pleasure, money – everything. To what end? To shore up my sagging ego? To make me, the leper, the "odd one," the outsider, more accepted? Perhaps to make others look bad (read stingy, selfish). God knows – I don't.

And what has this giving gained me? To many, I am sure, it's given me the name of a mark, someone to count on for a good time, a free ride, no strings attached. Others must see it as weakness, a lack of inner strength and security. And to the rest, I suppose, I'm a nice guy, but of no real substance or particular consequence.

For me, this "giving" has become a way of life unto itself. I do it automatically, unconsciously, and thoroughly enjoy a very large part of it. It has, however, protected the *me* I really want to give; the me that trembles to be held, that cries to be soothed. The me that aches and aches for some special being to share tomorrow.

Dear M.

This is how it came out, and I realize that even when I try to dig deep I still try to express myself in some fucking stylistic way that screams *taste*!

Maybe it's because I hate the living lie of my life so much that I don't know what natural is.

The thoughts above, however, I do believe to be honest attempts at coming to grips with some of fucked-up me.

May 1, 1984

Dear M.

I think spending so much time alone is a bit taxing and I find strange thought patterns running rampant in my head. You have recently received some of those odd juxtapositions of visual and felt emotions (the strange note about French Blue). I do apologize, and I hope you understand it is more important for me to write than it is for you to read.

Last night I spent a good part of the evening reading the May issue of *Playboy* (the only English magazine available in this area, other than *Time*) and I must say Reagan, China, and all that shit bores me.

Anyway, this issue has an incredible article on the young Kennedys, and John F. K.'s best friend, Lem Billings. It's heavy reading, especially for me as it exposes the nerve ends of youth and age attempting, through drug abuse, to consummate an impossible dream.

There is also an article on AIDS that, for the first time to my knowledge in a public forum, states the facts: that it is contracted via semen entering the blood stream, usually anally. Good reporting, I thought.

The thing they don't write much about in *Playboy* or anywhere is the male orgasm. Lots on the female, but not the male. Again, my self-imposed solitary confinement has made me realize an awful truth that, for me, and I would suppose many or most other men, whether hetero, homo, or whatever, the act of ejaculation does not in any way equate with orgasm. Certainly, they can combine to make fireworks if you're lucky, but I must say it's been quite a while since I had an earth-shaking, toe-tingling experience. Even with others during the act of pleasing, the functions of the body are not often in that so desired state which allows maximum sensation.

You see what I mean? My mind is truly weird! I also bought the cassette *The Best of Leonard Cohen*, and a song on it keeps haunting me. "Bird on a Wire" is the title, and I guess the truth hurts.

Good night.

P.S. The young doctor in the village looked at my X-rays and said he is not an expert but suggested an appointment with a lung specialist in Marseille. He mentioned tuberculosis, and I thought, Christ, not another version of Camille! That would really be too much. However, the blood still persists in my phlegm each day, so I shall go to Marseille and take the good doctor's advice and probably visit a steam bath at the same time.

(Killing two birds with one stone, so to speak.)

May 2, 1984

Dear M.

You realize M stands for mother, master, masochist, moral, mutant, military, masturbatory, marvellous, and more, more, more.

Oh well, on to less revealing things, like age.

Age is a very trying experience. In the world, my world I suppose, of Greek gods and tight buns, pectoral displays and baskets for days, tarnished mirrors and true vision are almost unbearable. If people live vicariously through me, I too have a very active vicarious life that is covered rather well by an extremely complex and thick façade. The scars and marks on my body are my obsession, and few people are allowed to see this visual obscenity of the physical. Heart surgery, gross drug abuse, and spinal fusion have left a spectre not unlike a hand-stitched quilt, but with none of the inherent beauty.

I suppose my retarded growth as an adolescent (I was five foot and skinny until I was sixteen) started the problem of self-image. I was not exactly stupid, so I, like many kids in those days, skipped two grades in public school and arrived at Bloor Collegiate, age twelve, with my dick the only sign of maturity. I found early on that laughing at myself and playing the clown was quite successful, and I became a sort of mascot for the football crowd (all giants in comparison).

I refused to go to physical training – PT as they called it – and invented all sorts of excuses. My treasured discovery of sex was *private*.

I am sure, even in those days, I sought some kind of help. I would jerk off at least four or five times in a row, and defiantly aim my semen at the wall beside my bed. Those stains were there for many years, wallpaper with daisies and ferns and a torrent of seminal fluid, the whole predating Jackson Pollock's paintings. My mother, Christian lady that she was, I am sure saw and realized the situation, but she never said a word. The rest of the family never entered that room except my older brother Bob, whose bed was on the other side.

My brother Bob was handsome. His face was much rougher than mine, with pock marks and a rugged expression. He chose at an early age to be "one of the boys" and hung around pool halls and beer parlours, but inside he was much more gentle than me. He died, an alcoholic (like my father), when he was forty-eight, and I don't believe he ever really understood life. He loved me, and the sense of loss I felt at his death was much stronger than at that of my father.

So, life goes on. One advantage that I have as I go into my "twilight days" (fuck! what sentiment!) is a natural leanness which helps the illusion of youth considerably. I have always loathed pudgy, flabby flesh, and associate it with eunuchs and the fleshy females of Rubens.

By the time I was out of high school, I had developed the image you met the first few times. Seemingly confident – my wardrobe not effeminate, but also not "butch" (unless there is a specific role to play). I also decided early not to pretend to be like everybody else, and in doing so I found a great deal of acceptance.

Most gays have had experiences with the nasties of the straight world. I have not. Through my almost blatant honesty, and my moral fibre (the Calvin in me), I have earned a great deal of respect and many people have cared for me (literally and figuratively). This is where my battle with Gay Liberation comes in. To change attitudes of society, one must work within it, not establish a new ghetto, a foreign embassy, a Berlin wall of misunderstanding. The key is mutual respect, built on some sort of trust.

My problem these days is everyone I meet and feel attracted to seems to trust me so much that I cannot reach out, touch, fondle, or instigate any kind of physical involvement for fear of breaking that belief. It's my fear of rejection – I suppose every single patient you have ever seen, and you, yourself, can relate to that. Rejection has no respect of gender – it touches and taints us all. Add to its inherent malignancy the debts owed to and sins committed against our Christian deity, and you really understand a portion of the fuck-ups of our globe.

If I am confused, baffled, and bewildered at my life and its complications, then Morriseau – Morrisseau (he added an extra "s" some five years after I "discovered" him) – is a virtual mix-master of emotions and personalities. I was teaching for the Ontario government in the summer of 1962 when I met him. Port Arthur (now Thunder Bay), Terrace Bay, Red Rock, and other places, all cultural wastelands, perfect for me, the seducer of the senses. The big-fish-little-pond syndrome helped me develop confidence, which later led to my teaching in so-called higher educational levels, giving university lectures.

Norval was thirty-two, the same age as me (he has since lost two years, but then almost all stars do). Lean, a bit savage, he was married and had had the first of his seven children. There was always a sense of duality about his being that transfixed the viewer. Highly volatile, a man of great extremes, he was always theatre.

About three years later, he arrived in Toronto on one of his famous drunken binges and brought with him a handsome young man, a "student" he said. That was my first visible indication of his bisexuality.

Much later he abandoned his wife and children (they lived on treaty money and welfare in Sandy Lake) and began an incredible journey into total sexual indulgence. I have often fantasized about his coterie of beautiful young men (all hustlers, all very well paid with thousands of dollars in cash which I provided from paintings sold), lots of drugs, and ritual pseudo-Indian ceremonies.

He began painting sexually explicit pictures and created a wonderful soapstone pipe for hash in the form of a giant penis. This, of course, as all his later *objets d'art* in a sexual vein, was justified by his being a shaman. The first object he ever gave me was the soapstone phallus you now own. No paintings, no drawings, but a big prick. He said no man was made big enough, so the shaman must create!

The wooden dildo he gave me later does, I believe, have some true history. The knot of wood from which he fashioned it is, I am told, quite rare, and these objects were part of some past ritual.

Anyway, there you have a *petite histoire* of your new objects.

May 3, 1984

Dear M.

Practically every passage of your treasured letter seems to have opened doors to the past. So many cluttered closets, all, in a sense, containing common threads – warp and woof – that, I suppose, total the fucked-up creature sitting here in glorious Provence, attempting to weave a carpet. Not a lasting or permanent carpet, but one strong enough to carry him through the rest of his gifted days. Each day is a gift, that I do recognize!

The mention of "prison" in your letter reminds me of Queen's University, Kingston, summer in the mid-sixties. I had taken over the painting course from Ralph Allen. Grant MacDonald, the wonderful, limp gentleman that he is, was teaching drawing. Someone took me to the penitentiary to look at the art of a prisoner who was hoping to do a mural in the dining room. Typical of me, before I knew it I started a series of drawing classes there – the first, to my knowledge. Every week, I and a guard who, thank God, was sympathetic (there really are such rare creatures) went to be locked up with twenty inmates behind several pairs of clanging doors. Many were lifers, in there for murder, armed robbery, etc. Most were grubby, unkempt, and rumpled.

One young man, however, was crisp, clean-shaven, and smelled of cologne. He had been arrested in Hamilton for possession of grass and, believe it or not, sentenced to three years. The other inmates told me, on the sly, that he was the head guard's bum boy and got special treatment. I felt sick and thought that if it had been another prisoner, such tribal law somehow could be justified. But for a married guard, with access to the world of freedom, to dominate and use an inmate disgusted me. I returned to Kingston the next year to lecture at Queen's University and went to call on "the boys." The young man had been gang-raped and murdered as a kind of protest against the system.

Back in Toronto, I called Joe McCulley. You remember him, perhaps; he was the former warden of Hart House, who then worked for prison reform. Over a drink, he explained to me that "these things happen." I was asked if I or any of my friends would want to be a prison guard. Idealism, my dear M, as you and I have learned, has no place in the jungle known as society.

Time: fourteen years later
Place: Grosvenor St. (the "track")
The Buyer: me
The Seller: Little J

After weekly and semi-weekly meetings with him, I received a phone call at seven-thirty in the morning of August 1, 1979, my forty-ninth birthday: Little J is in the Don Jail on a smash-and-grab charge with his lover, Jim.

Ten-thirty: I arrive at the Don Jail, find they have placed bail at $5,000, go to the bank, borrow the money, and have him released in my custody – to live with me until the trial.

Six-thirty that evening: drinks with Thelma Van Alstyne, the painter who lives in Port Hope. She was passing through and had two fresh canvases to show me.

Eight that night: I arrive at the gallery; it is dark. Suddenly, "Happy Birthday!" Over a hundred people were there! B, my ex-lover, and his lover, R, had arranged it all. R serenaded me. Tom Kneebone, Dinah Christie, Barb Hamilton, were all there. And me, crying. They all thought I was very surprised and touched, which I was. Zena Cherry wrote it up in the *Globe* with a photo. No one knew of the madness of the day!

Almost a year later, that same Little J blew my Rosedale Valley penthouse apartment to bits with a home-made bomb.

He also took four thousand dollars' worth of gold, silver, and valuables. But that's another story.

Strange, but I still care about him. That's masochism for you.

Dear M.

This note is in response to your remarks on the creative process. Over the years, through teaching, lecturing, but most of all *doing*, I have developed some thoughts that might be of interest. The basis for most of my insights is that you cannot separate art from life. My theories are simple, not pompous verbiage but, for me, truths learned from experience in both arenas, art and life.

Three basic ingredients are essential: Intellect (head), Emotions (heart), Technique (hand). These are the three sources from which we create our lives and, therefore, our art. In them we have the Father, the Son, and the Holy Ghost of creativity. They all are necessary for survival, communication, and life itself. The visual creative process, as I see it, is an attempt to communicate, feel, and express personal values not possible with the written word.

Problems arise and leave us with mediocrity when the three are too evenly balanced, too safe, too protective. But if one of the three becomes too dominant, it overrides the other two, destroying the value of the whole. So the dance continues.

Intellect: God knows why man, of all creatures, was blessed (or cursed) with this strange and awesome power! If we want an artist whose supreme challenge was the mastering and control of the mind, then Piet Mondrian is a fine choice. He began as a rather ordinary Dutch landscape painter, using the dung-coloured palettes of his peers, but soon, through his drawing, showed us an almost overwhelming sensitivity which he fought and struggled to control. He chose celibacy as a way of life and tried in vain, thank God, to eliminate from his art the heart and spirit of chance and feeling.

For many years, his later canvases – white-black with rectangles of only the three primary colours, red yellow blue – eluded me as art and I felt only their design. But no, dear friend, the passion of red, the blazing heat of yellow, the clarity of pure blue were imprisoned in cells of black bars, screaming for some slight release. Tension is created – a dangerous wire that often threatens intellectual purity.

Today's society, with its Ph.D-constipated tunnel vision, in some ways tries to achieve the same purity of non-emotional involvement. Your profession, through its applied knowledge, is constantly striving to control situations. But it is almost impossible to think, feel, and interact all the time, and calculation can be extremely destructive to the basic senses. So beware, dear M, beware. You have an obligation to the sensitivity within you (battered or not) to remain vulnerable – to touch, mould, and create, if for no one else but yourself and the power that gave you such gifts.

Emotions: I suppose if one were to think of an "emotional" artist of true greatness, Van Gogh would be the logical and correct choice. I recall a major exhibition of his works at the AGO (it was then the Art Gallery of Toronto). No one dared criticize them, but I felt that a few pictures lacked construction. A certain kind of fast, subconscious direction rendered them for me not totally successful.

In life, as in art, when emotions ride too high they do cut off intellect and hamper technique, sometimes to a point of total chaos. Van Gogh was a giant. Even the flaws I perceived in no way diminished the power, the energy, the *balls* of the manic creature striving for acceptance in the coldness of Christian society.

My grandmother had a saying: "You only use your fists when you run out of brains." You, more than most of us, constantly see abuse and distortion on the emotional plane of our existence. The channelling of this force is, we trust,

30

tempered with intellectual controls and techniques, learned and applied.

Technique: Well, here come the school books, the parental rules we are stuck with, the balancing acts of survival in a mass society in which we always feel a sense of being different – a kind of isolation and lack of acceptance. In an earlier note, I mentioned my decision to play the clown, to "accentuate the positive" as the Andrews Sisters used to sing. (Do you remember the Andrews Sisters?) Manners or the calculated lack thereof, costume, choice of vocation, avocation, all play a part in the final canvas – you.

There are many artists for whom technique would appear to be the pinnacle, the ultimate. Vermeer is one of them. But he, like all the greats, used his incredible knowledge to recreate light, to breathe life into two-dimensional space. A true visionary! Had technique alone been his forte, then he, together with so many Flemish artists, would have produced what I call sweat-on-a-fly's-ass pictures – perfect in detail, superb in structure, but without an ounce of feeling.

When you visit the AGO the next time, take a moment to look at four paintings in the Old Masters collection. The first, *Jar of Apricots* by Chardin, is a composition consisting of a myriad of oval forms, held firmly in place by a Mondrian-like geometric construction. That's technique! The wonderment of a moment caught in time–casual, informal, unpretentious. That's what makes it art.

The still life to compare it with by Van der Ast is of overblown flowers in a vase, with a shell and a chameleon. It is so bad and vulgar that it makes the neo-realists of this world look good.

The third and fourth paintings depict social events: Brueghel's *The Peasant's Wedding* is so lustful that you almost get a hard-on as you revel in its energy and passion. Scarlet carries your eye throughout the entire picture plane.

The fourth is by Arentsz. It attempts to depict the joys of winter sports–skating and so on. The period is approximately the same as that of the Brueghel painting. However, the clumsiness, the dismal colours and the lack of fluid composition render it totally empty – devoid of action, activity and, most important, spirit.

Well, so much for taking the world of art apart and attempting to put it together again. I would make a lousy art historian as I don't give a damn about most names or dates. I do, however, believe that I have the ability to allow each visual experience to register in some personal way.

The stone sculpture that sits beside your desk is a portrait of you. Let me try to explain: First, the material has quality. Second, you have given a great deal of attention to the surface, the polish, the external things. No abrasive elements are evident, yet there is an edge, a fine and well-defined line that dictates – and the word "dictates" is important – the reading of the entire surface. Though it seems passive, the surface is a taut skin that contains the spirit, the soul of the stone itself, and of its liberation. Third, the volume, which is much greater than we have been led to believe. Although weighty, as visually suggested by the material, the sculpture is poised in hesitation. It has what many great sculptures, such as *The Discus Thrower* and *Hermes with the Bow*, have given us in the past, a sense of *arrested* action, revealing the moment of indecision, the time before and after the tension.

I bet you never realized I had looked at that sculpture much! I have watched you, in your always correct attire, and your *alter ego* has told me more about your world and you than words ever could.

P.S.: Get off your ass and start sculpting. Please!

May 12, 1984

Dear M.

I have been painting all day and worrying about my house, Lou Paradou. I don't know what the receiver is going to do. Is Eva going to sell it or will she buy my share? Am I going to have to leave? I know I have to leave it for a while this summer because Eva has rented it. I shall come back to Toronto. God, how I wish it was settled and I knew I could live here for whatever life I have left.

Did I ever tell you how I found Lou Paradou?

For several years I'd been coming to France but, of course, as the grand Mr. Pollock of the Pollock Gallery, I went to the Riviera, to Paris, to Nice, Cannes, Monte Carlo. I knew nothing about the smaller, more beautiful, less arrogant areas of France. Then, in 1970, I got an invitation from Madame Pompidou, inviting me to the opening of the Didactic Museum of Vasarely. I had exhibited him in Toronto. Vasarely had been given the ruins of the château in the village of Gordes by the government of France and had spent over a million dollars restoring it. It was to be the museum of his major works. So I came to the opening.

The magic of this village! You drive down twisting roads, seeing nothing very much, then, suddenly, there it is, perched on the top of a hill and surrounded by the Luberon mountains. The cathedral and the château dominate it, of course. I had a wonderful time at the opening, and for the next few years I didn't go to the Riviera or to Nice or Cannes, I came back here to Gordes.

About four years after my first visit, I decided that one way to explore the area around Gordes would be to get a real estate agent to drive me around. I'd heard that if you go to Florida, or some such place, and you don't drive but want to see the area, you pretend you want to buy a house and get a local realtor to take you around.

In my fucked-up French, I told the real estate agent here on the square that I was interested in buying a house. He told me there was just one. I asked him to drive me there and he replied, "*Marchons!*" We walked for literally just two minutes from his office down this tiny, narrow, cobbled street – the steps double-width because they were built for donkeys. No car could ever get down it. And there, built in between the buttresses of the ancient cathedral, was my house. It was cold, it was damp, and I loved it.

It was owned by a *ménage à trois* from Paris: a husband, wife, and mistress, who had a very civilized relationship until, of course, it turned uncivilized. The wife and the mistress decided they liked each other and threw the husband out! He was selling the house cheaply because he didn't want them to get much money. So I was lucky. I wrote a cheque for $1,000 for the down payment, wired my bank not to let it bounce, and said I'd be back in a couple of months to finalize the deal.

The price was $36,000, but because of the tax system, they wanted $12,000 of it under the table in used French francs. I didn't like that idea one bit. But back in Toronto I ran into George and Alison Ignatieff at an opening at the Royal Ontario Museum. They have a house just outside Gordes, and they'd already heard from market gossip that I'd bought Lou Paradou. They assured me that this under-the-table payment was quite normal.

I couldn't afford to pay for it myself. There were no mortgages, so I had to pay the full $36,000 in cash. Eva, my secretary, who'd never been to France, and my friend Margaret Jones, decided to buy into it. I flew back with the money – $12,000 in used French francs in a briefcase – with my lawyer, Aaron Milrad, and his wife, because I didn't want to get screwed.

We arrived in Marseille – the drug capital of the world – with this briefcase filled with money. I thought they'd throw me in jail if the customs ever opened the case, but they didn't. But I slept with that case between my legs for five days. I wouldn't let it out of my sight.

We finally got to Gordes and the ex-owner, the real estate agent, my lawyer, his lawyer, and Nadine de Montmollin, a wonderful friend who'd flown in from Geneva to act as interpreter, and I all sat around and counted the money. Each one of us had to count all of it! Then it was put in a large manila envelope, sealed, and we all had to sign across the seal. Eventually, I got the papers and the bill of sale for $24,000 from the lawyer. But his bill was for a percentage of the full $36,000. Crooked!

The crypt of Lou Paradou had never been finished, the floor was mud, the walls were dripping where they were carved into the live rock of the mountain. We spent quite a bit having it dried out and properly finished. Then the roof had to be redone–in the old way, because the whole of Gordes is a historic site and nothing can be changed. The base of the house was built at the time of the Crusades, 850 years ago. There was an earthquake in the 1700s, unusual for the south of France. It was rebuilt then.

There are eight rooms on five levels. It's the prototype of the town house: tall and narrow. It's a splendid place. There's a spirit about it you can't imagine. It's tranquil. You should visit me here – an untranquil man in his peaceful, wonderful house. The weather is perfect now – the sun is shining. It's enough to gladden even this battered, scarred heart. But I do feel lonely, scared, sometimes.

Better stop before I get started on that again.

May 18, 1984

Dear M.

I think I spoke too quickly when I said the sun had pushed back the clouds. Heavier clouds have moved in, and for four days now the doors to a sunlit sky are closed. Rain was gentle on the first day, a little damp on the second, and is now just a bloody nuisance.

My feeling of aloneness is greatly enlarged when the front door is shut, and passersby can't nod *bonjour*. Well, if the vineyard folks are right, the mistral will blow this evening, drive the clouds back where they belong, and the sun of Provence will warm us all.

Good news, I suppose. I have not had blood in my phlegm for over a week. I have forgotten about the specialist in

Marseille, and as I feel well (I never did feel unwell) will go with the flow.

I am having a difficult time deciding on when, if at all, to return to Toronto. My return ticket expires June 28, but as I have had no response whatsoever to my letter to Eva, I feel a bit uneasy about leaving Lou Paradou. She stated before I left that the house was rented for June and July, and she and her family (friends) would be here for August. I know the chap who wants to come in June and said in my letter that was fine. He would like me to be here (he is bringing his mistress) to give a kind of tour of the area. I have no idea who was to come in July, but I said in my note that it should be cancelled. I also requested dates on her arrival in August. While she is here I can stay with Jean-Pierre.

A can of worms.

It's a bit like *Waiting for Godot*, and the inherent complications don't do anything to lessen the feeling of aloneness. At times I have no true sense of a physical presence. I float with a strange and not altogether desired weightlessness. (No, dear M, I am not near drugs, this is a kind of *déjà vu* or remembrance of a past laid to rest.)

Numb – that's the word – void of feeling or sensation, just a misty, musical presence. I look in the mirror, sometimes pinch myself (God! That goes back a long time: pinch yourself to see if you're real) and concentrate on feeling, smelling. Sometimes I talk to myself in French – anything to make me realize I did not totally self-destruct. I am still a presence with thoughts, ideas, and caring.

Shit! You must think I have gone round the bend. No, my dear M, these are real feelings, or lack thereof. I wonder if most people sense this time-space strangeness at some time in their lives. I remember when I was about fifteen and went to the dentist to have a tooth extracted. He gave me gas, and as I counted from one hundred backwards, the thought crossed my mind, Don't worry. You're not real anyway. You are just a character in someone's dream. They will awaken, and you will be gone. Weird!

I have often thought of that moment, and I suppose people who do go "mad" as they say, must feel similar sensations. Transitory, temporary, impermanent, float, fly (I just came back to earth. The word "fly" suggested zipper, cock.).

I guess I'm still around.

May 20, 1984

Dear M.

You ask how I first met Morrisseau. I just take it for granted that everybody knows the story of how we got together. I'm sure that, if I were to die tomorrow, the single most important thing people would remember me for is, damn it, the discovery of Norval Morrisseau. I'd like to think that I've done other equally important things. However, that's the way it is.

I met him in the summer of 1962. My gallery had been open for a couple of years and was struggling along. (The rent was forty-five dollars a month.) I was teaching courses at the YMCA, and Paul Bennett, the head of the Community Programs Branch of the Ontario government, approached me. I had taught a course for him the previous summer – teaching art teachers how to teach at a summer school in Guelph. He said he had a project he thought I might be interested in, teaching painting for six weeks in small mining and pulp and paper towns in Northern Ontario. He said I would have to teach two to three hours a day and that they would get me from one place to the next, by plane when necessary.

I thought it sounded really exciting and I felt I was becoming a professional, with the government hiring me to teach. Also, I'd never been up north before.

The first stop was Port Arthur, where I met a wonderful

37

lady named Susan Ross, a graduate of the Ontario College of Art, married to a judge, James Ross. She used to go live on reserves and do portraits and drawings of Indian life. She kept telling me about this Indian who painted on birch bark. I told her the last thing I wanted was an Indian who painted on birch bark. There I was, Jack Pollock, gallery owner, feeling sophisticated, professional, promoting modern art. Birch bark! It made me think of the cutesy birch-bark canoes they sell at Niagara Falls.

I purposely avoided him. In almost every town I went to someone told me about this Indian. I wasn't interested. I did not discover Norval Morrisseau, dear M, he discovered me, because, in Beardmore, I couldn't avoid him.

Beardmore was a ghost town. It had been home to a gold mine, but the vein had run out and now most of the main street was boarded up. But some people were still clinging on there. I was teaching three classes a day in the one-room schoolhouse. I was hired to teach just two or three hours a day, but you know me—what was I going to do with the rest of the day? So I taught kids in the morning, teenagers in the afternoon, and adults in the evening. Three full classes a day.

The second day I was there, the door opened and in walked this tall, young Indian man, aged around thirty. He was disgusting—drunk and he had pissed his pants—and he had a roll of birch bark and paper under his arm. He had heard this white teacher was up from Toronto and he wanted to show me his paintings. This was Morrisseau.

I couldn't avoid him – he was there. I had to look at the pictures, and I was stunned. They were brilliant. I looked at him and I looked at them and I thought—he didn't paint them! Not this dishevelled, unkempt creature. Some of them were on white paper, and the paper was pure, not a mark on it.

I was excited. I liked them very much and I told him so. I asked if I could go to his home and see more. He said yes.

Susan Ross had come to Beardmore for some extra classes with me, and her friend Sheila Burnford, who wrote *The*

Incredible Journey, which Disney made into a film, had come along for the fun. They drove me to Norval's house the next day.

His house was in the middle of a garbage dump – not next to it, but in it. I shouldn't call it a house, it was a tar-paper shack, half of it had a roof and half didn't because there was a huge tree growing through the middle of it. A little girl was sitting under the tree, Victoria, his first child. She was filthy dirty, covered in fly bites, and a chipmunk was playing over her knee. There was no stove, no water, no toilet, but there was a table set up under the part of the shack that had a roof.

As I walked in, he scared the shit out of me because he started chanting and banging a drum. He was having fun, really having me on – a brilliant, brilliant manipulator. But then he went over to the table and picked up a brush and did this magnificent painting–and scared the shit out of me again. I got goosebumps. I knew he was a genius.

I didn't know how to handle it, but I asked if I could exhibit his paintings in my gallery in Toronto. He just said, "Good. How many do you want?" I went through a stack of paintings he had and chose about thirty. He wanted me to pay him five bucks each. I had to explain that wasn't the way I did business –that I'd take them, get them framed, exhibit them, and keep 25 per cent of what they sold for. I sat down and made a list of the size, the material, and so on, signed it and handed it to him. He tore it up and said, "White man's paper's no fucking good. Take them." (Eventually, I made another list and left it with the mayor of Beardmore.)

I arranged that the show would be in October and asked him if there was anyone he wanted me to invite. Yes, there was, Senator Allister Grosart, who'd been the brains behind the campaign when Diefenbaker won such a raging majority. Norval had met him on one of the senator's trips up north. Norval wanted to be flown down for the opening and asked me to buy him a grey flannel suit.

So I took the pictures with me to Toronto, I contacted

Senator Grosart – and I still have his reply because it's signed by his secretary, Flora MacDonald.

The rest is history. I'll tell you about it tomorrow. Now I'm tired.

May 21, 1984

Dear M.

Back to the story of Morrisseau. That exhibition made both him and me. It brought him to international attention and it made the Pollock Gallery a public name. So, fame happened to both of us at the same time.

As soon as the paintings were hung, I phoned Pearl McCarthy, the art critic for the *Globe and Mail*, to come and see them. She was the first to write about Morrisseau and the first to call him a genius. Morrisseau flew in, I bought him the grey flannel suit and a tie, and he promised not to drink before the opening – and he didn't, he was very good. I didn't serve any alcohol.

The small works on paper were fifteen dollars; the largest paintings, about two by three feet, were three hundred dollars, framed. Within twenty-four hours the entire exhibition was sold out. Morrisseau became a *cause célèbre* and I became an important person. He was on every national television and radio show. *Time* magazine did a feature article with a photograph. He was an instant success.

The night after the opening I decided that Norval should stay with me. He had a CBC television interview at ten the next morning, and I didn't want to put him up in a hotel because of his drinking problem.

So Norval stayed with me. The opening was over, there was a red sticker on every painting in the gallery, everything was fine. That's when Norval decided that the white man didn't deserve any of his paintings and he was going to smash them all. Luckily, the gallery was locked and he couldn't get in. He demanded I get him a woman, and when I said I couldn't, demanded that I get him a man! Then he got up, left, and ran out into the street. We had this interview the next morning with Helen Hutchinson, and I had no idea where he'd gone or what I should do.

At nine-thirty the next morning, he came back. To this day I don't know what he met, but I think it was a bear. I've never seen so many hickeys. His whole neck was covered in huge bruises. He looked like the wrath of God. At the CBC, they had to do a make-up job like you've never seen, slapping pancake over the bruises. And he carried off the interview perfectly. I almost had a nervous breakdown.

He made three or four thousand dollars from the show, which I gave to him. Later I got news from Susan Ross that Norval had been handing all this money around and the entire native community was drunk. Two Indians had got so drunk, they had lain down in the middle of a road in the fog and had been run over and killed.

I felt guilty, awful. I decided that the answer was to set up a trust fund. After his second exhibition, which I held about a year later, I talked to Alan Jarvis, who was the ex-director of the National Gallery, and to Millie Ryerson, who ran the Artisan's Shop in the Village. We approached a lawyer none of us knew, who could act in Norval's best interests, and set up the trust fund. Norval would get something like five hundred dollars every two weeks – which was a fortune in those days.

The next thing I know, I got bills from the Hudson's Bay Company and from Eaton's in Port Arthur. When I phoned to see what the fuck was going on, they told me that Norval had come in with the *Time* article on us both and had told them to bill his agent. He had bought a silver tea service. He lived in a garbage dump, with no running water, and he bought a silver tea service! I passed the bills on to the trust, but the trustees couldn't cope. The fund lasted only six months, maybe a year. From then on, I bought each painting outright, one at a time, with the idea that he would never have a huge amount of money at any one time. Of course, later, I'd pay quite a bit at once, because I was buying a large number of pictures. I was building his reputation, the paintings were getting well known, but he'd still be selling them on the street for a bottle of booze. To this day, he's still doing that.

He's eccentric, mad, brilliant. He's an extraordinary human being. I love him and I can't stand him. He's caused me more problems than any other single human being on the face of the earth. Every once in a while he hates me, he'd screw me around. But he loves me. There's a bond between us. Amazing.

Enough of Norval. That's how I met him.

May – September 1984

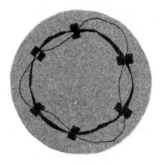

Dear M.

New paper – new day. The sun has been cock-teasing for two days now. It's time to shit or get off the pot!

I was sent the interview and the review of the William Ronald exhibit at the AGO. When he first painted in the fifties and early sixties his work was fucking good. The Holy Trinity of Ronald, Harold Town, and Gerald Gladstone is living proof that talent, or gifts, are cheap. Town is possibly the finest draughtsman Canada has ever produced. His technique is flawless. But for twenty years he has been too busy being Town to invest his art with any humility, introspection, or feeling. His mutton-chop sideburns, his piercing eyes, and his opinion on *anything* is standard Canadian fare. As for Ronald, the "savage" in his art was all he had, and when he took to capes, satins, and silver booties to attempt some stature of his own, he sold out. Gladstone was a hip young Jewish boy who welded not badly, and his early simple pieces, which Av Isaacs showed in his Bay Street gallery in 1961, were formal, but more. He then discovered his wit and lucite simultaneously, and proceeded to produce the elegant TV lamps (as I see them) of the late sixties and seventies. His chutzpah and his genuinely coarse personality wore thin, and I have no idea where or what he is today. (Sheila Gladstone, his wife, had a manic sense of creativity, and anything she created became distinctively her own. I don't know where she is, either.)

So the story goes, as I sit and live my death. My cock lies dormant, even from my own touch – again perhaps waiting for the stimulation of true humiliation, of true life. All here are friends, yet in their very closeness the odour of my own decay becomes more evident.

Macabre – that's one word for my outlook on the orbiting sphere we call earth. Yes, macabre, complete with clouds of bats' wings, thunderous silence, and the not-black-enough black of tonight. I am not allowed the wallowing I crave. The stars twinkle, the moon casts a cool, but accepting, glow. Most of all, the rejection I have set myself up for does not materialize. To me, you, Ron, Barb, and my other "fellow Canadians" live a kind of false reality. But you can, and do, accept what exists. It does not satisfy me and I continue my depth of probing – further and further, to what end?

I am, as I stated once before, radar – my eyes laser beams of lust and power, rendered impotent by my sense of morality. Castrated by Calvin. Laid low by Luther. One part screams I care! I care! The other part wishes to use the carnal past of me, and if abuse is part of using, to accept that fact. My scales have become imbalanced and the answer now is nothing. In nothingness I find a kind of empty peace, a hollow heaven, a sexless security. I cannot imagine this altered state continuing for long. Life must answer my questioning. Death must give a judgement.

I woke up this morning and re-read the previous pages. Wow! I guess I can get heavy. There is, however, a very real thread of my feelings in those words, a true attempt at explaining the unknown qualities of my existence.

So much for now. I am beginning to feel you will judge this epistle with detached scepticism. Be it so. It did come out of a sense of order, and I do believe it to be true.

P.S. Please, please write. And, please, no more Mother Hen. I like Calvin better.

Dear M.

I have just finished a picture for the Estaminet, the bar in Gordes owned by Suzanne and Max which I frequent when I get too damn lonely; they like it very much. A geranium, a red pitcher, and glasses. It's a good painting.

I am now going to start a series of boats *à la* Cassis which will be part of a show at the Musée municipal here in Gordes in September I've been asked to do. I must be planning to be around for a while, as I have the whole exhibition in my head. All I need is money to buy canvases and paint and enough strength to get me through each day. I feel I have a right to demand support these days, as I produce with a self-discipline I don't recall having had before.

Tomorrow is June 1. I wonder if the guy Eva's rented Lou Paradou to will arrive? My desire for company and my embarrassment about not being well create a kind of heaven-hell tension. Tomorrow they will do blood tests and I am expected at the hospital in Avignon on Monday. They want me to stay a few days. I sense a return to life-support of some sort. Yet, at a time like this, I don't see the purpose in survival. Not that a self-inflicted end would not cause problems, but I don't intend to negate the belief of others in my ability to cope. I shall live until a decision is reached by the sun, the moon, the stars, *et al.* I shall continue to attempt to justify each day with word or image. But I just wish sensation would return. I crave taste and touch and long for physical tenderness. My flesh feels anesthetized and I desire the tingle of response.

Externally, my image has been and is one of assurance and capability. I must admit that I am not sure I could break those barriers and just be – that's all – *be*. Instead of attempting to live up to what I have built as a false image, I would rather gently and carefully explore the regions of sensation I have buried. Pressure – release, pressure – release; tracing the flesh with fingers of exploratory wonder, softly, with firm but fine movement; arousing the dormant and seemingly deceased passions of my being.

The curve of warm bodies gently bonded and tenderly entwined is but a faded photo in my memory bank. The polaroid shots of my life – the one-night stands of splendid and excessive release – seem too distant to expect return exposures. The shutters of life tend to be stuck, immobilized by the strength of wanting. The aging films have become brittle and will probably soon refuse to activate the image, even if the shutter should suddenly release. So I sit, looking at the mental albums of my past madness, filled with vivid images of me in my many-coloured robes of experience. By comparison, they prove so clearly the greyness and lack of focus of the present. I need a Daguerre of the senses, a Kodak of the soul.

I am beginning to be part of the tapestry of the village. I have come to know more intimately its traits and the habits that give character to the cast of players. My life seems centred around the Estaminet, the bar where I try to read *Le Provençal* each morning while drinking my hot chocolate, where I lunch every day, and visit most evenings for a *pastis* before or a *poire* after dinner. My sense of belonging to this place comes through in the feeling of having been accepted by the clients. This is one level of Gordian society and I feel quite at ease with it. But having realized the need for some intellectual stimuli besides the company of my homespun friends, and also being quite aware of the value of association with those who belong to the "other" Gordes to my future success as a painter, teacher, etc., I just recently began to make an entrance into the world of the doctors and professionals. They are a snob element but very real. The way they dress, behave, and affect the air of urban living, has given the village a reputation for class and sophistication. Most would pale dramatically in a real urban scene but here the big-fish-little-pond syndrome seems to work quite well for them.

So it goes. I am putting down roots, trusting I will survive to become aware of new growth. I am pleased with most of the paintings I have sent to Canada, filled with imagery for tomorrow and tomorrow.

Dear M.

Well, I arrived here yesterday. My friend Gerry Conrath and her son Rob drove me. I was informed that my bed was waiting. As I was to call you at noon (six p.m. here) and it was only three-thirty, I checked into my room, had a cardiogram and an X-ray, and left. Rob and Gerry drove me into town and I phoned from the post office. It is directly across the road from the ancient ramparts of Avignon, a section that caters to the cruising, needy types I have so often encountered there.

If I seemed a little "ripe" with emotions when I called, please forgive. Faced with hospitalization, no one speaking English, and as yet, no medical history to give the doctors here, I felt very needy of our threads of contact.

I got back at seven. They had kept dinner for me; dinner being impossible pasta with the largest, hardest meat balls I had ever seen outside a bestiality porn flick. They told me I could have no breakfast as I was to have electric shock on my heart in the morning. I freaked out and was ready to walk out. Thank God Rob was here. They did not insist on shock and today are giving me digitalin in *liquid* form. Disgusting!

I requested Halcion for sleeping, but they told me they ran out four weeks ago and none had arrived. They gave me something in its place and, at three this morning, something else again. It is now about two in the afternoon and I am just coming out of a grey fog. *Petit déjeuner* was a large plastic bowl filled with hot water, a package of instant coffee, a package of instant milk, and a crusty roll.

I have stated I must leave the hospital on Friday, as friends are arriving from Canada on Sunday and the house needs a thorough cleaning. If they attempt to keep me here, Rob and his brother Chris have agreed to help me pull a little escape. We have the plan all worked out.

I look as close to "cute" today as I ever could, sitting here dressed in starched, pure white. Unlike most WASPs, I have no pajamas as I do not believe in night attire, unless it be a lace-leather costume, and that is not for sleeping. I do, however, own a wonderful *chemise de grand-père* and black ballet slippers, covered with splashes of red violet orange from my paint box. So I sit here in starched pure white, neatly groomed and terrified.

Hôpital de la Durance, Avignon
June 6, 1984

Dear M.

I thought of you earlier this week when I realized the mess Lou Paradou was in. The house is, as I have mentioned, medieval. The cave, or crypt, as it is known, is carved into the lime rock of the cliff. This room, like the kitchen beside it, is vaulted and carries a special aura. It is here that the life-size bust of some cardinal of Avignon reigns alongside a huge wrought-iron cross, and assorted other *objets d'art religieux*. As there is no window (a six-inch square hole allows air to change), the room is always dark, and although electricity exists, I light it only with candles (about twenty). The furnishings consist of a suite (small couch and two large chairs) which are museum examples of art deco. The upholstery is deco-patterned velvet in tones of brown and beige. The only problem is they need restoring as the springs have sprung.

The main room, which you enter from the street, is where I live mostly. A huge pine table, which seats twelve easily, dominates the space. It is from a monastery and is quite similar to the harvest tables of your ancestors.

The *premier étage* boasts a huge fireplace, a twin-bedded bedroom, shower, bidet (they are handy little items for men as well as women) and separate toilet (there is another toilet *en bas*, off the large room).

The salon with the fireplace is two stories high, and at one end stairs lead to a mezzanine, with a bed, which leads to a double-bed bedroom, which leads, by way of carved stone steps and a trap door, to a perfect small room at the top. It has a single bed and windows on three sides, which give a view of tiled roofs and, beyond, the majesty of the low mountain range, the Luberon.

The furnishings throughout are sparse and, now that I plan to live here, seem quite inadequate. However, one day at a time. I was quite reckless a few weeks ago and spent the money I am supposed to live on this month on two chairs from the Orient Express. That's me.

I have been living in only one part of the house: the crypt for drinks before dinner, the dining room, kitchen and toilet, and the first bedroom (twin beds) on the *premier étage*. This room is filled with clothing. Just about all I own is piled on one twin bed in semi-dirty array, while the other bed remains unmade and unkempt. (I straighten it each night before sleep and have changed the sheets four times since I arrived.)

My work – well, that's harder to explain. I have been busy with the *Lacoste* series, and the *Fenêtre* series. Both are abstract and I balance them with the simplistic, yet sophisticated still-life works which I call provençal. They are truly *hommage à Matisse*, and the shapes of chairs, shutters, pots, and plants are excuses to hang colour. They are not modelled or shaded, but are pure colour, interacting in joy and a sense of frolic. I do not know when I start a picture – abstract or realistic – what will appear. One line, one shape, one colour suggests another, and another, so the creative process is in total continuum until the end. I rarely correct, and destroy rather than overwork. But by now, if I don't understand the craft, then I never will, so my formal properties – composition, form, line, balance, and colour – are usually successful. But, as we know, craft does not make a work of art, so it is for others to view, accept or reject, and establish their value to the major role

of art – communication. I have never before felt this sense of
satisfaction from work completed.

Please God! Let some sell!

June 27, 1984

Dear M.

Received your letter this morning. For the past two weeks
Lou Paradou has been a kind of hotel-hostel, with all six
beds full and a constant cast of changing characters.

I have been giving conducted tours of everywhere from
Marseille to Aix-en-Provence to Les Baux, Apt, Avignon,
Roussillon, Lacoste, and Cavaillon. Through all of it, I
remain chaste and the grand host.

After all my complaints of being lonely, now I have a
strange urge to be alone. I don't believe I will ever be negative about self-company again. When Dennis and Helen
arrived they brought a letter from Helen Duffy and in it was
a crazed, child-like card from David Hockney, done in coloured pens, wishing me love and health. I have known him
for about sixteen years and was the first in Canada to show
his works in 1966. The *Cavafy Suite* – a series of superb etchings – hung on my walls at ninety dollars each, *framed,* and
no one bought. The same happened with Walker Evans' photos, Jasper John's *Numbers* and hundreds of others.

My sadness at your news of the death of Jerrold Morris is
intensified by my regret over the lack of support and respect
the community as a whole gave him. Jerrold's flirtation with
American Pop art was daring, but his true love was nineteenth-
and twentieth-century drawing. I know of no finer eye for
this specialized field, and the serious collectors who relied
on him will not find his guidance easily replaced. I have always
felt honoured that he liked and respected me.

In the late sixties, Av Isaacs (I do love him), Jerrold, Walter
Moos, Doris Pascal, and I became founding members of the
Professional Art Dealers Association of Canada (PADAC),

Toronto branch. (It originated in Montreal.) Built into its regulations was a form of ethics committee.

Soon after its formation, Mira Godard arrived in Toronto from Montreal and the "gentleman's agreement" that existed between the dealers to leave each other's artists alone became threatened. Tough, aggressive, and with an apparent lack of sensitivity, Mira began wooing and winning artists, well established by other dealers, to her stable. Ed Bartram was (and still is) a fine Canadian printmaker; Doris Pascal had championed him, but Mira got him. The ethics committee of the association said, and quite rightly, that it takes two to tango, so Mira was free to approach artists from other galleries.

Since 1966 I had been working with the Petersburg Press (Paul Cornwall-Jones) in London, England, exhibiting works produced by their superb studio. It had evolved into a contractual agreement wherein I was obligated to purchase three copies of all works produced by Petersburg in exchange for the exclusive right to represent their work in Ontario.

Several artists, such as the prolific Dieter Rot, Patrick Caulfield, and William Tucker, rarely sold, but by committing myself to take all that Petersburg produced, I had such important names as David Hockney, Richard Hamilton, Claes Oldenburg, and Jim Dine.

Aaron Milrad was a young lawyer on the move. I, along with David Mirvish, was one of his first clients from the art world. He collected art and was, I believe, concerned about the problems of exploitation of artists and dealers. At this point, he was the lawyer for the Professional Art Dealers Association. One day he arrived at my gallery to inform me that Mira Godard had new Jim Dine etchings from the Petersburg Press on the walls of her Toronto gallery. (Mira's gallery, by this time, was called the Marlborough-Godard, affiliated with the famous – and soon to be infamous – international Marlborough Gallery, based in London and New York.) I went to see for myself and was shocked – and pissed off – to find this news was true. She had purchased them from Petersburg on the understanding they were for her Montreal gallery.

Now, this was not the "two to tango" agreement that existed for the local art scene. I thought this was unfair and unscrupulous as I had a contract with Petersburg. So, naturally, I went to the ethics committee. I didn't attend the meeting when this was discussed, as I thought that would be inappropriate. Av Isaacs, Doris Pascal, and Jerrold Morris were, I understood, for me, but others, including Aaron Milrad, refused to act on my behalf. I had no choice – I resigned.

Walter Moos, who was president, sent Aaron and Alkis (a fine man – then David Mirvish's assistant) to convince me to return, but for five years I was not a member. I rejoined later only because several of the younger artists I was showing convinced me that, for their benefit, I should be a member.

During that five-year period, the Marc Rothko scandal broke. Rothko – a giant on the New York art scene – was a despondent, brooding genius. His death (an apparent suicide) started a blitz of theft, deception, and collusion between his estate executors and the powerful Marlborough machine. Paintings were removed from the widow's home, inventoried works went missing (many are still unaccounted for), and legal battles began.

One morning I wakened to find the photo of a familiar building on the front page of the *Globe and Mail*–Len Deakin's fine art warehouse. Len – a wonderful man (to Len, everyone was Uncle: Uncle Jack, Uncle Av) – pioneered in fine art transportation and storage. According to the newspaper, a collection of Rothko works had been found in Len's warehouse.

Rumours ran rampant. Mira removed the Marlborough name from her premises, but much of the international art she subsequently exhibited – and still exhibits – was by artists connected with the Marlborough empire. Frank Lloyd, the Marlborough Gallery mastermind was taken to court, and he and the gallery were fined over nine million dollars.

What a mess! All the result of power and greed.

Shortly after I rejoined PADAC, Doris Pascal and I were asked to prepare a pamphlet explaining what a print is. Canadian Artists Representation and many fine printmakers were concerned that buyers, out of ignorance, were spending good money on worthless reproductions.

Richard Sewell, co-founder of the Open Studio, worked with us, and after six months of talking and writing, we submitted a draft to PADAC. Sadly, the pamphlet was rejected by some members, as they represented artists who signed and numbered photographic reproductions, which were sold as prints.

A print is anything that is transferred from one surface to another (a good example is the fingerprint). But master print-makers produce fine graphic images – printed images – that do not exist in any other medium. The original prints are the work of art, pulled from a stone in the case of a lithograph print, or through a screen of silk for a serigraph print – there are many mediums, from woodcuts and linocuts to delicate etchings. But in the art world, the word "print" properly does not include a photographic reproduction.

It is difficult for buyers to determine what exactly they are getting when they buy prints. When I was teaching, I would suggest the potential buyer insist on a written statement to confirm the originality of the print – knowing the technique alone is not enough. "Lithograph" doesn't mean much – the newspaper colour supplements are offset litho-photo prints. Numbers can also be misleading – some artists in Canada and in New York, wherever, print an edition numbered one to one hundred on one paper and a separate edition of another hundred on a different stock.

There is absolutely nothing wrong in buying a Robert Bate-man print, or one by Trish Romance or Keirstead, or by any of the many other artists whose work is photographically reproduced, but the buyer should be aware of the technical process and of the lack of involvement by the artist. Supply and demand sets the market price.

Anyway, you don't need to hear all this. But our little pamphlet did lay it all out. PADAC agreed to publish it only after a great deal of rewriting, and, in my opinion, watering down. The print racket still goes on, often without the artist even being aware.

Another instance of taking a moral stand actually paid off! It was with the Art Rental of the Art Gallery of Ontario. Initially I supported it to the hilt, as I felt all the artists whose work they rented out benefitted from the exposure and education. However, I soon began seeing many international prints with no gallery credit in the Art Rental. I enquired and found that they were dealing with Walter Carson (a wheeler-dealer and a landowner in Yorkville).

I complained, and withdrew from rental all the works from my gallery (over a hundred). A special meeting was called, Clem Carson, Walter's ex-wife, backed me, as did Carol Rapp and many others. Walter's prints were withdrawn, and I believe they now only show, rent, and sell works they've gotten from artists themselves, or from their dealers.

So, dear M, you are right – I wouldn't, I couldn't, and I won't be dishonest. I guess Calvin is still there – somewhere. (Was Calvin poor? Just like to know!)

A few words about Doris Pascal. She was the singular driving force that propelled Canadian printmakers into the national and international markets; a truly wonderful woman. I met her when she worked briefly for an eccentric lady named Ruth Cohen (who opened The House of Prints) in my first small gallery, after I moved next door to "grander" quarters. Ruth had Picasso's *Vollard Suite*, his ceramics, the *Miserere Suite* by Rouault, wonderful Miros, Braques, Man Rays, Magrittes, etc., but she had no sense of business. Doris caught the bug of fine prints from her, and shortly thereafter opened her first gallery on Yorkville, with Sylvia Schwartz.

Doris's commitment and astute business sense made her loved by all. Tragically, when she could no longer physically function due to rheumatoid arthritis, her son took over and ran the gallery into the ground.

Doris and I had planned to get together before I left to come here, but, as you know, time ran out. I hope if I return,

I shall be able to see her, hug her and tell her for many, many artists, she was, and is, a queen.

Dear M.

Summer is at its glorious peak here. The lavender is glorious; I wish you could see the fields of violet. When dusk arrives, the dampness of the air intensifies the wonder of its scent. Heady and rich, lusty and robust, not the Yardley's smell of stale maiden aunts with faint moustaches and sallow cheeks, no, the heavy sweaty smell of life, pulsing, and continually moving in a vast and cloudless arena, dark and inviting.

(Shit! I got a bit carried away there!)

I am restless. My painting at the moment stinks. Nothing is happening, and a sense of panic is setting in, as my show here at the small museum opens September 15.

The pictures I sent to Canada are good, but I can't seem to get going. Granted, having no money for large canvas or more paints is a problem, but the real issue is that I am dry of ideas and have to break this depressive mood or get really down, one of the two.

At the moment I am in a sort of arrested action. I need a hot, horny fantasy to come true. I need to break the mould of containment, and let loose. In the meantime, I fuck up one picture after the other. In August I will have an *atelier* (a workshop) above the bar so I can work uninterrupted, and I hope money comes through so I can buy large canvas and paints (as well as eat).

These recent paintings don't have the denseness of the *Lacoste* series, or the freedom of the *Fenêtre* series. They all end up kind of neuter, so I tear up the paper for release.

I haven't written much either, as you have noticed. I suppose the "excessive" in me applies to my *not* doing, as well as my doing. I have started piddling about with "little" provençal pictures, and they are correct, but who needs correct art? They are the type of things people like, but I feel a repetition and craft I don't like. I just did the first landscape I have done in years. It is "twee," as my landlady in England would say.

I am really frustrated. I need a good old-fashioned orgy *à la Notre-Dame des Vapeurs*, complete with a cast of thousands. It may be just as well I am not in Toronto at the moment.

My fifty-fourth birthday arrives on August 1st, and I'm beginning to wonder how long the crotch rules? Masturbation at least once a day doesn't seem to help, and I have given up the notion of "walking into the sunset" with someone. It's just not natural. The strictures Calvin placed on us were attempts at redirecting the energies and passions of the mind and body. They insisted on an innocent and totally accepting belief. It would be nice to have that simple approach to life and living. The devout, born-again Christian seems such an artificially inseminated creature to me. Yet a Calvinistic morality pervades my being.

Who knows when it all ends, or where? I do know my body is very much alive and my desires are real and potent. Can that be bad? I don't believe so. It is, however, a bitch of a problem. Maybe an ad in the personal column of the local newspaper: "Aging satyr desires a host of young men to obey and service. Rewards in accord to performance and stamina."

Enough!

July 26, 1984

Dear M.

I found this note, which I wrote to Eddie Kingstone, my psychiatrist at the time, in 1980. It talks of my past excess, not, alas, my present abstinence:

The public urinal in Cavaillon is subterranean. It's dark, moist, and scented from the piss of a thousand bladders every day. It also has that seductive stench of sperm, spent and congealing, that can become the cologne of true lust and passion.

Today, I made an impassioned pilgrimage, and spent three hours in the bowels of male excretion. I entered one of the cubicles, removed all my clothing and waited. As men and boys arrived, I exhibited, teased, and serviced. My own ejaculation seemed totally secondary to playing the role of receiver of the seed of others. One, two, young, old, no matter, I was insatiable and revelled in my total abandon. To what extent the element of danger enhanced the heaven and hell of the moment I don't know, but I was recalling the glory holes of my youth.

What I wish to know is: Is it necessary to understand the hidden motivations for our actions, or is it sufficient to accept the fact that these desires exist, and occasionally (thank God I go public only occasionally) reach the point of absolute need of resolution? After the fact, I often shake with the fear of past possibilities, but for those seconds, moments, hours, I feel quite close to a kind of ecstasy. And, as Piaf said, *Je ne regrette rien*.

I wonder to what degree the pain-pleasure equation is inherent, acquired, and/or fashionable. Knowing very little of research in this area, I would suppose my intuitive feelings tell me it is a *mélange*, where each element plays its role. The degrees of involvement, however, are, I believe, a direct result of society and acceptance-rejection factors.

Although I know I have what is known as a high tolerance for pain *vis-à-vis* illness, I abhor the thought of having it inflicted upon me as a so-called stimulus or sexual aid. Restraint or confinement are also phobias which I suppose I should someday look into. I can, and often do, enjoy – as the British say – "Slap and tickle with mild bondage" (read the cards in Soho for Madame Sophie and her neighbours), and I enjoy the role of bossy teacher/master in the theatre of sexual fantasy, but I could not, I am sure, knowingly hurt anyone.

All this musing, by the way, comes from my frequent visits and wanderings through the ruins of the château of the Marquis de Sade. Many followers of fashion in Toronto would surely titter to know that their alligator T-shirts were born no more than one hundred yards from the château of this noble gentleman. (Trivia: Did you know that when the revolutionaries finally opened the doors of the Bastille, there was only a handful prisoners, one of whom was the Marquis de Sade, who was so obese that he had to be aided in his departure? So much for my glamorous image of a cross between Don Juan and Paul Newman!) When I return I shall buy a good, accurate translation of his writings and judge for myself his degrees of the deranged, demented, and destructive.

I feel strangely sure that were he here today and watched a few hours of prime time television, complete with our realistic documentaries on such diverse subjects as Viet Nam, Jamestown, Chad, the Manson story, and on and on, he would, by pure contrast, appear almost innocent, and find it very hard to accept the atrocities that we take for granted in our vicious, warring world.

You see, dear M, my letters to Eddie were just the start of my true dialogue with you.

September 9, 1984

Dear M.

It seems like several lifetimes since the last letter. I tried (unsuccessfully, obviously) to do myself in. My neck was in such physical pain that I couldn't bear life any longer. After I didn't appear in the bar for a day and a half, and the nurse couldn't get in to give me my injection, the doctor arrived with the police. I don't recall much for a few days; however, Gerry Conrath got me to a specialist in Aix and he put my head and neck in a plaster cast. Pain killers, sleeping pills; nothing worked, and after a week, I thought I would go mad. I returned, and they fitted me with a moulded plastic cast which adheres with Velcro. The pain has subsided, I have not had any medication for four days now, and I sleep.

I also have finished work for my show here, about thirty canvases (mostly small) and about fifty works on paper. They won't all hang, but I am very satisfied with them. Several of the canvases are really constructions, with pieces of old fence rails and real barbed wire, which I stole from the grounds of the famous Marquis. They are filled with tension and controlled violence. George and Alison Ignatieff were over yesterday, and he was knocked out by their power.

I've designed a poster for the show, which you will receive when I get some mailing tubes. It's the Canadian flag waving behind the wrought-iron bars of my window here, against a provençal blue sky. It's fucking good!

I now have debts of about three thousand dollars, and am literally being kept by the local bar and grocery store. Somehow, I know it will all work out. I feel energized and confident. Hugo Gallante, the best-known architect in the area, bought a small construction this afternoon for fifteen hundred francs, and he feels I will be very successful with my show.

Why do I have to get to rock bottom to truly create? It's a little tiring, you know! I am having slides taken of my exhibition, and will send you a set. The Musée municipal in Gordes has been renamed and is now called the Aumônerie Saint-Jacques. I wish you could see the works hanging. I think they will be very powerful.

September 16, 1984

Dear M.
It is ten-thirty in the morning. I have just finished cleaning up the mess of last night's opening. Over two hundred people arrived, and it seems all were impressed. I feel tranquil, spent, and somehow empty.

The gallery was a twelfth-century stopping place for pilgrims from the Crusades. It's a two-room gem. All the walls are stone, the ceilings vaulted, and each column bears traces of the unique and wonderous embellishments of the past. The larger room is filled with two series of pictures. The first is the *Lacoste* series, many of which have become constructions, complete with ancient pieces of wood, *objets trouvés* and the real barbed wire I cut from the barriers of the château de Sade in the night.

The other, the series *Fenêtre*, are abstract compositions, with the symbol of window bars – *épis* they call them here. They are decorative, suggesting leaves and vines, yet they are real barriers protecting the inhabitant and barring the intruder. Both series are a testimony to my survival, a celebration of life, and they are not "pretty pictures." I am content today.

I have titled the exhibition *The Two Faces of Provence*. The smaller room rests quietly, bathed in the light of the sun's golden glow and filled with still-lifes, boats, symbols of the simple and glorious beauty here. This is the one face. But the history of Provence is a history of war, famine, and the struggle for existence. The *Lacoste* and *Fenêtre* series are a kind of homage to that courage. This is the other face.

Roger Vincent, a warm and caring friend of the Ignatieffs and mine, who lives in the outskirts of Gordes, was a prisoner of war for four years. His wiry, sixty-odd-year-old presence is felt here, and I've named one canvas *La Guerre à Roger Vincent*. His family came to the opening and we all shared a few tears. He is not well, but will try to come some quiet afternoon, when there are no crowds.

The Ignatieffs bought a small work on paper, of boats, a little like the one I gave you. I have sold four other small ones and one canvas.

The prices here are about half that in Toronto, so I need sales badly, but the sheer miracle of the show's existence is buoying my spirits these days. My debts are over ten thousand francs. I have made twenty-eight hundred.

Dear M.

I sit here each day from ten-thirty a.m. to six p.m., custodian of an ancient chapel and the testimony of my survival. I realize the works on the wall came through me, and I am in awe of the process. Yes, I made the marks, the scars, the colours and forms that the works consist of, but they seem to extend beyond that. They might be really good! I don't know, except I feel slightly alienated from them, they intimidate *me*, the so-called creator. They are sharp and aggressive, offending me, and yet I find their emotion curiously contagious.

Heaven and Hell; Calvin and the Devil. Why must I bring myself, or be in some way propelled, into disaster in order to let loose, let go and allow God, or Satan, whichever, guide my forces and power, channel my energies, and produce works that cry, in fact, scream? Yes, the justification is the history of Provence. However *I* did them. Or did I?

Jackie, the little boy, seems to have been eliminated in this exhibition. There is nothing child-like in the tortuous twists of barbed wire, unless it relates to the unknown phantoms I was terrified by as a child, being erased by light and proven to be only shadows, spectres without substance.

Daylight, especially the sun-drenched provençal daylight, does bring an end to the spectres, and thoughts of you help me through the blackness of the night (that sounds fucking corny, like a bad country and western song).

My emotions feel like a tightly packed keg, waiting to explode. I need to paint; writing just doesn't satisfy my physical needs the same way. Energy builds and tensions soar, strange and wonderful, but also frightening.

The museum here is unheated, the summer has gone, and a damp cold pervades the stone. The sun rarely reaches the slit windows, and I feel I am sitting in a cellar, filled with the follies and visible facts of my being. A kind of homemade prison of the soul. Vinegar and sugar – bittersweet (shit, that sounds like Jeanette MacDonald and Nelson Eddy, remember *them*?).

Anyway, life seems to continue, and I get from one day to the other with minor joys and, thank God (and Calvin, I suppose), minor sorrows.

Finances continue to plague me, but that's nothing new. The villagers won't let me starve, and somewhere along the line, I know if I keep to the straight (strong word?) and narrow, my needs will be met. That belief probably comes from the old adage – "The Lord will provide."

Anyway, enclosed are doodles I do as I sit here waiting for Godot.

September 29, 1984

Dear M.

I think Toronto has finally written me off, as three weeks have passed and I've received no mail. I write about ten letters a day, just to keep from going nuts. Maybe one or two of them will warrant a reply.

I am being courted by the village weaver (I couldn't make that one up!). He is tall (over six foot), thin, dark, and quite good-looking, but all I see when I look at him is black lace and sequins (and I didn't pack my toybox!).

As you can tell by the tone of this note, I am feeling much better. No money, but I seem to be adjusting to poverty (with the occasional infusion of champagne).

The weather here is still moderate, but October is quite "iffy." Then comes winter, and no central heating. I suppose the winter will be long, and lonely, so I may yet have an affair with a drag queen. I've had everything else, God knows! Although I detest obesity, I am thinking the village weaver would be warmer with a bit more flesh on him.

He is making me a priest's habit, as I have wanted one for years, and they don't have them, as they used to, in the flea market these days. When it is finished, I will send you a photo, for your "Calvin" moments of reverie. (He'll roll in his grave!)

The figs are dropping off the trees and the almonds are filling baskets ready to be dried for winter cooking. Herbs of all types hang in bunches in the kitchen and I make tisanes daily.

So goes the life of a peasant. (As I write this, I toy with the massive silver bracelet on my arm, and the ivory and silver child's "dummy" that hangs around my neck. Some peasant!)

I don't know whether I told you or not, but about a month or six weeks ago I lost my leather cock ring (that had served his master lo these many years). Now my "Holy Trinity" has only the keys to Lou Paradou caressing from the pocket of my pants. Pity! Maybe Santa Claus will bring me another. (Maybe filled, *j'espère!*)

Okay Pollock, enough shit. Hope all is well with you.

September 30, 1984

Dear M.

Received your letter this morning. Several things struck me.

Your drawing: I am sure it is, as is most of your thinking and advice, weighed, measured, and attempting the impossible – perfection. Paul Klee said drawing was "taking a line for a walk." Don't hold the leash too tightly. Close your eyes and make some marks. Paper is cheap. So don't worry about creating a drawing – just draw.

You really suffer, as I see it, from an over-abundance of neat and tidy. Tight-ass, speck-on-the-fly's-ass studies can result from this introspective approach. Let go and let God! (For Calvin's sake!) Let the little boy M go outside the lines of the colouring book. (I believe colouring books to be obscene; they should be banned.)

So, grab charcoal (a pencil is too tentative) and mark – suggest feeling with the line, by the weight of line, choosing angles or curves. Take the same image (object) and do a yin and yang version. Fill the picture plane, don't do miniatures. The charcoal is an extension of the fingers, the fingers the hand, the hand the arm, the arm the entire body. Let it have its freedom. Rape and seduce, it's safe on paper.

Would that we all learn from the genius of someone like Miro, who never lost the child-like joy, the surprise of innocent discovery, that makes his works sing with truths so often obscured in others by convention and visual formal logic.

Many years ago, Anthony Caro was the dutiful apprentice of Henry Moore. He questioned the need of sculpture to have a defined perimeter (base) and took three-dimensional art off the sculpture stand and placed it on the floor. God help us all. Since then the young, the immature, the talentless have been throwing, piling, welding pieces of natural and man-made material in an all too often vain attempt to create.

I am reminded of a joke told to me when I was lecturing to a Rotary group once. (Yes, I did the Kiwanis-Rotary circuit.) You know the definition of abstract art? It's the same as jerking off. It's fun when you're doing it, but what do you do with the mess when you're finished?

It's very anti-intellectual, but the thread of truth runs through the laughter.

Many young "creatives" used to come to my gallery with their minimal-conceptual works or ideas. I would ask them if they knew the works of Marcel Duchamp and suggest they look at his growth and development through all the phases of his creative process as a textbook. He did it. He explored and attempted to realize his potential after travelling the well-worn path of tradition. Josef Albers used to say to me often (he, who spent thirty-odd years painting squares) that drawing was essential.

The main problem with technique is that one has to learn it, absorb it, and then consciously forget it in order to create. It's like language, where the vocabulary, the skills, the structure, make it possible for us to communicate. And, my dear M, no one can convince me that the purpose of art is not

66

communication. Self-expression is fine. Create for the sake of creation, okay. But when the chips are down, sharing that vision, telling that visual tale, being understood in an alien land. That's success!

The Art Gallery of Ontario, John Bentley Mays, and their ilk, don't communicate, they alienate and build barricades, making it difficult for those who come from the masses (and I believe there are more all the time) to learn and participate in the world of creative endeavours. It's not fair!

The AGO and JBM should be opening doors that are rust-sealed with past prejudice. The light of understanding cannot shine in Arian marble shrines. If the *Globe* and the AGO did not have such power, one could laugh it all off, as a bad joke, an immature prank.

One of the major problems I had over the years of teaching art is with the AGO. I enjoyed teaching for places like the Skills Exchange because the students there knew very little and were very eager to learn. I would teach them for four weeks, and for two of those weeks I would take them to the gallery to show them the works of what they call the Old Masters (very few of the paintings there are really by Old Masters), and I would take them through the Impressionists, the early Canadian works, and onto the contemporary Canadian painters. There would usually be a few paintings by the Painters Eleven, but that would be all I could show them. The AGO rarely has a group of contemporary Canadian paintings on show. They have a tremendous collection of some of today's artists, they have Coughtry, they have Rayner, they have Colville (there are gaping holes in the collection – the last Jack Shadbolt they bought, to my knowledge, was done in the forties or fifties), but they don't show them.

I think it a great disservice to Ontarians, first of all, who want to see what's going on in art today, and, second, to people coming from abroad who want to see contemporary Canadian painting, and, third, to me as a teacher. I think it is outrageous that these paintings, these teaching tools, which should be on display in a gallery funded almost exclusively by government grants – yours and my tax dollars – aren't to be seen.

Over the years very few curators of contemporary art at the AGO have looked at painting – I think paint frightens them, actually. Instead, they have favoured works by those artists I call conceptual minimalists. Minimalist art is difficult to explain to students – the reductive process, less is more, very simple. An example: There's a pile of felt in the National Gallery by Robert Morris. When I first saw it, I thought they'd just been unpacking a new work and had left the packing lying around, but, no, this was the art. The AGO owns a quite expensive work by Richard Serra–a huge pile of chicken wire. The sculpture is never the same twice, because each time you pick it up to move it, it gets dented. They also have Hans Haacke's *Snowcone*. It is a phallic shape that looks a bit like a septic stick that men use when they've cut themselves shaving. It plugs in and it freezes. These objects are in the AGO's permanent collection.

I do think that the gallery should exhibit everything that's going on in contemporary art – it is their mandate. But they do not have any right to eliminate most of what painters are doing, yet that's exactly what they do.

There are a few curators in Canada – Alvin Balkind in Vancouver, for one–who love paintings and do show them. David Burnett was a short-lived curator at the AGO who loved painting and set up some fine exhibitions of contemporary painting. But for the most part curators of contemporary art live in a kind of ivory tower, and although they give lip service to the public and invite you in, they don't educate you in all aspects of modern art, only in the narrow specialty of conceptual, minimalist art. It's a problem in museums and public galleries everywhere, but I am upset about the AGO because I am from Toronto, from Ontario.

I have talked to Bill Withrow, the director, many times about this, and his unvarying reply is that there is always an exhibit of contemporary Canadian paintings in the Art Rental service. But, first, that service is a commercial venture; second, most people visiting the gallery don't go to it because it is tucked away in the basement; third, most of the art in it is quite mediocre. It gives a distorted and not a true picture of what current Ontario painting is. I once suggested – and I still think it was a good idea – that artists and galleries should boycott the Art Rental. Then there would be no contemporary Canadian painting shown, period, and the gallery would be forced to hang some on its walls.

I have had this complaint about the gallery for years. Once I got up at an annual meeting and accused them of racism because there was, at that time, no such thing as a work of art by a native person in the entire gallery. Morrisseau was famous by this time, and other native artists had tried to emulate him and were known as the Woodlands School – some of them were very good indeed. Well, the gallery did look around, and in an exhibition in Stratford they found a Morrisseau painting from my personal collection, which I had had since 1964. That was the one they wanted – the only one of his works they wanted. I felt I had no choice – I had to sell it to them, even though I did not want to part with it. I've never seen it again. It's not hung.

Helen Band, whose father, C. S. Band, championed the Group of Seven, in her wonderful way has promoted native artists. She once put a lot of pressure on the AGO to mount an exhibition of Morrisseau's work, because he is the father of the Woodlands School. Roy McMurtry, the politician, got involved and helped put the pressure on. So, finally, the gallery put on a show called Norval Morrisseau and His Followers, or some such thing. They never contacted me – never. They didn't even use one of their own curators. They chose Tom Hill and Elizabeth McLuhan. I was appalled when I saw the show and came away convinced that they had deliberately put on a mediocre exhibition – even the works by Norval were not the best works they could have selected, and the whole thing was watered down by some paintings that were just bad imitations of Morrisseau's. What they should have done was a stunning Morrisseau retrospective – that has yet to be done.

The exhibition was panned in the press. John Bentley Mays quoted Roald Nasgaard as saying that they didn't want the show, but they had had to mount it. I thought it pretty disgusting that he'd admit that to the press. But, obviously, they now have a justifiable reason for saying that they will never have another exhibition of native artists.

So much for the bastions of Good Taste. I'll take the *pissoir* any day.

October 1984 – March 1985

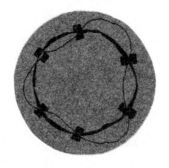

October 24, 1984

Dear M.

I arrived back from a short trip to Paris yesterday at five-thirty, and found my front door boarded up. While I was away someone broke in, stole my new cassette player (the second time I've been robbed of one) and a tumbler filled with coins (all the extra sous I had to my name, about eighty francs).

Jean-Pierre had nailed boards over the glass and had changed the lock, so I had to wait until nine for him to arrive home. The villagers are truly wonderful. The small restaurant Chez Tante Yvonne gave me a *pastis* and dinner while I waited. I am outraged, hurt, and wondering when this shit will turn to sunshine. I had to go to the *gendarmerie* today. They feel they may have some clues and believe it to be the same youths who vandalized the Bar Estaminet a few weeks ago. I didn't sleep much last night so I am tired.

I have enough francs to survive tomorrow, and will phone the bank to see if monies have arrived. If not, I will run tabs, and somehow make ends meet. I think I will get a dog. A *big* dog.

November 1, 1984

Dear M.

Today, I became a family man. How does that grab you? I have invited Marc, the twenty-three-year-old son of a local shopkeeper, his "woman" Sylvie, and her (not his) five-year-old daughter, Jessica, to spend the winter here.

As I write this they are moving in: a washer, a stereo, two dogs, two cats. (I always was a gentleman of excess!) The plan of the house gives them the two top floors as a kind of apartment, so I believe it will work.

He is out of work and her job finishes this week, so money is tight. I can help a little, and gain some company and a sharing of basic expenses.

I was not looking forward to the winter alone in Lou Paradou, and to try to find Mr. Right is, quite honestly, stupid. So, now I have a reason to cook–and I do love children –so I trust it will be a base for me during the heaviness of the winter.

I hope some money arrives soon, as the tabs at the bar, the grocery store, and Tante Yvonne, the restaurant, are mounting. I would have thought *something* would have sold, but I realize my new work is not what people expect. I know you told me to paint more saleable things, but shit, it's not that easy.

Anyway, each day passes, I feel very well physically, and try to produce a bit. No paints, no canvas, so I draw a little (not much paper) and write.

It is true when you say that I write like I paint. But for me to edit, reduce, expand, and all that crap, would eliminate any of the immediacy I feel. I could not accept another's analytical assessment and redigesting of what I attempt to communicate. The biggest problem, of course, is that I realize I am a lightweight in the overall scheme of things, and that hurts. My only consolation is that I *try* to create. I work at expressing my visions and feelings. If they are, as you suggest, quick and undisciplined, then *tough shit*.

In another twenty years no one will care anyway! I will not leave a major work in the history of anything. I just hope I touch someone, somewhere, in the ups and downs of my roller-coaster life.

(Sorry, got carried away again.)

74

Dear M.

I have just returned from the café, where I sat for an hour in the brilliant provençal sun and sipped a *café crème*. (*Café au lait* is *passé* as a phrase here, I find, and used only by tourists.) The temperature is about seventy degrees. I feel truly blessed by the weather. The lilac bush is in bud, and crocus are blooming. I have no idea what will happen to them when winter comes.

I have not been very creative these past weeks. I think my talents limited and of no real importance. Last night, to try and jolt myself, I started to write a kind of memoir of the early days – I am so frustrated because I have now pages of names, places, artists, and dealers, but cannot separate dates and times. I figure if I continue with loose observations and compile a list of people and places, I can, if I ever get to Toronto, put dates on, as I know the reference library on Yonge Street has a huge file on both me and the gallery.

Maybe through reviewing my past, I will stimulate some self-belief, so lacking, and so needed right now.

Where were you in the late fifties? I picture a WASP-Rosedale background for you. "Comfortable" was the word used in those days, I believe.

Enclosed is a *petite histoire*, a beginning, perhaps, of what might be an interesting personal observation of the art scene over the past twenty-five years.

Do you think it worth pursuing?

Douglas Duncan
The art scene in Toronto in the fifties was dull, and to most of the young, budding talents, seemed anything but democratic.

Laings Gallery, on Bloor Street, just west of Avenue Road, was the reigning emporium of good taste. Blair Laing brought us International Quality (well really not "us," as his mother, Mama Laing, hovered about, bird-like and dressed mostly in black, exuding a kind of neurosis, and seemed to make no one welcome unless they wore a three-piece suit, suitably padded with a chequebook). On the walls there were drawings and paintings by Augustus John, Ben Nicholson, Graham Sutherland, along with sculptures by Henry Moore, Barbara Hepworth, and other British greats. Italian Marino Marini's horse and rider images jostled with the splashy presence of France's Bernard Buffet. Krieghoff was relatively important, the Group of Seven had found acceptance, and people like Borduas and Riopelle were among the token Québécois. The Roberts Gallery, on Yonge Street, was what the Roberts Gallery is, a constant bastion of conservative establishment quality. Sure and safe, most pictures were scaled to the panels of Rosedale homes, and "over the fireplace" paintings were in much demand.

Birks, then Ryrie Birks, had a gallery on the second floor which specialized in European art of little or no true importance. Most pictures were landscapes or seascapes. Horses, sheep, and the occasional peasant figure would appear. All seemed varnished within an inch of their death.

The Art Gallery of Toronto (now the AGO) continued its club-like support of those who established it. Again, most of its choices were safe and sure, with the occasional international exceptions.

With the private gallery scene so sparse, it was logical that the societies would thrive, and, by a kind of collective bargaining, make their presence known. The Ontario Society of Artists (OSA) was the leader in this field, and their annual "open" exhibition at the Art Gallery of Toronto was supposed to be a highlight of the season. Judged in those days completely by insiders, this show bred patriotism, incest, and in many instances elicited justifiable anger. The old saying that it's who you know, not what you know, seemed to apply to most of these groups. They continued their back-patting ways, and so many young talents in a state of post-pubic searching found very little acceptance or understanding. However, just south of Bloor Street, off Yonge and up two

76

dreary flights of stairs, was a society of a different sort. The Picture Loan Society was alive and inviting, always pulsating with the energy and excitement of promise. The name, rather too proper and stuffy, belied the warm and casual atmosphere. The gallery served as a breath of fresh and vital air in the smog of accepted, safe, establishment taste.

Douglas Duncan, the proprietor, was as close to a saint as one could possibly be in the crazed world of art and artists. An independently wealthy gentleman, he had through education and art training earned the respect of his peers. His keen eye and articulate conversation bridged the gap between painter-client, producer and public, with an ease and graciousness that won the hearts of all.

The society worked, as I understand it, much as a library and exhibition space. I believe it started as a means of introducing art to friends but soon became a major fibre in the warp and woof of contemporary Canadian art. It survived over twenty years, but after Duncan's death in 1968, the magic and caring by necessity evolved into an attempt at solid financial security. This seemed impossible, and sadly, the doors were closed a few months later.

I cannot remember the first time I visited the Picture Loan Society, but I do recall the warmth, generosity, and concern I felt. Any private gallery visit in those days seemed an intrusion for those of us, insecure and penniless, who sought inspiration and encouragement. Climbing those dark, twisting stairs, I would be met by Duncan, his old-school appearance softened by upturned collars and sometimes by the threadbare elbows of his cardigan.

Though not at all affected, he created an effect of natural trust and comfort. Many painters now known and successful, and countless others overlooked in recent, trendy years, were striving to make a mark, to explore and answer the challenge of the new. Duncan seemed to understand. He took the time to look, listen, and somehow breathe art. Long, lean, and slightly awkward, his shock of sandy hair always falling in a rakish way, he possessed an aesthetic presence that was borne out by the quiet, yet strangely energized timbre of his voice.

This gallery was no palace of prettiness. There was no room for the ornate or precious. Several rooms were stacked with pictures, leaning against walls, tumbling from racks and closets. The atmosphere was that of a gentle cyclone, cluttered, unruly, and filled with the excitement of discovery. Even on special occasions, such as openings, the walls would be lined with works, askew, hung, and casually clustered, not quite organized. Dedication, and a genuine love of art, beauty and nature created the special presence felt by all.

Most patrons are, surely, patronizing. Nothing could be further from that truth in the unstinting support given his artists by Duncan. Never a businessman, money was not one of his gods; it was not a demi-god either and just seemed a necessary nuisance to be tolerated, and often forgotten about. The proof of this is borne out by the stack of undeposited cheques found after his death. To this day there are people who have paintings on their walls they rented but never purchased from Duncan. His erratic filing system relied on trust and goodwill more than on business logic. Alison Ignatieff loves to tell a story of her mother, Mrs. Grant, and Douglas Duncan. Mrs. Grant purchased a small picture, paid for it, and waited for its delivery. Over three years later, Duncan arrived at the house with the painting. He crawled with it on his hands and knees to the second-floor flat, sheepish and amidst gales of laughter. He loved the painting and had kept putting off the separation. Douglas Duncan's dream, and it was used as a magic key to knowledge for thousands, was to begin a dialogue, to attempt through confrontation and conversation an honest understanding of the visual experience in art, thus providing a forum for discussion and acceptance.

As I write this, there are hundreds of picture loan galleries across the country, many of them in our major public museums. They carry on the Duncan tradition, all are surely more solid business structures. But none have or can achieve the intimacy and the unique structure of the Picture Loan Society. Most Toronto collectors, many with little or no means in those early days of middle-class achievement, used Duncan's picture rental service as a major tool in learning and in building their collections.

David Milne, that lonely genius, haunted and often in self-imposed isolation, was sheltered from what he considered the "performance world of art" by Duncan. Through loans, purchases, and the greatest gift, moral support, Milne was protected and supported in the firm and solid way that only an independent and caring believer such as Douglas Duncan could afford. I recall a cold and dreary day in the late fifties. It was spring, and Jack Nichols, a teacher at the Ontario College of Art, was having an exhibition of his wondrous inky black lithos, which he'd recently completed while in Paris. I arrived at the Picture Loan Society, chilled to the bone, and was immediately offered a cracked mug of steaming tea. As I drank and feasted on the richness of Nichols' imagery, Duncan approached me, and asked, somewhat in the manner of a Tom Sawyer-Huck Finn disclosure, if I would like to see his latest discovery. I was then solemnly escorted into a small room, and there, on the floor in a shapeless cardboard box, was a glorious Jack in the Pulpit plant. The woody earth which contained it gave off a fragrance I have never forgotten.

Many years later I was in a posh gallery on 57th Street in New York City, and viewed a room covered with earth. No magic fragrance here, no tenderness or joy. Just earth, somehow antiseptic, rudely placed, and arrogantly attempting to assume a presence.

So much for progress.

Thank you Douglas Duncan.

P.S. That exhibition of lithographs and drawings by Jack Nichols has remained fresh and powerful in my memory. The lithos are, I believe, some of the finest prints ever produced by a Canadian. Their rich, mysterious surfaces speak of Nichols' personal twilight world. Circus figures, as tragic-comic symbols of life, became personages of depth and human feeling. They are not, as in the powerful case of Georges Rouault, heavy and compositionally lead-enclosed. Rather, they seem infused with a sense of weightlessness and levitation. They speak of light from darkness, knowledge from the unknown.

January 14, 1985

Dear M.

I am freezing! My hands and feet have not been warm for over a week. The acrylic is stiff and won't move on the paper. I sit next to the fireplace, pondering my life – past and present.

Your letter arrived Monday, but I have resisted writing until now, because, as you know, I am trying to get my shit in some sort of order. One letter a week, and try not to be too heavy. For the past two weeks I have survived very well – no money, bills outstanding, but no sense of panic or despair. I feel a lot more together (for the moment) and work at my "mad-motor" pace. Working from nine in the morning to eight at night I am painting a new series of pictures of bottles (I have finished over thirty works on paper and three canvases) and I am now working on a new idea of marrying barbed wire with flat floating shapes in colours that belie hostility and anger.

I know I should have arranged for representation in Toronto when I was there. I do not expect you or anyone else to devote valuable time to my problems. I also cannot expect Barbara Rosenberg to act as a warehouse, so I have to get something going. I am now waiting for replies from the Canadian Cultural Centre in Paris and from Hart House about possible exhibitions.

Sometimes the Man Pollock feels very much the child. I wonder if the Man M sometimes tires of his broad shoulders and of being so understanding? Although I feel depleted of true force these days, I would like to hold you to return some of the support you have given so freely to others.

The lifestyle I have chosen or that was chosen for me, seems to thrive on a youth-oriented ideal. Body beautiful is demanded; attire is allure. And, like most gay men, I have played the game – positive and negative, yes and no – projecting to the world at large the image I desire to have, but not what I truly *desire*.

Today I rest, scarred and marked by the ravages of my own indulgence. To me, you have remained whole. Interestingly, my sexual fantasies, my "jerk-off thoughts" rarely involve the people I know or love. This separation seems to be at the heart of my problems of true communication.

I have decided that all my signals point to not wanting to have anyone too close. No love affairs, no madness. I have become (or perhaps I am just realizing it) very self-contained. I am not sure if it is good or bad, it just seems to be the direction I have chosen, or that has been chosen for me. For the time being it works.

We both seem to have reached a similar point in life – the autumn of our days, or some such shit. Our paths, God knows, have been as opposite as possible. You, holding back, perhaps living a vicarious existence at times. I, jaded and filled with the emptiness of past excess, find stimulation and relief more and more elusive. You canter or jog. The hundred-yard dash is for me – breathlessly pushing beyond logic to "test my invincibility," as you once stated.

But I feel we both share desires – the largest, I believe, the giving of pleasure, assistance, and support to others.

I have often "taken myself in hand" with you as the object. But my respect for you would not allow me to continue the process. So I wallow in worlds of unknown steamy pricks and balls, not wanting to degrade our "special world." That, to me, is sick. I feel that at the base of this problem is my total disgust at what I feel, think, and crave. Calvin must be somewhere waiting in the wings!

Enough is enough!

Dear M.

Well, last night was interesting. Marc and Sylvie said they had friends arriving from Paris. Could they stay here overnight? Of course.

I got up this morning and two stunning black men – aged about thirty – were sitting in the middle of the floor in front of the fireplace, surrounded by what must be thirty or forty pounds of grass. They were separating, sorting, and weighing it.

Maybe that is why Marc does not work but always seems to have a little money. He and Sylvie inhabit the upper two levels of the house and I never go upstairs. Maybe Lou Paradou is the centre for grass in the region. *Mon Dieu!*

At the moment, I am, I suppose, what one would call "stoned." Sitting over hot chocolate, I thought – why fight it? Join it. So here I am, joint in hand (no, not *that* joint, yet), having just read your New Year's letter, which arrived today with your cheque for the deposit on the self-portrait.

I guess I'll have to invest in a full-length mirror to view the ravages of time, and attempt to achieve a graphic but not *too* obvious portrait of myself. (I am reminded of a song from my youth – "You have to accentuate the positive . . .")

I don't know the book *The Sexuality of Christ*, but the Christ-prick image has always fascinated me. The erection has been the prototype of great art and architecture of all times. Phallic church spires, pipe organs, glass and steel towers. Limp does not seem to survive in a world demanding hard and ready service. What flaccid architecture do you recall? Gaudi's buildings in Barcelona and Cardinal's in Canada, and Frank Lloyd Wright's use the earth and its undulating forms, but they were far from flaccid. Most buildings are truly erect. Most master paintings have a triangular method of construction, the zenith of which is the point, the thrust, which carries vision throughout the picture plane.

I have just realized that, maybe thanks to the dope, my feet and hands are tingling and feel a little warmer, while my crotch is getting slightly restive. I am aware of the silk lining of my leather pants against my thigh and the coarser surface of the leather against my trinity.

I am looking at the two young men (Nabeel and Jean) and thinking of Françoise Sagan's *Chocolate for Breakfast*. I look at their thumbs – the closest I can come to a measurement ratio for speculation. My throat feels very dry. I lick my lips constantly, getting into a kind of rhythm. I am aware of my tongue teasing my teeth and continue the game. A minute seems like an hour, and I become fascinated by the second hand of the travel clock in front of me. Countdown to the end.

I just found my left hand on my thigh. The leather feels chilled but blood seems to rush and warm a swelling in my loins. Pull yourself together, Jack, or pull yourself apart! The importance is in the pull. The joint passes and I twist from the waist, as my lower half is, at the moment, strained.

Jean gets up to go to the john. I hear the power and force of his piss stream and visualize the pipe through which it is rushing. Nabeel is grasping his crotch, but all the French do that. I try to imagine it is a secret signal, a tease that will lead to a please. The toilet flushes and Jean returns, tucking in his shirt. His fly is agape and becoming. He zips it up and I regain a brief moment of clarity. I *am* stoned! The feeling is strange and, although not unpleasant, not a barrier breaker either. I am aware of pulling (that word again) the centre of my concentration out of my balls and into my brain.

As I sit here contemplating this truly extraordinary scene, I have to stifle a laugh. Moments ago, I had visions of "Black & White & Hard Forever," but now the pants slacken; a return to reality from a supposed high. It dawns on me that I have not a cent of money and no wood left and I am harbouring a mini-drug ring in a twelfth-century house, complete with crypt. Now I am not sure *which* is the high.

"Oh, thank you, *merci.*" They have just made a pot of tea. Tastes gritty and slightly acrid. It is warming, however.

Sylvie and Marc are playing, teasing, and obviously warming up for later. Their bed upstairs has a percussion section, and I have always marvelled at the precise rhythm and the almost identical length of time it takes for their nightly romp. I look at Nabeel and Jean. They are or could be instructed to be more creative and imaginative than a thing that goes bump in the night. I think they already are. A bit of the old, racist stereotypes of jungle and savage flash through my mind; all the trite images from colonial days – Leo, king of the jungle, knows who lays down the laws. God is black. The blacks don't know what we know; they still suffer from the Sunday School System. This idiocy feeds my fantasies of missionaries-savages, daddy-little boy, foreman-hired hand, boss-worker, master-slave.

My hands are cold again. The left one finds its way to my crotch, feeling heat coming through the leather. The fingers start to move to improve circulation. It does, it does!

All this is happening at the same time as my eyes are fixed on the pattern of the cloth on my table – black, plum, scarlet, green, ochre – an ancient provençal design, much like a Paisley print from Liberty of London. There is a tiny cut through the fabric, and loose threads challenge the totality of the design. At this moment, I recognize the greatness of Proust.

I have stirred an erection while drinking the visual cup of colour. I find it impossible to record the multi-levels at which I sense the things around me. I taste the tea again; it is lukewarm and strong. The major smell is of burning wood. I think about incense or cologne but prefer this raw, natural odour of wood.

Marc is taking our guests for a short drive in the country. I wonder if black balls shrivel faster in the cold than white ones. I make a note to check it out – sometime. Balls! That reminds me of the leather thong I fashioned from the cuff of my pants, after I lost my cock ring. The steady pressure suggests I put it on. It is stuck in my pocket, pressing against my growing cock.

I hear the door slam. I stretch, allowing my hand to retrieve the thong from my pocket. I smell it. It smells good and is pliant from lubricants as diverse as Vaseline and suntan lotion.

It smells wet. I stand up and put my crotch near the fireplace opening. The leather heats up and so do I. I turn and start massaging my bum. It wasn't bad thirty years ago. I remember my Aunt Sadie, spinster sister of my mother, always saying, "Jackie has a bum like a tame bumblebee." Some bum! Some bee!

I sit down on the couch and put my feet close to the fire. The soles of my boots bubble against my cold toes. The bubbling spreads and I feel the tingling and teasing heat. But my mind has forgotten my prick; it rests semi-dormant, the leather thong still twisting between my fingers.

Potheads Don't Do! That slogan from the sixties flashes across my brain as I realize that I will do nothing for the moment about my dangling dong. I'll just relax and enjoy the flames. God, the pleasure-pain syndrome is everywhere! The fire is beautiful, hot, and desirable, but potentially destructive. What allure! What presence! What ultimate power!

The second hand of the travel clock becomes the world again; the world as it turns, twinning tease and torture. At one moment we cling desperately to the stability of the present, then we wish for release from the simple act of decision-making. So, I rest, trying to return to logic so that my letter can end on an up.

January 16, 1985

Dear M.

The two "night visitors" are still here, as is the stash of African weed. I feel Lou Paradou is no longer my place of peace and quiet. Another mood, another spirit, has entered it, and I am living a kind of alien existence.

I left Canada for the peace and simple life of Provence, striving to come to grips with whatever life I have left, and I find myself in the midst of a drug ring. Fortunately, it is not "the drug of my choice." I have no idea how I would have handled that.

85

The menagerie is getting on my nerves. Dogs, cats, people, no hot water half the time, and yet I fight confrontation. But, I have no money, and they do buy pasta, soup, and potatoes, so I do eat. (An added insult to me is that God would send me a couple of "pot heads" who don't drink, so don't buy wine.) I don't know how long they intend to stay. Let's drop my "nightmare" for the moment.

You must have been around Toronto in the fifties. Do you remember the TSO Prom Concerts at Varsity Stadium? The Chez Paree, the Concerto Café with Greg Curtis playing the guitar and singing? The Casino trying to become legitimate and show-casing Billy Daniels, Johnny Ray, Eartha Kitt, and others? La Colombe was a tiny French restaurant on Gerrard Street, owned by Rita and Henri La Goff.

The Bay Theatre's darkened tiers were quite another story —wet-dreams material made real. What about the old restaurant that was for men only and served soup-kitchen food? Dessert was always in the washroom.

Anyway, those days were memorable. Philosophers' Walk on warm summer evenings; Queen's Park and the bandstand that was destroyed to make room for the equestrian statue that now stands there. Glory holes at U. of T., the Rex, Rio, and Gay theatres. Oak Leaf, Continental baths, cab drivers, store clerks – anyone, anywhere – and, of course, High Park.

I worked briefly for M.J. Crozier Company, designing and sewing original women's hats that were sold at Holts, Creeds, and at The Room in Simpsons.

I had met G on Bloor Street and was having a "steady" (as steady as I could be) affair with him. He was living with his mother, brother, and sister and was the breadwinner in the family. He had been in the war and was ten years older than me. He was possessive and jealous. I was highly charged and devious.

We went to Florida, New York, Rochester. I was accepted and loved by his family but couldn't continue the façade of "oneness." We "saw" each other for seven years. Then, after a few wild years, B (ten years younger) came along. It has been almost ten years since he and I broke up. I have been alone, since then, and now it seems that state will be permanent.

What the fuck. Here I am in glorious Provence, realizing that you have to eat the cherries to be stuck with the pits. My heavy and constant past appetite seems to have caused an avalanche of pits.

January 18, 1985

Dear M.

I did it! I composed a letter – the first I have ever written in French. I told Marc that the grass had to be removed immediately, his *noir* friends had to be out by tonight, and he and his family had to look for other accommodation as soon as possible.

It worked! I went to Tante Yvonne's for soup (on the tab) and returned to the hustle and bustle of packing. They have all gone – dogs, cats, the lot.

The fog persists and the air is thick like carpet underpadding. Visibility is nil, and the valley below is a solid sea of wet grey. The stone of Lou Paradou seems to be permeated with the dampness, and only my bedroom, that stale and musk-filled prison of my escape, is warm, thanks to the electric heater, which seems to bake and intensify the scents of toe jam and spent semen.

I've written another *petite histoire* for you, and will send it with this note.

London, 1956

Fog, dampness, and in 1956, London. I had arrived on the maiden voyage of the *Empress of Britain* (by destiny more than by choice). My original booking was a Greek freighter, which quietly sank in the Montreal harbour two weeks before my planned departure. The travel agent felt duty-bound to help me, as my trunk of worldly possessions was already in Montreal (on shore, thank God) and so was able, at no extra charge, to book me on this posh and elegant floating hotel. (My cabin was rather close to the engines in the bowels and I shared it with an Englishman of dubious background and rather lazy habits of hygiene.)

But there were bars, festive meals, a pool, a cinema, and for five days I pretended to be grand.

"An art student, how interesting!"

"Slade? Rather a fine school, old chap."

And on and onwards.

A purser and two of the stewards made midnight madness a remarkable crotch memory.

Finding a studio place in London was not easy, but the *Times* ad section put me in touch with Flo, a wonderful woman who owned a three-storey house on Fernshaw Road in Chelsea. The going rate was five pounds a month. I could only afford three, and explained this. As her sister and her two children had been evacuated to Ottawa during the war, Flo was happy to welcome a Canadian, and I moved in.

Chelsea; King's Road before it became Peacock Alley; the pensioners in their red-jacketed, aged wisdom; Fulham Road; the World's End pub and the Black Cat Coffee House, which two friends of Flo ran. After three disastrous days working in the Brompton Hospital for consumptives (they gave me a body on a stretcher covered except for enormous white waxlike feet to take to the freezer), I took off and, depressed, returned to Flo. We talked. She had heard me singing about the place, and next thing I knew, I was standing in the coffee house, emoting à la Belafonte "Scarlet Ribbons," "Yellow Bird," and enjoying it. I was accompanied by a skiffle group.

Enter one Brian – handsome, older, and visually crotchbound – mine.

A brief fling, a long lunch on board a large houseboat docked nearby, and I was offered a "position" using techniques and talents not too related to my choir studies at Perth Avenue United Church.

Brian ran a discreet, well-organized operation from the boat. We, the commodities, were fitted (so to speak) with clients for mutual satisfaction and, for me, substantial financial gain. I am, as you know, dear M, a giver, and I was (damn it, still am) a horny beast of lust, so I thoroughly enjoyed my brief career as fantasy fulfiller for the mostly upper-crust clientele of the boat-bank.

It was a school of higher learning in the age-old profession, and I quickly learned about "slap and tickle," the erotic naughty-boy syndrome, and found that no such thing as deodorants for men existed in the British capital.

Priests were plentiful. One fine "servant of the Lord" became a regular. I would be dispatched to his lofty and beautifully appointed church late at night. I was costumed as an altar boy – black gown and white lace surplice – ushered into the sanctuary and stood on one side of the altar, he on the other. I urinated in a chalice – he, never touching me, masturbated, and that was it. He was about forty, handsome and kind, and one night, after the ritual, I asked if I could, another time, touch and truly service. His reply to me, sad and never forgotten, was that his interpretation of celibacy was no physical contact with another, and he had worked out a solution, this strange erotic vignette, that he could comfortably live with. The compassion I felt for him was tempered by my anger over a man-made structure that denied the natural functions of man.

That period of my life was the only other time I wrote letters. They were not like these I write to you – crazed attempts at self-knowledge – they were links to my friends and family, and, as now, I would wait for replies.

One week, two, over a month, and no note, no card, no communication from anyone. I finally sent a telegram to my sister, angry, then went to Canada House, thinking perhaps some mail would have been addressed there. One of the joys of an embassy in a foreign country is they have all the newspapers with news of home.

This particular day, on the front page of *The Telegram*

(Toronto) was a photo of my sister Gladys and an article stating she had been killed in a car accident.

Gladys was a year and a half older than me. We were very close. She, the first to know of my "alternate longings," accepted them and continued to love me. She had three small children under six and was eight months pregnant with her fourth.

I had to go home and, in my inimitable style, decided to hitchhike from London, England, to Toronto. I made it.

London to Liverpool: two nights on benches in the train stations, days haunting the docks. Finally, a captain of a Norwegian iron ore ship, the *Sally Stowe*, offered me passage in the cabin-suite occupied by him and his wife. I played at assisting the sailors (no, not that way). I peeled potatoes, tried to tie knots, and became a kind of mascot to the crew. The crossing took twelve days, the last two were horrendous thanks to a battle between the tail end of a hurricane and the *Sally Stowe*. Finally, we arrived at Wabana, Newfoundland. The chef packed me a big lunch, and I was on my way, by ferry, to St. John's.

My sister Audrey's husband, Harold Barrett, was born and raised in St. John's and I spent a few days with his delightful maiden aunts. Then onward, and four days later I arrived in Toronto, tired but well.

I have always enjoyed hitch-hiking and still often find myself on the twisting roads of Provence, thumb out, in anticipation of the journey.

March 28, 1985

Dear M.

One year ago today I arrived at your office with a bunch of mimosa and a strange green plant. One year ago tonight, over fifty people came to wish me *bon voyage* with champagne in plastic cups. I left, leaving behind a mess of tattered ends, bits and pieces, and taking with me the firm knowledge that when I expired I would, at least, be away from those who care.

Yes, I truly did expect to die. I had spent the monies I had; I had given as I always have given. Now I am in some kind of shock, realizing that I have survived and may be around for a while, but with no idea how to handle the future.

It has been over two years since the receivers, the landlords, and all the powers that be collided and collaborated to plunge me into a deserved Hell. I cannot place blame or guilt on anyone or anything but myself. The mess with Eva, B, Lou Paradou, the receivers, seems to be something that will not end this side of my grave. It goes on and on; no answers, no explanations, just continuances and the gnawing unknown. A sense of true worth escapes me and whatever I do never seems enough.

Talent is something I find more and more confusing. Work? Well, I have established some patterns that seem to be productive. But my general state of mind is without self-respect or pride.

Lou Paradou is like a large garbage dump at the moment. I have not had a clean sheet or towel for over three weeks. The refrigerator is empty except for a few disgusting bits of mould-covered leftovers. My priorities are strange since, although I wallow in this filth, I paint on pure white paper and insist on cleaning my brushes more often than I clean myself. I shave about once a week, bathe every three to four days, and recycle my clothes. Why should I bother to keep clean?

That's a shitty attitude and I know it. My self-respect should make me try to live in cleaner surroundings. Respect for Lou Paradou should make me, at least, sweep the floors and take out the garbage. But I sit here and vegetate when I am not painting, still waiting for the eternal sleep or whatever.

The mistral has been blowing again for a few days. Maybe tomorrow the long-awaited spring will arrive for a longer stay than the one or two brief glimpses we've had so far.

I know that most people who know that I am still alive feel that because I am in glorious Provence I have no major worries or needs. But the opposite is true. My worries and needs here are deeper, more real, and can't be temporarily erased by excess, except by painting and writing. Even jerking off has become a bore and I wonder if a great deal of my problems stems from never having truly understood the functions of that Holy Trinity between my legs.

Power-playing quite often covers up gross insecurity. Masters are mostly terrified of being slaves. By over-reacting they somehow succeed in the game of bluff. But you don't need this crap, and I wonder why I bother to write it. Perhaps, in the process of putting it down, I might understand it better and accept it a little.

The new paintings are going well. I am concentrating on a still-life of boats, feeling a bit like a whore. But they are strong and bright and, I think, better than before. The *Fenêtre* series still fascinates me, and the bars on my window, the *épis*, have almost become a logo, a signature.

My show in Marseille opens on April 17. I would truly love it if you could be there. It has been a long time since we had a true consultation and I am in great need of a shoulder. Maybe the waters of Vichy would be good for all. I promise a tidy, neat Lou Paradou – clean sheets and some good food.

April – December 1985

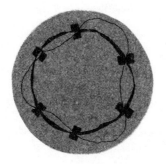

Dear M.

This morning is glorious! Sunny, warm: the mistral has cleared the sky of all but the wondrous blue of Provence. My peach tree is bursting with flowers, and the world seems at peace.

How I survived the winter I don't know. I have never really known true aloneness before. After B and I parted, I lived a lot of the time by myself, but steam baths, orgies, "drugs and sex and rock and roll," as the kids say, protected me from loneliness – and destroyed me. Here, although the villagers are truly caring, I have lived alone, been alone, and had to put up with me alone.

I am not as bad as I thought. The real problem has been to do things for *me*, not for others. I still have to clean the house, and get laundry done, but this morning I feel a little more like doing it.

I spent the weekend finishing a large still-life and looking at the recent paintings I have done (about a dozen new canvases and thirty works on paper). These are the results of the first year of my life I have dedicated to painting.

Most of the new still-lifes are complicated. Many have paintings hanging on the wall behind objects and plants. They are more planned and take a little more concentration, but I am not sure they are any better than the earlier ones. The new series of constructions are small (8" x 10", 10" x 12") and give a sense of playfulness. Old hinges, bits of wood, worn-out paint brushes and empty tubes, all combine with canvas and paint in a light-hearted view, the opposite of the *Lacoste* barbed-wire heavies.

The show I have been asked to do in Marseille is two weeks away, and I have to decide what to exhibit. The two large *Lacoste* ones are important. I now have about thirty *Fenêtre* series on canvas, and about twelve still-lifes.

The consulate feels I should attempt an exhibit in Toronto, but where? (Perhaps the Club or Roman baths, as I have exposed there so often!) Kidding aside, I have no idea of who, if anyone, might be interested in showing the works of this degenerate has-been, now living a pure (well, almost pure) and celibate existence.

You are supposed to be the man with the right words at the right moment. Look in your crystal ball (or balls) and see if there appears to be a logical path for me to follow.

Remarkably, I can still feel a sense of purpose and have not lost my sense of humour. I had trouble smiling most of the winter, but it seems the sap is starting to run, and I might be catching spring fever. It's about time!

As Tallulah Bankhead said, youth must have its fling. I wish someone would fling a youth at me!

P.S. Add this *petite histoire* to your collection of versions of *moi*.

Brother André
Brother André, as this tale has been labelled, happened when Eva and her husband, David, and Phillip Ottenbright (now manager of the Mira Godard Gallery, but then working for me), and I were on a holiday in France and staying at Lou Paradou. Eva and David had the twin-bedded room on the *premier étage*, Phillip the large double bed on the third floor, and I was content in the tower room.

We had been touring that day, and after a wonderful meal we retired for the night. It was after midnight, a full moon bathed the upper room in a cool yellow light, and the canopy of stars seemed endless.

I had probably drunk too much coffee, because I couldn't get to sleep. Then, from the darkness, I heard a voice, "*Attends, attends*," and a whistle. I sat up, looked across the ancient tiled roof, and in the window of the presbytery saw a handsome young man, the upper part of his body visible and nude. He pretended to be calling his cat.

I whispered, "*Bonsoir*." He smiled and returned the greeting. "*Il fait chaud ce soir*." "*Oui*," I said. "*Je suis un peu amoureux*." He replied, "*Moi aussi*," and stood up to show a large and beautifully erect penis.

He was only about ten feet away, but we could not connect, so I stood and fondled my ever-growing member while he ejaculated in an arc of moon-lit liquid over the roof. He then whispered to meet him at the door of the presbytery at eleven the next morning.

The tower room is made accessible by a trap door, always open, and the carved stone staircase, which leads through the large bedroom to the mezzanine. When I went down the next morning, Phillip asked who the hell I had up there and how did I get him in. He had heard my fucked-up French whispers and couldn't figure out how I had sneaked someone past his room. Phillip knew me well, and when I explained the night's unfolding, he broke up. Then I had to enlist his aid in occupying David and Eva while I kept my date with the youthful spectre of the night.

I arrived, discovered he was the brother of the priest and visiting from the north of France, working for the summer. We tossed, tumbled and took off, and I met Phillip, Eva, and David on the square for lunch.

After a day tour of Les Baux, as we were returning, David said he wished we could eat at La Mayanelle, a good restaurant in our village. He had been trying for a week and it was always full. I asked him to stop, went in, and soon arrived back at the car saying we had a reservation for nine that night. We were given the finest table on the terrace, overlooking our wondrous valley, and enjoyed a bottle of champagne and a superb meal.

The maître d', smiling and knowing, was Brother André.

I dined out on that and other *petites histoires* for quite awhile. Tony Calzetta (a fine painter now represented by Mira Godard) titled a large abstract painting, *Brother André.*

So it goes.

May 21, 1985

Dear M.

Today I am feeling content. Yesterday I received your letter in which you say you might be able to come to Gordes, if only for few days, later this year.

I know you will love Gordes, and the villagers will love you. They love me, even though they call me *Monsieur Bizarre* because I dress in black leather most days. That's a bit kinky for a little village in the south of France.

There are several good restaurants in the area, and there are also some wonderful, little, local bars. The Cercle républicain, which is at the top of my street, is a very old Communist bar. It's the only private club in Gordes. Private club! You pay twenty francs a year for membership! All the old guys, the veterans of World War II, are there at six-thirty, seven in the morning having a drink (booze, not coffee) and they're there until evening.

The *haute société* of Gordes I have little use for; they're big fish in a little pond, and they're forever trying to artificially inseminate Gordes with chic. They hold endless cocktail parties – and that's part of what I wanted to escape when I left Canada, so I stay away from them.

When you are here, you must meet Monsieur and Madame Vincent. They live in Les Martins, a tiny hamlet about two kilometres away – the place where George and Alison Ignatieff have their home. The Vincents are a tiny couple, both under five feet. She looks like an older version of the Campbell Soup baby: a wonderful woman and a superb cook. Behind their house they keep pigeons, rabbits, goats, and a donkey. They make *chèvre* and pigeon pie and all sorts of wonderful, peasant dishes. They never buy any food – they grow everything they need. A wonderful couple. He worked in the sulphur mines when he was a child, and during the war he was a leader of the Resistance. He was arrested and incarcerated in a concentration camp for four years. They put him in a cage where he couldn't stand up – for over a year.

They hate Germans here, and it's understandable. It was a centre of the Resistance. Chagall was hidden here for the first year of the war until they got him to Marseille and then to America. Charles Étienne, a great French writer – Jewish – lived in my house. One of the reasons they love Canadians here is because our troops would fly over and parachute in supplies. They would land in the Luberon mountains where the forests were so deep the Germans would get lost. But the provençal men, including M. Vincent, knew every little road. So they'd get the supplies and keep on winning the battle.

The real tragedy was that two days after Armistice was signed, the Germans, in total frustration, bombed the village on market day and killed over two hundred people. No wonder they hate the Germans here.

There's another bar I'll take you to, the Estaminet, run by Suzanne and Max and their boys. Suzanne runs the bar most of the time and Max and the three kids work in the bakery. They start work at midnight, work all through the night making *baguettes* for the morning, then start again for the evening *baguettes*. They go dry so quickly, you wouldn't serve anyone a morning *baguette* for dinner.

The Estaminet is the bar for the young people, teenagers really. I like going there so I can tease them, and they tease me right back. One young man is really beautiful. His name is Pascal, but we call him Frisé because of his blond, curly hair. He has a body like Adonis. He has about six words of

English and asked me once to teach him some more words. I told him that when he meets English tourists, he should just say to them, "Bend over." He tried it on the tourists who came to the bar. Of course, they just looked at him as though he was out of his mind. We all roared. But he figured it out and one day he just came up to me, turned round, and bent over in my face!

They're good kids. They take out my garbage every week. Frisé comes by every few days, and I let him try and paint. A wonderful kid, the whole village adores him.

Well, dear M, these are some of the people you'll meet. Now I'm off to the Estaminet for a drink.

June 11, 1985

Dear M.

You ask about my one-man show in Marseille. Well, I was very proud of the show. I had over fifty paintings and constructions hanging. The opening was very well attended – hundreds of people came. It was a gala event. The local newspaper gave the show a rave review. I never sold a single picture.

That was depressing.

June 16, 1985

Dear M.

I am sitting in the Hôtel de Brest, in Vichy, the day after my opening, trying to cope with time warp, disappointment, and strange vibrations.

The past week to ten days has been quite bizarre (read: typical Pollock). Thursday past, the day before my friend Alex (who snores) was to arrive with his son, the electricity was cut off. The same day, my butane tank for the stove ran out, and I had about ten francs in my pocket (about $1.50).

I should have been depressed, gone into a funk, but I laughed (perhaps a bit hysterically). I went to the local Co-op (grocery store), got a tank of gas, and provisions for a grand meal (seven courses), including four-dozen candles, and charged it. Alex arrived, not only with his son, who is a sweet young man (twenty-six, and street-wise), but with his daughter and her husband, who are in real estate.

Candles burned, I prepared dinner and all of them were truly impressed. The daughter and son-in-law rented a chic room in a local hotel, Alex and Chris stayed at Lou Paradou.

The next day (Saturday) I took them on a tour of villages in the area, ending in Cavaillon, for a drink in Le Pub before dinner at Lou Cantalou (five courses, forty-two francs).

In Le Pub I met my friend Christian and told him my story of the electricity. He paused, went over to another table, and returned with a friend. They asked how long I would be in Cavaillon. I said we were eating next door, and we arranged to meet after dinner for a drink. Chris (son of Alex) wanted some hash, and so I mentioned it to Christian.

After dinner, we returned to the bar. Christian and his friend suggested we drive to Gordes, to my place. They had hashish and also the tools and special equipment to turn on my electricity. It turned out that Christian's friend works for the hydro here. So, at midnight, we were sitting in Lou Paradou, with lights, and smoking up. Miracles don't cease!

Alex had brought with him over five hundred dollars from the sale of some of my paintings in Toronto, so I bought stretchers for my recent canvases, wood for frames, and glass and clips for the works on paper. I still had no idea how the pictures would arrive in Vichy.

I arrived home about midnight one night to meet Penni (a young lady) from Boston (*very* preppy) whom Chris had picked up at a concert. She was hot to trot, he was more than willing, and she owned a station wagon. The rest is, as they say, history. They fucked, they loved it, and she decided to come to Vichy for the opening. We loaded the station wagon the next morning and arrived here in Vichy at five that evening.

The Centre municipal is a beautiful space, but the France-Canada Society, which is putting the show on, is what one would call retarded. No invitations were printed, the posters (which are beautiful) were not put up (nor printed with info). I was truly upset.

However, we got the show hung (fifty-two works, over half of them new). The opening was attended by about seventy-five people. Gerry Conrath, her husband and mother and father-in-law came from Aix. The consulate, Terry Cormier, arrived and speeches were made. The mayor of Vichy welcomed me, and bought a small collage with Canadian stamps. They had invented a cocktail in my honour, which was truly disgusting: dry white wine, and maple syrup imported from Canada for the occasion. I decided that I should get pissed because I was so upset, but no amount of booze made any difference.

This morning it is cool, grey, and I feel more relaxed. I also realize that Vichy *is* a *station thermale* – the average age must be seventy. My hotel is one of many with full *pension* and I have just finished lunch in a room full of face-lifted matrons. Most tables were covered with pills, eye droppers of strange medication.

Oh to be a gigolo! I hope I find an aging queen with lots of loot, one foot in the grave and the other on a banana peel.

July 4, 1985

Dear M.

It is ten days now since I hitch-hiked into Apt, planning a drink in the Café Grégoire, which is a hangout for pimps and punks, and a quiet dinner chez Daphnis (La Taverne du Septier).

While sitting at the bar, a beautiful young man, clad in jeans and wearing dark glasses, said hello, and asked if I recognized him. He removed his shades and I realized he was Alain, the chief waiter at the Mayanelle restaurant in

Gordes. We had a drink, and a few other young men joined us. We ended up at a small *crêperie* called Le Gamin for dinner. There were six of us, all the others young and very attractive. At ten, I suggested I call a taxi for Gordes. Alain said no. He would take me home on his "moto." I suggested he may want to stay with his young friends, and he said *no* again and that from the first time he had seen me in the restaurant (over six months ago) he had *desired* me.

My sex life in Gordes has been, as you well know, entirely masturbatory, so I felt excited, and truly blessed. When we got to his bike, he insisted I wear the only helmet. We mounted, and he said to hold on tight to him, and placed my arms around his waist. He took my hand and placed it where he wanted it, and as we began the journey I discovered an enormous erection. About two hundred metres out of town, at a speed of no more than perhaps twenty miles an hour, the bike hit some sand at the edge of a curve.

I recall tumbling off. The next thing I remember was limping to the prone body of Alain – calm, still, and like death. I knelt and touched him, called his name, and felt he was warm. His pulse was beating and he still had an erection.

I stumbled into the traffic and stopped a car. The police, ambulance, etc., arrived and soon we were in hospital in Apt.

I was bleeding rather badly but insisted I was fine. Alain, they said, was in a coma, and they prepared to transfer him to the reanimation unit in Marseille. At four in the morning, after having my exterior wounds cleansed, I arrived home, alone, in a taxi.

I didn't, and couldn't, sleep for two days, partly because my ribs were paining me tremendously. I went to the local doctor and discovered four broken ribs, and my left index finger broken. The hospital in Apt had not done X-rays, as I had said I was fine. When I finally called you I was, I thought, in slight control.

I have refused all pain killers and tranquillizers, and just seem to exist in an aura of pain and guilt. I realize that firstly, it is not my fault, secondly, that giving the helmet to the passenger is the etiquette of the road, but this twinning of passion and pain, desire and disaster, is truly a nightmare.

Yesterday, Jean-Michel of Murs, a small village close by, offered to drive me to Marseille to see Alain. The trip was filled with pain, and seeing him was truly frightening. He is beautiful, and, as I said on the phone, lying nude and tanned on the whiteness of the hospital bed, he looked like Christ in a *pietà*. The specialist stated he was not in a coma, but unconscious. His brain and body both function, so please, God, it is a matter of time.

Dearest M, my life goes on and on, and I seem to be confronted with more than my share of trials and tests. I am tired, weary, and although *not* suicidal, do not really care about being alive tomorrow. My attempts at a *vie simple* seem totally impossible, and I suppose I resign myself to the fact that I am in some way possessed, poisoned, polluted, and will never find peace this side of death.

Most of my previous trials have had an element of humour, possible to explore (sometimes after the fact). This horror is too real – too much to absorb – so I sit, and cannot paint or feel.

I hope this letter makes some sense. I am truly thankful you are there, and only hope we all survive (Alain, you, me) until you come here in September. I cherish the idea of your visit.

August 4, 1985

Dear M.

Well, I survived another year! My annual Birthday Bash was larger, more strange, and wonderful than ever! About one hundred people came, all in costume.

Togas, tights, clowns, saints, and sinners, all combined to create a strange Fellini-like ambiance. Sam, young man from Saskatchewan, wore a crown of real thorns (complete with drops of real blood!), brief shorts, and a T-shirt with the slogan "I just don't love you anymore. Yours sincerely, Jesus," and a bullet belt.

There was dancing in the crypt. Anne de Boismaison-White sang a complete aria from God knows what opera. Christian from Cavaillon sang Edith Piaf, and the children (yes, there were about ten children in clown costumes) sang provençal folk songs. For a brief moment I felt as though we were part of "The Sound of Music."

The fête lasted until dawn, and when, around nine, I tumbled into bed there were probably sixteen or eighteen people bedded, single and coupled, throughout the house.

The next day, having slept for over twenty hours, I felt rested and also a strange sense of time warp. Eight of the remaining nine young people packed their back packs and left, hitching to such varied places as Rome, Aix-en-Provence, and Berlin.

I've been thinking of death a lot, and I am amazed by its inevitability, frightened, as we all are, of the totally unknown, and yet feel a long sleep is somehow earned by those of us who live on the edge.

AIDS is certainly a big news item these days. Rock Hudson's visit to France was duly reported in our local press. The fear must add a tremendous weight to most sexual encounters, and you are probably striving to give support to many who have seething loins and terrified minds. The Moral Majority has a great tool in this nightmare, and I fear a backlash.

I find that my masturbatory fantasies are much more real and satisfying than most of what I may encounter, if it should happen. Freedom of excess within the personal and private realm of one's thinking seems more potent and charged than the interaction of two. Egotistical? Selfish? Probably.

Casts of thousands, impossible worlds of carnal lust—they all exist in the imagination and fire the crotch in a way not possible with others. Excess—I suppose that's what I am about.

My sense of mediocrity is at present overwhelming, and I feel that my personality far exceeds my talents. Art is life—

creation is often environmental. I suppose as a work of art my life is a masterpiece of the excess. A kind of trashy novel of sensational experiences.

I am not suicidal, but I feel totally burnt out and lacking spirit and energy. Yes, I can, and do, perform, but at what expense! I don't know – I just keep on going – to what end I am not sure. Is there masturbation after death?

August 5, 1985

Dear M.

Birthdays. My god, the fêtes here are marvellous.

I recall my fiftieth birthday – I guess everyone of our age recalls that birthday especially. I was here at Lou Paradou and decided to invite several friends over from Canada to help me celebrate. David and Eva Quan came; Michael Kierans, a great harpsichordist; Johnny, my dear friend and former coke dealer; Marg King, who used to work in the gallery part-time; Helen Boyd, who later worked as my secretary; Grant Lay; and two or three other people arrived whom I didn't really know very well.

The night before my birthday, Grant, Michael, and Johnny drove me into Cavaillon to the bar for a drink. Then it turned midnight and, technically, it was my birthday. We drove on to Avignon because Michael persuaded Grant and Johnny that the three of them should find a young man to bring in my fiftieth with me. We toured the old ramparts, but there wasn't anyone there to our satisfaction. We drove to the train station and there, standing outside, was a stunning young blond man, knapsack on his back.

Michael said, "Stop the car!" The car stopped, Michael got out and spoke to the young man in fluent French, the young man nodded and smiled and came back to the car with Michael. He was ushered into the back seat beside me. He was Austrian, eighteen, a student, hitching around Europe – and he was coming back to spend the night with me! Michael had clued him in completely.

We got back to Lou Paradou to find that everyone else had gone to bed. The only room left for me and my "present" was the crypt, right off the dining room. So in I went with this beautiful young man, not really expecting anything to happen. However, he was very desirous and active. He had what I call "helium heels" and his legs went in the air! I didn't know what to do; I had no lubrication. But on the table was a jar of royal jelly. Grant, who is a health fanatic and enjoys the best of foods, had bought it at great expense from the beekeeper just down the road from Lou Paradou. I looked at the jar, I opened it, and I dipped my wick, so to speak, and proceeded. It was very lovely.

When we woke up in the morning, everyone was sitting around the table in the dining room, having breakfast. We scurried and put on some clothes and tried to walk out gallantly and casually into the dining room. There was a moment of stunned silence. Then we all got over feeling awkward – until Grant made toast. He said, "Oh, I must get my royal jelly." Before I could think how to stop him, he went into the crypt, got the jar, spooned some out onto his toast, and ate it.

I never said a word.

September 13, 1985

Dear M.

I am at a loss for words (a rare experience for me, as you know). Your presence here in Gordes was very special. Seeing you as a real human being, even for such a short time, helps me realize why I continue to believe that some sense of self-worth is essential to life. But I seem to have somehow created the image, not the reality, of self-sufficiency.

I wish I had a positive grip on my life, but I seem to float, procrastinate, and, although, as you said in a letter, I do get some things done, they just don't seem enough. I wonder what the hell to do next.

No crystal ball will help. I know the answers to all our problems lie within ourselves. I just hope I continue at least to survive.

Sex, the once masterful role of my life, is now reduced to mentally sucking, giving oral pleasure, and truly enjoying it, but with a limp, large dick. It seems able to rise only to the solitary occasion – and it sure does rise, often as many as four times a day, when I set the ritualist stage for masturbation: leather thong tied around my cock and balls, a single candle burning, Vaseline (lots of Vaseline), first on my nipples, then my dick, slow, teasing strokes and fantasies – fantasies built on the realities of past experience.

It would be wonderful if I could find someone who could understand, be patient, and maybe return the true joy of sharing. I feel, however, that is all in the past. Why the fuck does everything have to be so complicated?

You are right. At the base of my problems lies a spoiled brat. Having wonderful people caring just makes me feel more seamy and more perverse.

Maybe, had there been more time during your visit, I could have unwound a little more. I was very nervous, and wanted you to experience a taste of my Provence. Surely, if you enjoyed your stay here, you can plan a longer visit sometime. Maybe I will have my shit together more.

October 18, 1985

Dear M.

Today is grey. The first mistral of the season approaches, and the air is filled with change. I have worked like a soul obsessed since your too-brief visit. Over sixty black-and-white drawings, plus a new series of still-life paintings with sunflowers. (No, I will *not* cut off my ear or anything else.) I have never felt comfortable with sunflowers, as Van Gogh has made them his. However, last Sunday, I was given some late-blooming sunflowers. They are wild and their petals dance; not the hard, circular centres of Van Gogh. I saw them and was hooked! The series (six so far) are, I think, some of the best things I have done. I sold two of them, so the voyage to Canada in November is now possible. I am making handbills for the village for an open house next weekend, and hope to sell a few more works.

So, here I am, surrounded by the musk and age of Lou Paradou, giving myself a pat on the back for merely surviving. Not many needle addicts do, you know, and, although purity remains a fantasy, I have come a long way from the bottom. I have always envied the temperate in you. You seem capable of measurements of time and emotion, and excess is rarely indulged. The flip-flop of my behaviour is truly exhausting, and I do wish we could exchange a few genes.

I expect to be in Canada by the 15th of November, with a return ticket. I shall stay three weeks, a month at the most. One thing I intend to do is some research for my memoirs. Until you mentioned Hugh Conover, I had completely forgotten the T. D. Gallery. Janet Conover worked for me at one point in my checkered career, managing my ill-fated gallery in the Toronto Dominion Centre. She and Hugh are good people.

I had two locations on Elizabeth Street, then Markham Street, and Phase II, a first, a loft gallery on Portland Street. Then Dundas Street, then Scollard. Then, then, then – my not so graceful fall from grace. God, I cannot believe it all happened to me.

November 1, 1985

Dear M.

I wonder – when I come back to Toronto, will I have been forgotten? Out of sight and out of mind? It's been the fate of several people who have contributed a great deal to contemporary Canadian art, some of them giants in their time. I think especially of Barbara Wells and Dorothy Cameron.

Barbara founded the Artists' Workshop, in 1951, I believe. The Workshop was originally held in an old coach house off

Sherbourne Street, and then it moved a couple of times. It was one of the few places in the 1950s where artists could gather – a centre of the art scene long before there was an art scene. It filled such a need. Barbara offered classes for those who wanted them, but it was the chance to draw nude models *without* instruction that became so important to many artists. It was the only place, other than the Ontario College of Art, which was stuffy and very constipated, where you could do this. Jack Bush went religiously. John Gould went religiously. Many artists, such as Graham Coughtry, could frequently be found there. Students would find themselves next to Jack Bush, or Thelma Van Alstyne, or some other fine artist, and by osmosis an exchange of ideas and attitudes would happen.

Later, the Workshop became the Three Schools of Art, and the original concept, sadly, was destroyed. Barbara later ran the Wells Gallery in Ottawa, but has now retired. I just wonder if people do remember Barbara. She is such a fine lady and contributed so much.

Dorothy Cameron's first gallery was the Here and Now Gallery on Cumberland Avenue, where she pioneered such artists as Louis de Niverville. She then moved the gallery next to Av Isaac's gallery on Yonge Street. It subsequently became the Carmen Lamanna Gallery and is now an autoparts shop, or some such thing.

Dorothy is a wonderful, vivacious, bright, outgoing, fun person, who has an extraordinary eye for art. She discovered Josef Drenters, a marvellous sculptor. She showed Rita Letendre, Ron Bloore – she married Ron. But one doesn't hear of Dorothy Cameron any more.

Dorothy, tragically, made the news at one point, when the powers that be in our crazy, Protestant city brought a charge of obscenity against her. (I was a witness on her behalf in court.) She had put on an exhibition, Eros, of erotic drawings, paintings, etchings, and sculptures. She had covered the windows of the gallery and posted a sign warning that the show was for adults only, because she had anticipated there might be a problem. There was: with some brush-ink drawings, black and white, by Robert Markle, of women in positions suggesting that they were lesbians.

They crucified her. She was found guilty. I think the trial broke her spirit somehow. She was never the same; the gallery was never the same.

The irony is that, at around the time that Dorothy was charged, I was showing in my Markham Street gallery John Bennett's erotic paintings called *The Ladies*. They were huge, of women with their legs aspread, vulva for days. I had no problems. A year or two later, in his shop next door to my gallery, B had purchased and was exhibiting *Bag One*—the first and only portfolio of lithographs by John Lennon, done just before and during his courtship with Yoko Ono. They were highly explicit—oral sex abounded. We expected to have problems, but there was none. The police arrived, but they laid no charges.

I said then that I thought that obscenity is in the groin of the beholder. And I still believe that. I do not believe that art should ever be censored. People are free to go into a gallery or not, as they wish; buyers (including public galleries and museums) are free to buy or not, as they wish; artists must be free to paint or sculpt what they wish, too. In those days, what was truly obscene was the Vietnam War. We tried to make those points: PADAC banded together to support the right of the artist to freedom of expression.

The other obscenity charge I remember was against an exhibition of Mark Prent's sculptures at Av Isaac's. I could see the thinking behind that charge a little more readily because Prent's sculptures are really quite graphic and vicious. But I think Toronto has grown up a lot since then. Now there seems to be a more sane view of art and of what art is. Except that I hear the censors are now going after films and videos.

What madness!

Dear M.

You can't go home again! (He was right, whoever said that, the bastard.)

Three weeks, three minutes, three years? God, time goes quickly these days. I have finished four small stamp collages and am working on the design for the Outdoor Art poster. Sleep is intermittent, and I am suffering jet lag here. Of course, here I can relax, and rather than being on stage, can be Jack (whoever he is).

My brief stay (perhaps, to you, not so brief) in your home was very cathartic, and helped me put many things in perspective. In the past I have been lonely, whereas here I am simply alone. The masochist in me all hangs in there. I realize now that I've spent two years trying to sever a cord that should have taken two minutes. Then the guilt, the shit, the snowploughs of running away. For what? I wasted almost four years of this precious thing we call life.

I am truly thankful that with your help, and the support of those who should have given up long ago, I made a decision. I left. My grandmother used to say, you burn your ass, you sit on the blister!

Well, it hurt for quite a while, but the blisters turned into lucky horseshoes, and the rest is history.

I love you.

I think perhaps this past few weeks have shown you the sentimental slob I really am. I know that the leather I wear, the barbed wire in my pictures, scare the shit out of people. They don't realize that they are symbols, maybe protection for the skinny little kid that used to hide from PT at school.

Our dinner that last evening was so special. I wanted to ask you to show me your etchings again (now there's a line), and I wanted to tell you to continue to draw and sculpt, but I was afraid of making a fool of myself. Also I was terrified of fucking up this special friendship. It is really interesting, the only time I thought seriously of cocaine while I was in Toronto was my fantasy of sharing it with you, breaking the barriers, damning the dams, and going for broke. Broke – well, that gets me to where we left off. How the hell will I survive? Do you think all the accolades and applause will turn into what the bank, the hydro, and the wine merchant needs?

It was so strange, I couldn't ask Av or any other dealer to look at my work. I sat chatting with Walter Moos for almost an hour, my portfolio with all the small works between my legs, closed. (Is that Freudian, or what?)

Maybe someone will see the works at the Koffler Gallery. Paul Fournier, whom I truly respect, told me they are fine paintings. Karen Wilkin, who curated the Bush show, said they were highly contemporary and very fine art. (What the fuck is *fine*?)

I must say that having visited about twenty galleries in the short time I was there, I rest content about my own work.

Who the fuck knows what art is anyway? I can tell when it touches me. I can feel when I get a physical reaction. The juxtaposition of the portrait which hangs on your wall and the head of the sculpture on the table beneath, is really a lesson in seeing.

But back to you, dear M. I don't know how to handle my sense of knowing that you're the big one, you're the heavy, you're the support system for me, and for how many many others I don't know. But, shit, I'm a giver, and I bleed sometimes because I can't say how I feel, I can't handle you the way I feel you need.

Okay – enough – time to shut up. I will if you make me the promise you'll start making art again.

P.S. I'm sending you this piece I wrote after I got back to Lou Paradou. It is good to be back in Provence.

Coming Home
Coming home is always a delight and wonderment. The train station in Avignon is always filled to overflowing with a myr-

113

iad characters – wealthy northerners (most Parisians) jostle with hair-covered hippies left over from the follies of a flower power culture, Algerians, Moroccans, their swarthy skins cracked by the constant battering of the sun, their smiles revealing decay and gold.

En face – the ancient and time worn ramparts which surround the old town. Periodic *portes* lead in through winding streets and, magically, you arrive at the two main squares: place de l'Horloge and the place du Palais des papes. Street musicians, artisans, dope peddlars, all mix with the mélange of tourists and tokers. Cafés are crowded and the spirit is one of joyous celebration. Avignon, along with Aix-en-Provence, feeds the visual thirst for the past.

On the Route Nationale, leading out of the city, there are small industrial buildings and blocks of apartments in the limited style of most French contemporary architecture, and the south of France's answer to Yorkdale – the Cap Sud mall.

Passing small towns and hamlets you arrive at Cavaillon – the marketplace for the wonderful produce of Provence. The local papers exclaim over the first asparagus of the season, the first strawberry, the first melon.

It's a very unpretty city. The story goes that the city council, along with the wealthy export industry, commissioned a large sculpture to be the focal point of the roundabout that acts as a hub for the central core of town. The sculptor (no one seems to know his name) created a huge and realistic melon, which, being what it was, resembled the *moule de femme*, or female genitals. All were shocked, the project was rejected, and in place of what I feel would have been an amusing image, there now sits this enormous and ugly many-pointed star.

Wealth is in abundance in Cavaillon, so fine restaurants – Nicolet, L'Assiette au Beurre, and my favourite, Fin de Siècle – do very well, as do the specialty boutiques and gourmet shops on the small rue des Piétons.

Le Pub, a small, crowded bar, is the centre of activity for most of the young people in the area. Leah, the owner and barmaid, is an extraordinary woman. Dark, tall, and full of vitality, she is *pied-noir* (white French from Algeria) and runs a very tight ship. My bank (God, that's another story, my bank and me) is in Cavaillon, and I am usually in town once or twice a week (by thumb, of course). Le Pub is my local in Cavaillon, and I enjoy the visual delights of the young bikers and beauties there.

The ruins of Roman arches stand guard at the foot of the mountain (one of the Luberon range) that rises right behind the market square. Tuesday mornings all is feathers, fur, fake jewels, and fashion. Stands overflow with the vibrant colours of the local produce, while a dozen or so black Senegalese attempt to flog fake ivory, Zippo lighters, and more discreetly, hash.

The Fin de Siècle café is the focal point of this seamy end of the weekly market. A true treasure, a survivor of La Belle Époque, it plays host to the hustlers and the raunchier youth from the Vaucluse region.

David Bowie, Mick Jagger, stringy-haired youths, their ears pierced, their jeans faded, torn, and often filled with the tease of tightness. These are the *vilains garçons* of the area, their cheeks often hollow, their eyes often glazed and wandering.

Strange that on the *premier étage*, the Fin de Siècle restaurant holds court in a haughty and *haute cuisine* fashion. It is festooned with rich gold and burgundy velvets, fine lace table-cloths, gleaming crystal, and silver for days. Although not high on the Michelin Guide list, it is mentioned with favour.

As is the case with many fine smaller restaurants, it is a family affair. Son Hugues and his mother attend tables with attention to details. Daddy's in the kitchen, and Grandma prepares the vegetables, and so on.

The food is superb, and a complete menu can be had for under a hundred francs (wine extra). Rich *pâté de grives* (those tiny birds, not much more than sparrows), a casserole of *moules* in Roquefort cheese, breast of duck with raspberry sauce, fine lambs' kidneys in Dijon mustard sauce, salad *tiède* with lardons and chicken livers, plus a dessert menu of over forty sinful and seductive sweets. The cheese tray is exclusively *chèvre*, but what *chèvre*! Over twenty varieties from fresh and creamy to bullet hard and tangy, from pepper-corn-covered to a pyramid aged in ashes. Their wines are fine and reasonable (I usually have Gigondas), and soft classical music makes for an atmosphere of quiet elegance and calm.

Gerry Conrath and I discovered the restaurant about four years ago, and now I suggest it to all who enjoy fine dining at an affordable price.

An interesting aside: One evening earlier this year I was in town, at the pub, when a large black Harley Davidson pulled up, and a young man, leather clad with chains and mirror sunglasses, passed by me on the way in, saying *"Bonsoir M. Pollock."* I looked and tried to figure out who he was. Then I recognized the small gold earring, and discovered it was Hugues. I had only seen him before in the black-tie elegance of his role as maître d' of the Fin de Siècle.

We became friends, but still observe a kind of formal etiquette when I arrive with guests for dinner. (Lots of fantasy for foreskin foreplay.) He has, on several occasions, taken me the eighteen kilometres to Gordes, but since the Alain incident I have no desire to ride on a bike. As I wrote at the start of this letter, coming home is a sentimental journey.

Now, leaving Cavaillon we pass through Coustellet, and then after twisting between fields attended by gnarled and ancient olive trees, we take a turn and there it is – the jewel in the tiara of Le Luberon – Gordes.

Leading off the square – *en face* to the Cercle républicain (the only private club in the area), is an ancient path, its steps wide and flat for donkeys of burden in the past. On the right is the Musée municipal – a twelfth century chapel – superbly restored. It was here, in 1984, I had the first of my exhibitions in France. It was here, on the wondrous washed ochre stone walls, that I first showed my two faces of Provence – one the simple and beautiful joy of the commonplace in still-lifes of an almost child-like colour, and the other, the haunted, twisted constructions using *objets trouvés* from the ruined château of de Sade, aged wood, remnants of hinges, and the highly symbolic barbed wire.

Now, through the Porte de Savoie, an arch from the eleventh century, and there, on the left, Lou Paradou, the strange and supportive pile of stones I love.

It's good to be home.

Dear M.

Well, I suppose it had to come. The letdown. It's eight in the evening and I have not done a thing all day. Xmas cards are half finished, an article for *Canadian Art* just about completed, and I feel heavy, and for the moment, not capable of going on.

I sold five pictures while I was in Toronto and spent half the money before I arrived back. Does that make any sense? No. One of the purposes of the trip, as you and I had discussed it, was to flog my wares, as winter in Provence can be hard.

God! How juvenile I am when it comes to structure, responsibility, and discipline. I have always said, "The Lord will provide," and gone on my merry way of excess and indulgence. Well, I'm tired of living on the edge, but I see no alternative.

I am just plain weary (I slept ten hours last night, so it isn't lack of rest).

I think of you, Barb, and Ron, almost everyone I know. You all have a kind of structure, a bank account, and a respect, sometimes awe for money, and it brings a measure of security and some kind of stability.

I give lavishly (that fucking word, *give!*), because it makes me feel good. But is it truly giving when those people to whom I "give" end up concerned about my well-being and my income?

You, dear M, explained it best when you said that if I continue the way I have in the past, then I cannot cry for

117

help and understanding. You're right. But I need help in channelling my talents (if that's what they be).

I was reviewing my past year and a half in Provence, and I have worked, produced, and I think grown, artistically speaking. But what good is a product when there is no market? As you know, I would love to give all my pictures away, pay for a vanity press edition of my writings for friends, and just continue to produce.

But my name isn't E. P. Taylor or Eaton, and I am stuck with the miserable fact that I have no respect for money (I suppose that relates to no respect in *me*).

My Toronto visit endeared me to hundreds, *again*, and I was pleased to present the image of a whole me. I loved the theatre of the visit, and if you had ever doubted my star quality, you now know a little more how it works. But those hundreds have no idea of the fear, the needs, or the insecurities of "little Jack Pollock," the kid who never grew up.

You, more than anyone, have had a chance to be exposed to the strangeness and oddness of my being. I think I'm an arrested spoiled brat. Daddy, what do I do now?

I have a lot of strength and, I feel, common sense to give others (I can feel like "daddy" too). But the pisser is the advice I give, I don't take.

I suppose that's logical.

December 21, 1985

Dear M.

I awakened to sun, joy, and positive feelings. I have, however, just returned from lunch at La Mayanelle and M. Mayard, the chef-owner, had been talking to Alain's mother. He will never be completely whole again. He has a limp and his brain will always be slow.

I have written him, and sent him a "Toronto" T-shirt. I was so sure he would be well. I don't know how to handle the nightmare of that experience. His sister has written me and said he is *très touché* by my letters and he does remember me. He also retains his English, which he was studying.

God, M, why him, not me? I know–fate, destiny, all that shit. But he gave me his helmet. He desired me. It's as if the poor little bastard had a date with the devil!

No wonder celibacy makes sense!

Sorry to dump this extra but telling you about it helps.

December 24, 1985

Dear M.

It is Christmas Eve and tonight I have been invited to share the holiday festivities chez Jean-Michel et Françoise.

Eric's sister, Sophie, came down from Paris, and as the heat in Wendy and Eric's house is on the fritz *again,* Sophie will stay here for a few days.

So, tonight Jean-Michel, Françoise, Guillaume, Eric, Wendy, Sophie, Daphne (from Apt), *et moi* will celebrate with dinner beginning at midnight. (I would like to have attended Mass, but the Tomchaks don't believe.) Mind you, I have no idea what I believe, but I must say spirit has something to be said for it.

Anyone who knows me and saw me during my visit to Toronto must thank you, dear M, for a good portion of my survival. The old story of transference of affections was played out over a year ago, for me.

Now, I want to transfer affection the other way. I want you to need me a little. I want to feel your presence because you want it. I don't feel like a patient at all. A dreamer, yes, a loner, yes, a daddy and a little boy, yes, but not a patient.

I am not old enough for a rocking chair and shawl but I'm not a young stud either, and I look at the choices I made and wonder why.

You tell me so much, quite often, by what you don't say. But that's a bit of a bind for me, who splashes all over the place.

Neat and tidy, trim and tucked in. That's the way you

have toilet-trained yourself, and I wish I had some of that structure. You once said that none of those who admire me would want to trade places with me. I agree, and I wouldn't want anyone else to go through my shit. However, if miracles were possible, I'd love to trade some of my demented dimensions for some of your rigorous rules.

When things get really heavy here and the mistral of the mind takes over, I re-read one of your earliest letters in which you said, "Don't die!"

Thank you. I also won't choose to die! In answer I say, "Please live!"

December 27, 1985

Dear M.

Your second letter arrived today and I feel slightly dissolved. I'm afraid the more you see of Toronto, the more my name will crop up.

The year 1980 is one I would rather forget, although it ended with the publication of my book of poetry, *We All Are All,* and an exhibition of its original drawings at B's small gallery on Queen Street.

I flew to Paris with a friend. I was drug-ridden and in the early stages of severe endocarditis. I arrived in Paris delirious and, although I don't remember, apparently functioning well enough to insist my friend rent a car and drive it to Gordes.

Once here, I was taken to the small hospital in the village from where the young doctor, fearing for my life, shipped me to Avignon in an ambulance.

I recall very little, but I do remember waking up and finding myself in a white iron bed, the windows barred, and the ghost-like figures of white-clad nuns hovering about. Xmas and New Year's were spent in and out of consciousness and, around January 10, I insisted on going home – home being Toronto.

Nadine de Montmollin, my dear friend, was visiting the Ignatieffs and came to see me at the hospital. She spoke with the doctors, but they refused to release me unless a registered nurse accompanied me on the plane and a hospital in Toronto confirmed they had an ambulance at the airport and a bed for me.

Nadine contacted B and, one day, when I climbed momentarily out of unconsciousness, there, at the foot of the bed, was B with R, his new lover. R is a registered nurse. He had arrived to escort me home, give me my injections, and so on. As you well know, R had a difficult time with me as the ex-lover. All I could think of was, he could kill me if he wanted to and I was not so sure I would have blamed him.

To make matters worse, on the plane (as I was on a stretcher I had to buy seven seats for almost $8,000 – R had booked the tickets on his American Express card), who should be there but a friend whom B hated, as did many of my friends as they blamed her and others for my "fall from grace." You know, no one is to blame but me.

Sunnybrook: a patch-up job, and into the crazed world again! More cocaine, more needles. Then the discovery that there was a hole in my right heart valve, surrounded with infected scar tissue. Then osteomyelitis; then fungus in my blood. Six months in Sunnybrook. Open-heart surgery: December 16, 1981. Dead for eight hours. Back on the road again and again needles. Then the shrink ward and then you, and now – Provence.

You end your letter with a reference to the nightmare of disorder and aggression. Then you say, "speaking of which, all psychiatrists should spend a week or so with their patients." Interesting linking of thought process. Disorder, I know, abounded while I stayed at your place, but I hope my aggression was understood to be only my survival tactics. I do have a "mad motor" and the brakes are very difficult to locate most of the time. If I don't keep positively active, then the negative takes over, and you know the results. I feel possessed. Your inquiry whether I feel there is a foreign power within me strikes a familiar chord.

I often feel tainted and worry that the others around me

might become contaminated. I suppose that has been the reason (or a reason) for my having cut off good people by my self-induced destruction.

As I write this, I am reminded of Utrillo, the French painter who was hooked on absinthe. His mother, Valadon, would lock him in a room and, when he had finished a painting, she would treat him to an absinthe.

If I had my druthers, I wouldn't mind being locked up, so to speak, allowed to write and paint, then given a small amount of coke by nose (my nose is bigger than my veins), and allowed to masturbate for two, three hours, then sleep.

As I must be in control of all situations, my attraction to cocaine makes some sense. It is the only drug I know that breaks barriers, yet leaves the user totally aware of reality – heightened.

Strangely, and this might come as a bit of a surprise, I often wanted to be passive-anal when I was on coke and would indulge in elaborate preparations for the act. But I would choose that position and would be still, in my mind, top man. I loved it. Now that's justification for you!

December 28, 1985

Dear M.

The colour of grey lavender hangs heavy in the sky. Clouds don't threaten rain but they are oppressive and unrelenting. Today was the memorial service for Frisé. He was, as you know, a volunteer fireman. All the firemen in Gordes are volunteers and they're all young men, with just two older men in charge. There was a fire this summer in the Luberon, just beside the village, on the road to Murs. Frisé was driving one of the trucks when the mistral turned. The fire swept across the road and engulfed the truck. Frisé was trapped inside and burned to death. What horror! He was an angel, adored by everyone.

I stood with three hundred villagers in front of the *station des pompiers*. Just as the procession was about to begin, Jackie Chanon, the doctor, arrived and sent two young men volunteers off in one of the emergency fire trucks to assist in a road accident. The wail of the sirens set my teeth on edge.

About twenty firemen, dressed in their formal attire, then led the way, banner flying and large blankets of floral tributes held high, as we walked to the cemetery, about half a kilometre down the road.

I wore my black leather and was the only one bearing a personal floral tribute of three red roses. I fell into line beside M. Mayard, the owner of the Mayanelle restaurant. He had adopted Frisé as his son. Alain also worked for him. He is probably about seventy now. His daughter had married someone who was not interested in the business. He seems like a sad man, resigned to his fate. We embraced and I could feel the tears flow. Although I almost caved in during the ceremony, I survived it.

The graveside moment was brief. I left my flowers and we returned to the château, where, in the great hall, the mayor presided over a ceremony, bestowing gold medals of honour to M. Mayard and to the two young men who survived the horror of the blaze. Patrick now has two plastic hands, Christian, his visage ravaged by scar tissue, has the distant look of slight retardation. (He was in a coma for two weeks.)

I have been working on a collage as a memorial for Pascal (Frisé's real name). It is a painting within a painting and uses Red Cross stamps, images of gothic church windows, and of the raging inferno of a fire. These images are suspended in a tranquil, simplified landscape with a large *épis* on one side.

Bracing myself, I took the painting, titled *Requiem for Pascal*, and headed for the Cercle républicain. The fire chief was there, along with six or seven volunteers from the brigade. I told him I had a gift for the fire hall. He led another small procession of *pompiers* to the hall. We went into the ancient, one-time chapel that now serves as the room for the volunteers. I unwrapped the picture, attempting to explain it in French. I broke down and we all embraced.

We hung the painting and then I returned home to a wonderful meal prepared by my friends. It is ten-thirty. I am going to bed.

No, M, just blessed sleep.

December 31, 1985

Dear M.

New Year's Eve. I feel a bit like Scrooge with ghosts of the past cowering in the shadows. All seasonal celebrations produce a kind of artificial reality. For me, living the strangeness of my being each day, fêtes have been most times anti-climactic.

Do you remember as a child, fighting sleep, so you could go out on the verandah at midnight and bang the hell out of pots and pans on New Year's Eve? My father was always passed out drunk much before the witching hour, but mother would patiently allow us the pleasure of released aggression.

Not many New Year's Eves stick in my memory. One, when I was, I guess, nineteen or twenty, was with G in Buffalo. I must have mentioned G before. He was ten years older, had been in the war. We met in Queen's Park, and had a relationship for over seven years. Anyway, he had a car, so we drove to Buffalo and checked into what seemed then a very grand hotel. We went to a couple of bars and finally bought two barbecued chickens and two bottles of champagne, returned to the hotel, and had what I recall as a highly erotic (and tasty) grease-covered entry into the New Year.

Strange what one recalls!

The only other one that really stands out was in the early seventies – George Cohon (MacDonald's of Canada) had listened to my wistful longings one evening at his home about, as a child, always wanting a pet parrot and monkey.

Well, Christmas Eve came, I was about to close the gallery, go home to our (B's and my) townhouse on Davisville, to prepare for our annual trek to Peterborough for Christmas Eve and morning with B's family, then back to Toronto for my family celebrations.

A distraught cab driver came to the door of the gallery and demanded Mr. Pollock. He then produced a huge cage, complete with a monkey! After a moment of shock, I opened the card, and after giving the cabbie a large tip – wondered what the fuck to do with this incredible gift from George.

B was not amused. We had Charlie (a standard poodle) and Mr. Chips (a Yorkshire Terrier bought at Harrods) and the last thing we needed was a monkey!

Sophie, our Polish cleaning lady, was staying at the house overnight to look after the dogs, so we arrived home and presented her with "Harry," as I'd named the monkey.

He was a cute little bugger, and I began to get very attached to him.

B would go to the cage, rattle the bars, and make faces. Harry, who knew who his friends were, would turn around, put his prick between his legs backwards, and piss! The week went by – I fed him and cleaned the cage, and he would come out and rest on my arm like a child. The dogs were very inquisitive, so we kept Harry on a high table.

New Year's Eve arrived. We were, as usual, doing a number. Dozens of bottles of champagne were stuck in a snowbank outside to chill. We were in the kitchen preparing the food when suddenly all hell broke loose. Harry was out of the cage! Dogs barked crazily, the draperies in the living room came crashing down, and B went white with fear. He listened to old wives' tales, and one was that if a monkey bit you, you died!

Well, Harry made his frenetic way to the kitchen, perched on the fridge and viewed the scene. I quickly found a blanket and told B to take two corners, I taking the others, and we tried to snare him. He pounced, and landed on B's balding head, shrieking! He finally landed in the salad greens and discovered green onions. He smelled one, then rubbed it on himself and went into what I can only describe as a drug-induced euphoria. B by this time was almost in cardiac arrest. I watched and then made a path of green onions to the open cage door. It worked.

Harry left for the Toronto Zoo two days later.

But I did like him! He had a mind of his own. (By the way, it is true they masturbate a lot.)

So much for silliness. I wanted to let you know my life has had its lighter moments.

P.S. Going through the hundreds of clippings and photos I brought back from Toronto, I found these photos, which might amuse you.

The two interiors are of my apartment on Rosedale Valley Road, before the bomb and my rather hurried departure. The two drawings over the "crate" (a superb canvas by Claude Yvel, Paris, which is now touring Europe) are by Dame Laura Knight and are sketches of Pavlova, backstage. The double portrait is a wash by Cathy Senett-Harbison. She is now Cathy Senett, as her husband and father of their three beautiful children decided to run off with a librarian in Guelph.

Anyway, Cathy has invented the wonderful Wrinkles puppet dog that is the rage among kids now. I am the godfather of their eldest son, Aaron Albert, who must be fifteen now. I have no address for Cathy, but I gather from a *Maclean's* article just sent me, she is on the way to being a millionaire!

The small oil to the right is a superb Christiane Pflug, *Two Pigeons*. I had to sell it. Below is an early pencil still-life by Phil Richards, now with Mira Godard. Two of my collection of over thirty pairs of Staffordshire dogs can be seen.

Life certainly does change, eh what?

Now to the naughties! Drugs and sex and rock and roll.

I was going to burn these, then thought you, too, have a fireplace, so after viewing another slice of my life, you can

126

help me exorcise the strangeness of my being by burning these photos. All three of these young men were, and are, good people. Donald (now forty, I suppose) was truly disturbed. Once when I was in the middle of a class with my "ladies," the phone rang. It was Donald saying he had just been stabbed. I finished my class quickly and went to his apartment on Spadina. There was no answer to the buzzer, but someone came along and opened the main door. After pounding for awhile on his front door, Donald crawled to the door, bleeding badly, and terribly drunk.

The trick he had picked up was a bit more sado than Donald had expected. He'd pulled a knife. Thank God Donald was strong.

He decided about four years ago to live in Lisbon, and I don't have an address. I hope he is well.

No wonder I live in Gordes!

January – February 1986

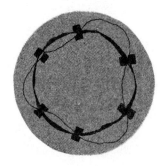

January 15, 1986

Dear M.

Perhaps now is the time – it's as good as any – to tell you of my total rejection of you as my shrink when you were suggested by my previous psychiatrists Eddie Kingstone and Robin Hunter. I yelled, said I was not going to see any psychiatrist, and almost refused to see you. I was feeling rejected.

I did test you initially, and I am sure that during my visits I was very theatrical. My great joy, and continued good fortune, is that you didn't give up on me. Thank you.

I find it amazing how we revert to our child-like/childish practices of acting out pain, guilt, rejection, and, as children, use any tool in the kit, including others, to help bolster our sagging selves.

I have never understood analysis as a treatment; never saw the point in going back, always reliving the past and trying to become aware of the social pressures that moulded our mouldy existences.

Both Eddie Kingstone and you (especially you) have attempted to help me get from yesterday, through today, and, with luck, into tomorrow. Surely that's all we have.

I think you will be pleased with my new work. The bottles are shapes (no bottle is complete) and excuses for problem-solving re negative-positive space and, of course, my first love – colour. The new barbed-wire pictures are strangely peaceful.

I draw-paint strands of barbed wire in black, then construct a simple abstract composition around them, using two, sometimes three, colours. They are soft colours, rich, and the torn paper shapes float. I am pleased.

January 19, 1986

Dear M.

It is eight-thirty Sunday morning. Vivaldi is on France-Musique. I have had my soft-boiled egg, *pain au chocolat*, and *chocolat chaud*.

I have just finished a large (three foot by four foot) canvas in the new barbed-wire series. That makes eight in the series so far. Their floating shapes intersected with painted strands of barbed wire fascinates me.

The overall appearance is of beautiful colour and torn, irregular forms. The barbed-wire makes its own statement, almost subtly, and with a kind of vicious subservient air. They (the pictures) suggest the glossing over of violence by the cosmetics of socially acceptable conformity. Strange!

Yesterday, I worked on some more small works on paper with pieces of bottles (just the necks, really) creating negative and positive shapes. A friend from a nearby village, Howard Apell, and his wife dropped by yesterday to see the new work. Howard is American, retired, and now pots and specializes in bottles. He was excited by the new work and we are talking about having an exhibition here in Gordes, called "Bottles," with my small works on paper, and his clay bottles. It sounds good, and may be a way to get some money in.

I have no canvas left, no paper, no white, nor several colours, but I do not feel depressed or any sense of panic. The taxes, the telephone, a new water and electric bill—they all sit and wait. Tough titty, said the kitty, but the milk's still good!

At last winter has arrived. Cold, but not bitter, and still, thank God, the sun. The mistral came and blew for three days. (I haven't blown for three days straight in a long time. If I recall, it was quite exhausting!)

Jean-Michel is one of the "innocents" you mention in your letter. His almost too-knowing understanding of me leaves just enough doubts about possibilities to make it continually teasing. Also, the final safety guard of my "Calvin closet" allows a verbal freedom that would not exist otherwise.

The attraction for the unattainable or the "just possibly" is the juice that keeps me going. Fate or destiny, as I have so often said, quite often somehow gives me what I need. Not necessarily what I want.

My sentimental and romantic spirit often does get carried away in writing and doesn't allow for the self-centred and detached me that demands my needs be met. If the lesson, or one of the great lessons in life, is to learn to live with another as one, then I surely have fucked up. Visits are fine and dreams of walking into the sunset are, I suppose, needed, but the day-to-day business of life is such a self-centred thing. And the professional do-gooders are more selfish than the rest. Their needs, like mine from time to time, are greater than most.

Extreme goodness covers for extreme feelings of insecurity and lack of self-worth. Christ, it's so easy to say – so facile to articulate and to understand – but doing it, making the balancing act work, that, dear M, is the problem. Certainly by now I should realize that I have worthy qualities that have earned me respect. Surely I should be able to say my work is good. But this child of the doubting twilight constantly needs support, touching, and to know that he is not alone in his questioning.

January 22, 1986

Dear M.
The sun still shines. Today is slightly chilly, but Lou Paradou is comfortable. I am a little heavy these days, for no particular reason.

With limitless hours for contemplation and introspection, I review much of my life, and realize how much I truly miss being where the action is – and the centre of it. The theatre of my past life gave me many roles to play, and they all aided my avoidance of the real. Tragedies and farces are extreme, and I seem to have been a perfect character actor in these extremities. Living a relatively simple day-to-day life, playing a down-played role, is much more difficult. Excess is easy – moderation is *merde!*

Is truth stranger than fiction? In my case, surely. This crap crops up, as I attempt to begin some kind of biography. The truth – unvarnished, and raw – is almost impossible to believe. I don't believe it all happened to me. But it did, and I suppose continues to be a circus of unrealistic proportions. Things haven't just happened to me; they have exploded, detonated, blown up. Any one of a couple of dozen disasters in my life would give someone else the reason for a book. For me, writing the truth is tantamount to writing a Cecil B. DeMille epic. If this sounds egocentric, I really don't mean it to. I just don't know where to begin.

Maybe I should start with the realization that I have never been able to give myself completely to another to love as the great romantics loved. Why? As a child I learned the lesson of rejection. My father never touched me. When punishing me he used a cat-o'-nine-tails, so that, even then, no physical contact was possible. No wonder that, at twelve years of age, I feigned homesickness and climbed into bed with my scout master during a weekend outing. The poor bastard never had a chance. I have often thought of him and realize that if that had been discovered, he would have been crucified and I would have been pitied as an innocent.

Later, when I was thirteen or fourteen in Woodbridge, I would walk across the swinging bridge to the barn dances in Fundale Park, position myself by the steamy, piss-filled trough and wait for men, many in those days in uniform (1943-44). They were hot and heavy, and most girls in those days didn't go all the way. I did. I suppose it was my contribution to the war effort.

Then high school, and on and on and on to a cast of thousands. The devious and cunning world of youth sets patterns that are all but impossible to break. High Park, Queen's Park, washrooms, glory holes, excess, excess, and to what end? Hollow physical gratification, the giving of pleasure more important than the receiving of it. The wheels turned, the patterns became a way of life. Now, I crave acceptance, pray for contact, and masturbate into oblivion.

I have always felt that teaching and communication have a lot to do with the seduction process. My success (and I was very successful on the lecture circuit) was partly due to my slightly *risqué*, suggestive style. Sure, I knew my subject, and could be articulate, but I believe the little devil inside, the imp, the seducer, was what made me different from most of the others.

My ability to draw unexpected responses out of others charged my batteries and, I think, inspired many of my students to take a chance – live a little – and break from the moulds of academic thought. Calvin must have been in my closet all the time because, strangely enough, I never took advantage of a student nor did I ever seduce anyone in the art world.

In the early days of my career (art career, that is) many of the major figures in the art world desired me. They were in positions of authority and advantage. I could not, and did not, use them. My success, whatever, was not built in the dark and bedroomed corners of that world.

It is interesting that my initial reputation as a speaker-lecturer was because Alan Jarvis would call and ask me to substitute for him whenever he was ill. I was terrified, as crowds used to come to hear the urbane wit of the ex-director of the National Gallery and they would find me instead. My good fortune was that later they started asking for me, because of me. But I have always felt a little sad that Alan's misfortune was a rung on my ladder. He had played the establishment game too well, and was a product of its fickle and unfeeling edge.

Nadine de Montmollin was his secretary in those days, and more than once, she has told me, after my first visit to his office (we were arranging the first Toronto Outdoor Art Show) Alan said to her, "Watch that young man. He is going places!" God knows, no one knew the places I would go!

I had it all, and obviously didn't feel I deserved it, so set about systematically to destroy the belief of everyone who cared for me.

Controls, like excesses, are patterns learned. Base insecurities are responsible for most of life's choices, positive or negative. Responsibility for others (me, students; you, patients) is heavy at times, but also very rewarding. I miss those responsibilities, and often wish I were back in the swim. If only I could count on the water wings of common sense!

My need to give is very hampered these days, and although the canvas and paper are willing recipients, they are not flesh and blood. They submit, but very rarely fight back, and the stimulation of exchange is not there.

So, back to the drawing board, on with the show. (No audience, just another dress rehearsal – alone.)

January 28, 1986

Dear M.

These days, I sit and wonder what madness is. Where does one draw the line between being withdrawn, eccentric, alienated, and being just plain nuts?

Doubts about everybody and everything crowd my head, and most of all, I feel my work is absolute shit. Yes, I go through the motions, I set myself problems and try to solve them. They work as problems solved, but who cares about that? I am building up another stack of "Pollocks" and I am tempted to burn them, tear them up. But I recognize that I am just a basket case of inner rage, and any destruction

136

of objects would be at best a temporary relief. I suppose it all comes from a lifetime of avoiding confrontations, problem-solving, and responsibility. External pleasantness and constantly taking the easy way out have a habit of building up inner anger and frustration. I don't even know what my hostility is about anymore. Sure, finances are tough, but that is the result of problems, not the cause.

I feel retarded in any kind of adult behaviour. Since I returned from Toronto, I have made a conscious effort to be in control. I eat well and strive to paint and write every day. I've finished writing a piece on the Gerrard Street Village, which I'll send to you. But none of it seems to relieve the pressure cooker of my head. Sleep is intermittant, frustration is constant, and I want to scream, break out, explode. I doubt all the caring I'm shown, and most of all, I doubt my own worth. I crave escape, but from what, and to what? God knows, and He ain't telling. No solution would be more than momentary, it seems. I remember my grandmother saying, "All these things are sent to try us." Try us for what?

It would be wonderful to believe that the hair-shirt, the pain, the isolation, was all for a higher, wondrous goal, but that, dear M, for me is the stuff that dreams are made of, and these days nightmares seem to be very à la mode.

I realize that I am building a great case for another "fall" – a descent from grace. And I could even justify it to myself. I think many people are waiting for me to fuck up, and the horror of it is that there has always been a morbid fascination for everyone in destruction. Death-defying acts are usually sell-outs, and, just as Madame Defarge watched heads roll, her knitting needles clacking, we all seem to be mesmerized by failure: not just failure, but grand, outrageous, excessive risk-taking. No-net, high-wire acts. Russian roulette.

This is what I seem to have been doing all my life—providing a perverse theatre of border-line destruction for others too timid (or sane) to do likewise. The worst part is I know it. I am not, unfortunately, stupid, and I'm aware of the daily death-defying acts I have continually performed. But I am tired. The carousel goes too fast. The needle seems to skip and scratch the record. (Shit, how's that for association?)

Anyway, I want off.

However, I go on. I continue to try and "put something in the pot" (whatever the fuck the "pot" is).

It is almost the end of January. Winter has finally come with the biting, bitchy mistral, and cold, damp greyness. However, February is shorter, and please God, the almond trees will give witness to survival. I am determined to see them.

Gerrard Street Village

The year 1960 was an end and a beginning for me. I had returned from London, England, in late 1956, had worked as a kind of colour consultant with Glidden Paints at Bruce Dougall Supplies at Bathurst and Bloor, and had ended up (or down) in the Toronto Psychiatric Hospital. Late spring, my nerve ends patched, I wandered the downtown area, seeking a place to call home.

Toronto, in those days, resembled a gangly, awkward adolescent. Sunday sports had at last arrived. The Silver Rail on Yonge Street made instant history as the city's first real cocktail bar. Beer parlours still had their Men's Room – with the added delight called Ladies and Escorts. The Victory Theatre (Spadina and Dundas) was a strip joint, and the infamous Casino attempted legitimacy with live shows of such performers as Eartha Kitt, Billy Daniels, and Johnnie (Little White Cloud That Cried) Ray.

In the midst of the hustle and bustle of downtown there was an oasis, a small area overlooked by most, tolerated by some, and supported by few. Gerrard and Hayter streets – between Bay and Elizabeth – were the remnants of a Bohemian past. Greenwich Village, as it was rather presumptuously known (Av Isaacs even called his gallery the Greenwich Gallery), was an aging spirit. It consisted of one- and two-storey workers' cottages, held up, or more properly propped up, by each other. Long gone was the ghost of Ernest Hemingway, who was supposed to have lived in the area, but a kind of independence and creativity flourished. Shops selling old collectibles – often posing as antique – jostled with Albie Frank and Florie Vale's studio-store-front operation. Barry Kernerman was a pioneer in the area with his Gallery of Contemporary Art, where he showed Painters Eleven artist Kazuo Nakamura, as well as Pre-Columbian *objets d'art*.

The old village was like a magnet, and I found myself outside a one-storey shop – empty – on Elizabeth Street directly across from the rear entrance to the General Hospital. It was for rent, and forty-five dollars a month, even in those days, was a bargain. So, in May 1960, I moved in. There was one large room, a partition at the back, a toilet, a sink (cold water only), and a trap door leading to an earth-floored basement, which housed an ancient wood-coal furnace.

The electricity had been cut off, and Hydro demanded a fifty-dollar deposit before they would restart it. After paying two months' rent, I had eighty-seven cents in my pocket, so for a few weeks I lived in the natural light of day and at night somehow managed in the dark (the odd candle provided minimum illumination). My mother donated a roll-away bed, some sheets, blankets, and a pillow; my sister some odd cups, plates, and a hot plate. I was in business. The window on the world, a large bay window with small panes of glass, dictated the future it seemed, so I placed a painting in it, and the Pollock Gallery was launched.

I had to survive (what else is new?) and I found a job teaching evening classes at the old (and infamous) YMCA on College Street. Then, somehow, the Ontario government heard of me, and I started to do classes and seminars for them. I began "showering with friends" and my rounds of the baths accelerated, as cold-water sink baths were not too pleasant. Once a month or so, I would rent a room at the Y and through the halls of open doors, whore. The proximity of the rear door (good choice of phrase) to the General Hospital, made visits by interns, doctors, and orderlies (a kinky lot, by and large) frequent and clandestine.

Two of the earliest and most consistent of my supporters in the village were Maggie Milne and Jack Grossman. I met them first at La Colombe – the tiny French bistro run by Rita and Henri La Goffe. It was on Gerrard Street, just east of Bay, and had an ambience and cuisine not duplicated in Toronto since. Onion soup thickly crusted with *croûtons* and cheese, *pot au feu*, and other simple French dishes, made it a haven for intimate dinners. I traded pictures for meals often. Jack and Maggie were regulars there.

A major problem, that of living in a fish bowl, thanks to the window on my world, was solved when Maggie made curtains out of bed sheets. I could then retire in relative privacy, roll out my bed, and sleep. Jack had a wonderful way of being there at the moments I was desperate. He would, in his slow, casual way, offer me a cigarette. He smoked Phillip Morris, which I hated. If I took one of his smokes, he would know things were bad. He would continue his village prowl and return with a sandwich, coffee, and a pack of my brand of cigarettes.

Pauline Fedio's large and spacious studio was a centre for tea and talk. Thelma Van Alstyne's studio on Hayter Street was filled with the incredible colour of her special world. Albert Frank and Pauline Fedio seemed to share honours as reigning monarchs. For me, however, there was only one king: Ken Dawson. Wonderfully haughty in appearance, clipped and articulate in speech, he suggested British aristocracy. His artificial leg lent him a rigid posture, and to everyone's delight, he was capable of the greatest sailor jokes in history. He sold second-hand things, but, unlike some others in the same trade, would readily admit to their recent demise as objects of affection. He painted a little, and lived alone above his shop. Harold Town was a friend, and a fine early portrait of Town's captures some of Ken's spirit.

Town worked in the village, where he produced his single or autobiographic prints, monoprints done on lithographic stones. They were exciting and adventurous, as were the powerful expressionist collages he showed at Laings a little later. I recall the hot and sensual pinks, not unlike the flesh of Rubens, and an egg carton not seeming to belong, but asserting a note of surprise and respect.

I don't believe Canada has produced a finer craftsman. With great sadness I watched him become the darling of the Women's Committee of the Art Gallery of Toronto. He was expected to be outrageous, and he was. I somehow feel he was so busy being Bad Boy (turtleneck sweaters at black-tie functions) that brilliant technique was all he produced for many years. I understand the AGO is planning a retrospective of his works. The Art Gallery of Windsor played host to the last major survey, but a total lack of editing, plus an installation that was eccentric to the point of absurdity, did little justice to the man or his gifts. I hope he shocks the pants off all of us and returns to an inner struggle and dialogue with the canvas. I long for the power and imagination of his early works, and would be disappointed if we are left with the cleverness and "look Ma, no hands" whimper of his *Horse Variations*. I guess we'll wait and see.

The most solid establishment in the village was surely Mary John's restaurant, on the corner of Gerrard and Elizabeth. A soup kitchen in the thirties, in 1960 it served fine home cooking, lots of it, at prices that even I could occasionally afford. The service was "family personal," and the ambience totally without pretention. Floors slanted, red and white chequered cloths covered tables that always seemed to have one leg shorter than the others. I can still see the highly varnished posters of exotic travel on the walls, painted around by many coats of cream enamel, and the whole stained with the tobacco smoke of countless dialogues on art, music, theatre, and the meaning of life.

While the art establishment embraced the Group of Seven and the Roberts Gallery, a new breed of collectors began to feel and answer the challenge of the time. Avrom Isaacs had opened his frame shop on Hayter Street and was showing the works of audacious and bright talents like Graham Coughtry, Rick Gorman, Michael Snow, Joyce Wieland, Robert Markle, and Gordon Rayner.

Michael Snow always showed restraint and a cerebral approach that anticipated his later career. Joyce Wieland, his wife at that time, was "naughty." Fingers, flowers, and *peni abundi*. Alan Jarvis, a great champion of the contemporary scene had a fine wit, and he emerged one day from a Wieland show to remark, "Phallus in Wonderland!"

The great romantic of the group was surely Graham Coughtry. Using a layering of paint not unlike the glazing techniques of the past, he fused figure-ground with tremendous passion and authority. Another bright memory for me is his exhibition of huge (size was beginning to be accepted) black, white, and grey brush drawings of Larissa, his wife. They transcended the bawdy and radiated a monumental presence. Rayner, along with Snow, was truly inventive and his assemblages were to precede many of Robert Rauschenberg's.

Av Isaacs's move to real gallery space on Bay Street, next door to John Bulloch, tailors to gentlemen, was, I believe, the beginning of the contemporary art scene as we now know it. Abstract expressionism spread like a brush fire, and few of us resisted its seductive and lavish use of paints. Emotions quite frequently took over from compositional considerations, but the colour, the sweep, and the sense of immediacy was contagious.

I remember Av's early exhibition of Gerald Gladstone, young, brash, and volatile. His welded steel sculptures had a rawness that spoke of the man. Crude, angry and rusted, they posed problems non-existent in his later work.

Victor, the tall, elegant, black picture framer, moved into Av's old space. He carried on Isaacs's tradition, and showed pictures by young talents, often framing their works for free. Shichan Takashima was one. She became a close friend and would often visit my gallery.

That first year, I made the acquaintance of a strange artist, Frank de brun Valerius. He was mad and would drive about the city in an ancient Rolls Royce, complete with a chauffeur and a Royal Dutch emblem on the fender.

According to his own publicity, he had been portrait painter to Dutch royalty, as had his father before him. He was working on a new series of pictures describing the Old Testament and wanted a show. Jack Grossman drove me to his home on John Street in Hog's Hollow, and we wined and dined royally, on massive silver serving plates and goblets laid on heavy carved oak furniture. We all got a bit tipsy. Valentina, his wife, did a "seven-veil" dance, ending nude.

Well, the time arrived for his show – the pictures were not all dry, but they were delivered in the Rolls. Jack and I hung the show. It opened with little fanfare, and for a week or so I slept and cavorted beside a huge (and, in retrospect, very vulgar) rendition of Lot and his daughters making out. We sold two or three paintings. Valerius was around for a couple of years, on and off. He had the wild look one would expect from a Van Gogh – but he was truly egocentric and nuts. A good craftsman, but what a warped vision! Years later, I received a letter from him. He was hiding in the jungles of Guatemala, and told tales of torture and deprivation. Valentina became a respectable librarian.

Quelle histoire!

Winter came, and so did the cold weather. I roamed the area for wood, broke a few fences, and tried to keep warm. That Christmas brought the finest, most original (and needed) gift I have ever received: a ton of coal, delivered by a dusty man, complete with a Christmas card from the patrons of La Colombe – my needs have always seemed to be met, dear M.

As I sit here, in Provence, writing down these memories, it seems life goes full circle. Lou Paradou has no central heating, and as electricity is very costly, the fireplace becomes the centre of activity. Last night, I wandered the village in search of wood (finding an old door, and two chairs).

Spring came – new shops opened and the village started to become active. Karelia Studios, Marilyn and John Brooks' first Unicorn Shop, Marti's Village Bookstore, all joined with veterans like Evelyn Hunter, the photographer, and Pauline Fedio, the sculptor, and a sense of us all being family grew. Natural disasters happened, and all pulled together to help. When the bailiff came for me, the villagers rounded up the rent, and I sold a sculpture a few days later to repay them.

Then the rumours started: We were all being evicted. The enemy—the Toronto General Hospital, which owned most of the property—wanted to tear down our homes, galleries, and shops and build a nurses' residence. No leases were renewed and all was temporary and testy. We, the villagers, had an impossible dream that we could stop progress, we thought we might be able to stave off the bulldozers and keep that tiny pocket of history.

We would meet at La Colombe, or Mary John's restaurant, or at Pauline's studio, or that of Thelma Van Alstyne. By this time, Bob and Lucille Andrews had arrived on the scene with their restaurant, the Limelight. Brian Milligan, a young accountant type whom I had met in Toronto Psychiatric Hospital (he was depressed and a teenager), and Derek Stephens, whom I had met through a strangely flaming queen somewhere along the line, were partners with Bob and Lucille.

Evelyn Hunter, the photographer, Marilyn and John Brooks, David Smith (*Mr.* Smith), and I, along with many others, decided we needed to make the public aware of our existence. So the idea of a festival was born. "Springtime in the Village." One idea cascaded over another and we decided on pots of geraniums (a dozen per shop) and daisies as our motifs. (Mine were planted in an old toilet bowl outside the gallery.)

We applied for, and were granted, permission to close Hayter Street for a weekend, so we could have fashion shows, entertainment, and a street dance. Barry Zaid, a talented young artist-designer, did a poster.

I decided we needed something out of the ordinary for publicity and suggested we paint a daisy chain on the sidewalks surrounding the area. I made large stencils of daisies, and at midnight, the night before the festivities, Bob Andrews (of the Limelight restaurant), B, and I started to paint a continuous daisy chain on the sidewalks of our designated area. The police, during regular patrol, took us into Fifty-two Division for defiling city property. I explained it was water soluble paint (not stating that, when dry, it was waterproof) and we were released.

The next morning both the sun and the press were on our side, and the festival was a tremendous success. Hundreds of people arrived, everyone had fun, and a village association was formed. We danced barefoot. I was on the front page of the *Telegram* with Jean Hall, the big blonde painter.

The Junior Chamber of Commerce honoured us with a trophy for "Beautifying Toronto" and we started collecting signatures on a petition to save the village. For the next eighteen months we gathered the names of great and ordinary folk. In the interim, there was the Toronto Outdoor Art Exhibition – and my tour of Northern Ontario, when I met Norval Morrisseau, that strange and solitary genius who, through breaking taboos, gave the world the gift of his truly unique vision. But that story, dear M, you've read already.

February 4, 1986

Dear M.

Your paper sounds fascinating, and I am very proud of you for your continuing attempts at justice. I remember our discussions of the black situation, of prison reform, and it is to your great credit that you continue your attempts to educate and enlighten.

"We all are all," my personal motto, includes the potential for violence – violation – as well as for caring and caressing. I was giving a seminar at Binghamton, N.Y., when Robert Kennedy was killed. I spent four days in a motel room, watching with morbid fascination the rituals of death. But what hit me most was the ability of most people to dismiss Sirhan Sirhan as a nut case. In my final lecture I stated that we all had the potential for murder and that Sirhan Sirhan was as much a product of our society as the rest of us. Thus we all, in some way, share that guilt, that violation.

My learned art (strange word) of not getting angry is excused by the fact that very few persons or situations deserve my anger, as it is, for those moments, all-consuming. The truth is, I am terrified that I, like everyone else, could let anger reign and that destruction would follow.

I was fifteen or sixteen. It was New Year's Day, and Mother had invited the family – her mother, her maiden-aunt sister, and my "girl friend" Leslie, a girl I had gone with through school. At the dinner table, my father, drunk as usual, turned to Leslie and said, "God! You're an ugly bitch!"

Apparently, I attacked my father and was in the midst of choking him to death, when my brother and others pulled me away. That's scary! Love is blind and often senseless and so is true rage. I recall very little, except a doctor, an injection, and me moving out of the house to live with my grandmother and aunts for a short time before I went on my own.

The scene: the Clarke Institute of Psychiatry. For days, the competent (?) and confident staff have been working on getting me to show anger. They have bitched, criticized and complained. All I do is paint, go to the common room for the obligatory hour, and rest.

I love jelly beans, and friends who are in the know have brought me four bags of them, plus two tins of fancy cookies. The head nurse, a large lovely black lady, passes my room and stops. I offer her some jelly beans. She accepts. I give her a bag for the nurses. An hour or so later, I am in the common room with others when the junior shrink comes over and demands to know, in front of all, why I am trying to buy favours of the nurses with candy.

I don't know why, maybe it was because he accused me in public, but I got angry. I went to my room, returned to the nursing station, and then proceeded to bombard it with two or three pounds of loose jelly beans, plus the cookies from the two tins. Having created absolute chaos, I returned to my room, smashed four canvases and was put on twenty-four-hour watch for three days. No way would I assist in cleaning up the debris. My grandmother's saying: "You only use your fists when you run out of brains."

Thinking of Leslie, I am reminded of her graduation, which was a formal affair. I rented a tuxedo (the first time), bought a corsage, and we went to dinner at a little restaurant on Bloor Street, near Brunswick Avenue. The Candlelight Café – you may even remember it – had checkered tablecloths, Chianti bottles with candles, and Wiener Schnitzel. The bill arrived. I went to the john and, how I don't know, managed to wipe my ass with the only ten-dollar bill I owned and then flush it down the toilet. Thank God, I knew the owner! These days, this seems to make a statement about my attitude to money.

So much for silliness.

Later, I wined and dined Eartha Kitt at the Candlelight Café one night. We kept in touch for years. She sang for one of our street festivals in the village and, much later, when I was a "guest" of the psychiatric ward of Sunnybrook Hospital, I was given an evening pass to go to the Imperial Room at the Royal York Hotel to celebrate Eartha's birthday in grand style. Front row table, champagne, and the glory of a talented lady.

February 10, 1986

Dear M.

I have begun to sort out the years of photos, clippings, and notes I brought back from Toronto. As you know, I have never been organized and it shows in the clutter. Anyway, among the bits and pieces, I found a quote – I don't know where it is from or who said it – but it hit home: "Every man comes to that time in his life, and it varies for each of us, when the human being gives himself over to his genius or his demon, according to a mysterious law which orders him either to destroy or surpass himself."

Somehow, it makes me feel a bit better about yesterday,

today, and tomorrow. Tomorrow's the tough one: the unknown and unexpected.

I also came across many articles and reviews of the famous Morrisseau book, which almost did me in. It is a beautiful book and, in late 1979, I was sent on a promotional tour from coast to coast by the publishers. In twelve days I did over sixty interviews for radio, television, and newspapers, and signed books in bookstores in ten cities. My memory of Prairie places such as Calgary, Saskatoon, and Edmonton is of anonymous hotels, limousines, PR people, luncheons, dinners, and my constant companion – cocaine. I know I could never have survived the ordeal of the trip, been on time for every appointment, and could not have thought up new angles for each interview (a "hook" was what they called it), without that stimulant.

Johnny, the one who committed suicide just before I left for France, had given me a wonderful new toy – a Vick's inhaler. You filled it with coke, and one tip would produce the equivalent of a line. All across Canada, I had a "cold" during the interviews and advertised Vick's on local and national television, using their inhaler. Happily all the articles and interviews were positive – I had "sniffed" my way to success, so to speak. God! What one recalls!

That tour brings to mind another tale that, as they say, you can't make up. I had just come out of the Clarke, after a three-month "rest cure," realizing that I had to re-enter the "scene," the art scene, that is. I had been invited to attend the AGO members' preview of an exhibition of Inuit prints on a Thursday evening in early fall of 1977.

I toyed with ideas of what to wear, and finally decided on a sleek, black Pierre Cardin jumpsuit I had purchased in Paris the year before. A black and beige foulard and black boots completed the look. As I glanced in the mirror on my way out, I saw I looked well and rested.

I arrived at the Art Gallery and found that the new addition by Parkin looked bunker-like and defensive. The old marble remains seemed so "establishment," they looked almost Fascistic. I entered, was greeted warmly, and wound my way to the bar. There, standing not two feet away from me, was a handsome young man, wearing the same jumpsuit! I thought, this only happens to dizzy blondes in B movies. Extending my hand, I went over to him and laughingly suggested we tour the show together as the Bobbsey Twins. No hand was offered in return and his icy stare made very clear the young man's distinct displeasure. Tough shit, I thought as I mingled with the crowd, catching up on news of art and artists, gossip about auction prices, and the rise and fall of reputations.

After an hour or so I'd had enough. So, into a cab and home, feeling empty. The apartment looked like a sophisticated stage set, but I didn't feel the play was mine. So I stripped, showered, and pulled on my raunchy torn jeans (I always get a hard-on from the tightness of fabric on flesh). A T-shirt, my leather vest (today, I'm wearing the same leather vest), and scruffy work boots finished the costume.

Another cab to the bus station at Bay and Dundas. Next door, under the shoe-shine shop and a tacky pawn shop were the Terminus Baths. Not on your guided tours of Toronto, this pit – dark, dank, and totally unsanitary – was just what I needed. I'm sure you're aware that these holes, like any other institution, have clearly defined rules: open doors, prone bodies, costumes, toys.

I walked around the narrow, sweaty corridors, dim in their red glow – true labyrinths of lust. Through an open door, I saw a body, a welcoming hand, and entered. After an hour or so of sweaty, liquid encounter, we both rested with a cigarette.

He: "Do you live in Toronto?"

I: "Yes – and you?"

He: "No, I am here for the night on business."

I: "What kind of business?"

He: "I am a newspaper art critic. I just attended a show at the AGO."

I: "Funny, I was there, too. Maybe you saw me. I was wearing a black –"

He: "Fuck, was that you!"

To my utter amazement, the young man who, minutes before, had been a warm and tender servant to my needs, became hostile. He flung open the door and ordered me out. As I left, I saw his jumpsuit hanging against the wall on a peg. So much for the Bobbsey Twins, I thought, as I prowled, probed, and searched for further contacts.

A few months later, I arrived in one of the cities on the Morrisseau tour. It was midnight. The publicist for the tour handed me my schedule for the next day. Nine o'clock – first thing – an interview, coffee and rolls served in my room with, guess who? I didn't know what to do. So, in the bar, over a double Scotch, I told the publicist the jumpsuit story. She nearly shit but agreed to "host" the morning encounter.

The next day, she arrived just before he did. He never hinted at the past and I signed a book for him. As he was leaving, he asked what I was doing later. So we finally kissed and made up.

So much for now. That's your bedtime story.

P.S. Next on the agenda is a bedtime story entitled *Le Lièvre* (The Wild Hare). Keep tuned to this station.

February 12, 1986

Dear M.

Hope you liked my bedtime story. I am going to try and get *Le Lièvre* off to you this week.

Last Friday night a few of us went to a night club in Saint-Rémy. It was Carnival in Rio night, and the place was jammed. Costumes ranged from elegant to the absolute end in transvestite tacky. But it was fun!

It was one of the rare occasions in my life when I have been in the presence of drag queens. These burlesques of women, with their posturing and pimping, their padding and wigs, bring out pity and rage in me. I have always wondered at their role in life. A man who chooses to desire another man does so because he is just that—another man. If I wished softness, curves, and the female sensibility, I would choose women. These sad creatures to me are true caricatures of themselves—and an embarrassment to most homosexual men.

I remember at the Clarke once I stated how I hated faggots, and Cindy, one of the nurses, said, "I'm Jewish, and I hate furred and jewelled Jewish Princesses." But I have to recognize them as part of what I am.

I have never liked the gay scene, can't stand faggots, and was never part of a bar-and-booze life (St. Charles, Parkside, and so on). Rather, I enjoy, and have enjoyed, the mixed blessings of tease, dry fuck, and seduction. Sex, if and when it happens, is quite often anti-climactic to the fun and games played out beforehand by both participants.

The dream of most homosexual men is a relationship with a straight guy. The foolish ones, in my mind—the prissy faggot types — attempt to lure them by simulating the feminine. It makes me barf. I am embarrassed by the "get-you-Mary" shit. I find them truly nature's misfits. (Christ — listen to who's talking about *misfits*). The others, as we are all well aware, try to appeal to the animal, the lustful desire for pleasure and release that cuts through sexuality, as Judeo-Christian teachings have defined it.

I think at the base of my great problems (sexually) is the gnawing belief that I am not truly homo, as they say, but unique. (What a crock of shit, "unique.") However, if I can justify my prejudice in not wanting to belong to that club, so be it.

Strange thought patterns seem to weave in and out of my head these days. Rape, forced sexual intercourse, abuse as a turn-on. These things are totally beyond my comprehension — I always had a problem with penetration — because the thought of causing pain made me flaccid, not at all what was desired. Different strokes . . .

I have had a flu bug for a few days, and while resting read a dialogue on male sex offenders and the different proposed modes of punishment/treatment. My brief experience with prisons tells me that they are not places for the angry and crazed, who, granted, in a fit of passion, often commit such acts.

One side of the argument–that it is possible for an offender to violate only once in his life, and thus he should not be removed from society – is juxtaposed with documented facts that most offenders have a history of abuse. Somewhere between the two lies the truth, and the major task as I see it is to broaden the definition of society so that frustration, fear, and the sense of not being normal is relieved and allowed a voice by understanding and acceptance.

The female of the species presents difficulties for those of us who through choice – genes, accident, or whatever – feel strongly for each other, man to man.

I believe many (actually most) homosexual men feel bitterness, rage, jealousy, or plain antagonism toward women.

The emergence of feminists, especially the radical ones who don the army-boot, masculine image to pound their message home, and blame men for all failures, gives men a much more public forum to use as a battleground.

The problem here is one of stereotype and escape. Just as the "prissy" types can be used as objects of ridicule in the gay liberation movement, so the strident over-aggressive feminist can sometimes defeat the purpose of their exercise.

I believe and I know most women to be good, and composed of the same many-faceted intellectual and emotional baggage as men. We all are truly all, dear M. If I believed in support of some "seeming" male position (seeming, because definitions of male and female are today obsolete in many ways, as they have been twisted by social and religious forces for their own purposes), I would not air my beliefs and attempt to gain support in the club house – the old-boys' school. I would offer a paper to a feminist conference. I would challenge the feminist separatists to start a true communication. Dialogue; that's where growth and change – political, social, and, primarily, personal – begins.

None of us has the right to violate another (active participation and willingness are not violation). Wife battering and child abuse will not just mysteriously go away. Nor will the anger, hostility, and castrating humiliation of female rage (more often using sexual denial, and verbal rather than physical) evaporate.

We, as human beings, must recognize our dualities, our similarities, and our differences. Only then can an open respect for the unique qualities of each person be nurtured.

Our society has become so warped that rage, frustration, and the horror of rejection are built into our psyches. We can be, and often are, born insecure, born angry, defiant, and our tiny hands are clenched, not open.

My feelings are still that, if through personal fantasy and role-playing, just as through sports and other physical encounters, we can release tension, with it will come a much-needed compassion for others. The old-boy system, still apparent in courts, politics, and business, is an outgrowth of the locker-room, boy-scout buddy system. It has often worked well, and will always have a place in society.

Until we allow true openness in our private worlds to the theatre of fantasy, real whorehouses, which cater to what society labels "kinks," are necessary. But society disapproves of whorehouses and because of this there is a noticeable growth of sexual imbalance. It is easy now for the alienated to become criminal and commit true crime–the violation of the individual.

Pollock–shut up!

Maybe the fever and the constant coughing has made me slightly unhinged. Sorry about that.

Le Lièvre
When nights are frosty and the roads are covered with a silver dust of ice, I remember a wonderful trip with Grant Lay in the seventies.

153

Grant was possibly the best travelling companion I have ever had, a fine driver, and though much more controlled and circumspect than me, a willing partner to many of my explosive escapades.

Rituals and hard-ons being what they are, many evenings (often after midnight) I would get the urge to prowl. The ancient ramparts of Avignon were the meat rack of Provence. Sensibly, they were partitioned off with areas for straight whores (one always wore white "mink" – probably rabbit – mini shorts). Others wore trench coats, ready to beaver flash at a moment's notice. Then there were the male hustlers (some dressed as sailors), the transvestites, and tacky sequin queens. My usual haunt was the male, male-hungry horsetrough.

Grant, maintaining a sense of dignity I have always lacked in the crotch area, wouldn't join me on the ramparts. He would drive me to the walls, we would designate a time, and if I was not lucky by then he would be waiting to take us home to Lou Paradou.

This specific night, not long after midnight, I was standing by the medieval stone buttress of one of the gates to the ancient city, pissing (or a reasonable facsimile of it). A hand, a voice, a squeeze, and what I interpreted to be "your place or mine?"

I said I lived in Gordes. He offered to drive me home so I contacted Grant, who was waiting in the car in the shadows, and said I had a ride.

My new-found toy guided me over to his *Deux-chevaux* (the lowest on the ladder of four-wheeled vehicles in France). It had slung canvas seats (only two), like deck-chairs, and a crawl space behind them. In one of the seats was another young and attractive male. I was introduced and manhandled, so to speak, into the rear of the car. They babbled in a quick provençal patois that I only grasped threads of. We took off, and he drove like one driven.

I looked from the window to see us ascending a twisting

and ice-clad mountain road. Canadian art gallery owner, raped and killed in the Vaucluse – Canadian artist robbed and beaten. Really, I am not paranoid, but I did feel nervous.

Then, exclamations of delight and excitement led my eyes to the road ahead of us. Caught in the blinding headlight glare was a huge wild hare. The driver went bananas, the car slipped and slid on the ice, and I thought we would end up a pile of rubble in the valley below.

A slight bump, and the car skidded to a stop. There on the road was the body of the hare, unmarked, but very still, very dead.

"*Un cadeau pour toi,*" the driver said as he handed me the enormous furry trophy of his chase.

For the remaining ten kilometres to Gordes (yes, they *were* taking me home), I shared the rear crawl space with this bloody carcass. (It wasn't actually bleeding, but it was bloody long – over four feet stretched out – and cooling fast.)

We arrived at Lou Paradou and as I unlocked the door, hare in hand, I yelled for Grant. He came down the stairs and I offered him the prize. "A present for you!"

He stood stunned, and refused to go near it. He just said, "You're going to be busy tonight." Then he went upstairs to bed.

I *was* busy.

They left around five the next morning and I fell into a deserved, deep sleep.

Around eight I heard cursing and a crash. I had placed the hare on the kitchen floor (cold and tiled) and Grant had stumbled over it while attempting to make coffee. I dragged myself downstairs, and over breakfast we discussed the future of my *cadeau*.

It is illegal to kill game in France, as it is in Canada, but I had the solution. Les Vincents, who live in the hamlet of Les Martins, five kilometres away, would love the gift, and all would be well.

Wrong. That solution was just too easy! Just as we were

preparing to depart for Les Martins, a knock on the door announced Jean, my bed-buddy-cum-hunter from the night before.

I'd forgotten in the midst of coming and going and coming the previous night (really that morning) that he had told me he was a chef at one of the fine hotels in Carpentras and that he would come back to teach me how to prepare *civet de lièvre*.

Grant shrugged, got his coat, and went for a drive. I, exhausted and hungover, had to assist as Jean produced large knives, a cleaver, and began skinning, gutting, and chopping the beast.

He then demanded four litres of red wine, two carrots, two onions, and produced from his bag of tricks a bouquet garni, all of which he put in my large soup pot, which he then placed, covered, in the crypt. A bowl of the animal's blood (yes, dear M, blood) was sprinkled with vinegar and placed in the fridge. He washed up, said he would be back in two days, and left.

Two days later, he did come back, just before noon, with a beautiful blond youth who he explained was a *sous-chef*, who would clean my kitchen properly. He was and he did.

The hare was inspected and tossed about and they left, saying dinner would be Tuesday and I should invite a group of friends as Jean would prepare a banquet. After a quick conversation with Grant, we both came to the conclusion that none of my village friends were quite suitable for such a soirée, and I suggested that Jean invite a few of *his* crowd.

"*Oui, merci!*" he gushed and said he would invite two *étoiles*, dear friends.

He winked, patted the young lad on his very firm bum, and said he would be here the next day to begin preparations. Grant and I looked at the darkening pot of flesh and wondered how it would taste.

The following day Jean returned and started preparing other exotica for the feast. He quietly worked, and quietly I became worked up.

I suggested I would have a shower and went upstairs, expecting him to follow. Almost a half-hour later, the hot water turned cold. My skin shrivelling, I dried myself off, pulled on my jeans, and descended into the kitchen. Jean was facing the sink, his back to me, naked, except for a tiny apron. He had a large knife and was cutting *crudités*.

Grant had left earlier, Jean and I came and went, and the show moved along. Kitchen callisthenics!

When Grant returned, Jean mentioned a nightclub in a tiny hamlet near Orange and suggested we go. After several attempts, we finally found the hamlet, no more than five or six houses, and the ruins of an old château.

About fifty cars crowded the roadside and all the available parking space. A large wooden door with a sliding panel, reminiscent of the speakeasies of bygone days, was lit by an amber light. We knocked, the panel slid open, and I said we were friends of Jean.

"*Les Canadiens!*" a voice exclaimed, and the door opened.

The large stone room was dark, vaulted, crowded, and the air was filled with smoke and a scent that reminded me of the strange Woolworth perfume Evening in Paris. We were ushered in and seated on the floor, front and centre of a small makeshift stage.

A master of ceremonies (so to speak) arrived under a spotlight and apologized for the delay, but he was pleased to announce the arrival of the guests of honour for the evening – *Les Canadiens*. The spotlight shifted, and Grant and I were bathed in light as applause, whistles, and screams made us more than welcome.

To understand this scene properly, you must have an image of Grant. He's not large, but he is finely toned, quite conservative, and at this point, truly embarrassed. I laughed and waved a regal hand of thanks.

Drum rolls, and the show began.

One after the other, almost a dozen tacky queens minced, mimed, and impersonated a galaxy of stars, beloved by the limp of wrist. Edith Piaf, Diana Ross, Judy Garland, Marlene

Dietrich, and so on. They were all there in their rumpled satin, shining sequins, and rhinestones, and fuck-me pumps for days. Both Grant and I attempted to appear impressed, but secretly wished out of the entire venture.

After the finale and curtain calls, the spotlight changed to a mirror ball. A large circle was formed and Jean insisted Grant and I join in. The music started and a small towel was passed from one man to the next. When the music stopped, whoever held the towel entered the centre of the circle. The music started and stopped again, and a second man stepped forward. The two of them knelt on the towel, fondled, kissed, then the ritual began again. Like spin the bottle from my public school days! Grant wisely declined to join in, and after I was caught twice, we decided to leave.

Jean came over and introduced us to two of the transvestite queens saying they would be coming for dinner the next evening. *Les deux étoiles! Mon Dieu!* I hastily suggested a late hour for dining, and we escaped.

On the way home we wondered how the *deux étoiles* could be slipped into Gordes without the villagers noticing. What would they wear? Would they stop in the café on the way for a drink? God! I didn't need it.

The next day, Jean came early. Grant went for a drive and came back with an attractive young couple he'd found hitch-hiking. They were German-Swiss and laden down with back-packing equipment. They were searching for the academy of tapestry weaving and Grant told them I would probably know where it was located.

Over a drink by the fire on the *premier étage*, I discovered they were in the wrong village. They wanted Cordes, not Gordes. As it was getting late, and they had nowhere to stay, I casually suggested they could stay the night. Then it dawned on me: this innocent young couple would be part of the evening spectacle.

As we talked, the conversation turned to cooking, and I told them, in abbreviated form, the story of the past week. The young man asked if we liked herbs. (He spoke little French and less English.) Yes, we grow a lot in the area and I cook with them constantly. No, no–*herbs*. The penny dropped and we were soon smoking a joint of grass, which they had grown in their garden at home.

At nine-thirty that night, we heard the click of heels on the ancient stone steps. Our guests had arrived, complete with pancake makeup and artificial eyelashes batting like flyswatters in a swamp.

We ate a superb meal of pâté de foie gras, escargot, and the *civet de lièvre*, a true masterpiece of provençal cuisine. The sauce was black and pungent, the meat moist and gamey. Steamed whole baby potatoes, tiny onions, delicate carrots from Vichy, a marvellous green salad, a rich and cream-filled dessert, plus three wines and a champagne.

The conversation was hysterical, a kind of *Cage aux Folles* wit took over the entire evening. They, the stars, in satin and tailored pants, large earrings dangling for days, and shoes with rhinestone buckles and heels that would topple the tower of Pisa, dished dirt and camped their way through the entire performance. Grant, the young couple, and I, suitably laid-back, watched the theatre of it all. Well after two in the morning we went to bed, while the stars and Jean went out on the town, dancing.

I have never seen or heard of any of them since. I often think of going to Carpentras and seeking Jean out, but I think I'll let sleeping dogs lie – so to speak.

Crazy, eh what?

February 18, 1986

Dear Ann Landers.
Today I became the proud owner of a born-again Christian Great Dane puppy – two months old. I may have mentioned it in one of my other requests for advice. (You are so sensible – I advise all my friends to "just drop Ann a line.")

A little background – Michel is a former bank robber who spent eight years in prison. He came out, and moved in with his brother's ex-wife and her two children (one by the brother, the other, another). Michel had a profound religious experience – saw the Light, so to speak, and set about converting Kaki, his "wife," and the two children. Last October, I invited them all to dinner, and realized it had become their mission to save my soul. They've not had much success. But what they *have* saved is one of the puppies from their champion black and white Great Dane bitch. The couple, Michel and Kaki, have separated. She's gone back to her sluttish ways (Michel's words, not mine) and he onward and upward toward heaven. And the puppy has come to me.

Damian, as I have chosen to name him, is very handsome. When full grown he will stand over a metre high and weigh over two hundred pounds. A big boy!

Now, Ann, onto my problem: Aside from the obvious – another mouth to feed – and feed – and feed – and shots – and ears to be clipped – I feel I have a strange responsibility for his continued moral upbringing. Granted, I have an idea that the crypt could serve as his bedroom, but, as you will see from the enclosed photo, Mommy seems to be a bit of a tart also. I feel an obligation to set standards. Do you know of a Canine Christian Centre in the Vaucluse region? Evelyn Waugh told me of several in California, but unfortunately he is no longer with us.

Also, Ann, should I continue to allow the mother visiting rights? She is, I fear, capable of corrupting his innocence.

Living in such a small community presents many perplexing situations, and I am aware of various deviations from the norm that exist here. Should he just, as the saying goes, "live and learn"?

He seems to grow before my eyes and I would appreciate any help you can offer – quickly.

February 21, 1986

Dear M.

Here's another *petite histoire* for your collection:

The Toronto Outdoor Show

At about the same time as we were trying to save the village from the Toronto General Hospital, some young painters (whose names I've long lost and forgotten) tried to display their talents on the fence surrounding City Hall (the old one). Police forced them away, the press duly reported the incident, and an idea was born. Murray Koffler, partner with Eddie Creed and Issie Sharpe in the new Four Seasons Hotel on Jarvis Street, contacted Alan Jarvis, and the Toronto Outdoor Art Exhibition was born.

Alan, a dear friend of Joe McCulley, warden of Hart House, enlisted the aid of his undergraduate secretary, David Silcox, and myself, and we all pulled together to pull it off. It was no mean feat. For Murray and the Four Seasons it meant costly car jockeying for all guests, constant food and bar bills, and publicity and advertising costs. For me, I had to round up artists, invent ways to display works, and organize space allotments. Ben Vicarrie was the PR person for the Four Seasons then, and we worked closely together.

It came off – one day of rain, which created temporary disaster, but then the sun came out. John Gould, Ken Danby, Takashima, Van Alstyne, Hanni Rothschild, Jack Reppen, and dozens of others combined to make it a great success.

It was during this mad weekend, late at night, I met B – alone, young, and innocent – on the corner of Jarvis and Carlton.

I was haunted, broke, trying to live up to the image I was creating for myself, hanging out in the Four Seasons, where I had run up a bill and had no way of paying it. To B, once he got over my brazen come-on, I was a somebody. God! Had he only known the hell I would put him through while he gained his "education" in the so-called finer things of life!

My mother came to the rescue, loaned me money, and I

found the building across the lane from me was about to be vacated. It was more than big enough for B and I to live there together.

It was very old, run down, and had been for many years an old man's home for the sadly alone Chinese in the city. We (the village) had bought geraniums for them at festival time, and painted the front of the house.

Anyway, the rent was sixty-five dollars a month for three stories in rough shape. B (God bless him) and I worked our asses off, completed a gallery on the main floor, and lived on the second. Ethel Raicus, a fine painter, rented a studio on the third floor, and we survived.

B had been working in Eaton's in the shoe department, but now found a job as waiter at Bob and Lucille's Limelight restaurant. We struggled and often had no money at all. (So, what else is new?)

Time passed – a young artist, Alan Weinstein, wanted an exhibition. He was from a wealthy family, and was also, I felt (and still feel), talented.

B decided to do me a favour and surprise me with a newly painted gallery floor for this exhibition. He went to Crippled Civilians (what a disgusting name) and bought battleship-grey floor enamel. Well, it wouldn't dry! So, on opening night for Weinstein, the floor was covered in brown paper, and a few of the beminked and bejewelled ladies found their expensive fuck-me pumps stuck to the oozing paint. Betsy Kilbourn (now an Anglican priest) was art critic for the *Toronto Star*. She came, her heel went into a knot hole, and she hobbled out on one shoe.

Winter was tough. Ben Vicarrie got me a commission to paint a thousand (yes, dear M, 1,000) hand-made watercolour Christmas cards for Procter & Gamble at fifty cents each. I was in the midst of them when two police officers arrived at the gallery, asked my name, and promptly arrested me on charges of "uttering."

Months before, while on a walk with B on Yonge Street, I had seen a sweater. B had loved it, and I'd paid half in cash, and had written a cheque for the balance. The cheque had not been deposited for about a month, by which time it was latex. Yes, they had sent me notices, which I'd filed with all bad news – under piles of crap.

Well, the police meant business! I asked them if I could go to the restaurant to tell B. No. They said I had to come immediately. I picked up a jacket belonging to B, locked the door and was duly processed at Fifty-two Division.

After photos and fingerprints, I was in for a gruelling questioning as B's I.D. was in the jacket and they assumed I was using an alias.

At eleven-thirty that morning, I was in a jail cell – iron bench, and open toilet bowl – desperately shaking the bars and demanding a telephone call. (I had always read in mysteries that everyone was entitled to a telephone call.) No. The cells were filling up with sad drunks and sadder whores. Finally, at around three-thirty in the afternoon, I was taken to a room and there was David Black, a young lawyer and one of my clients, who got me released and took me home.

B had come back to the gallery, heard the gossip that police had taken me, called David, and the two of them had tracked me down.

Eventually, the charge was thrown out of court. I asked for the record to be cleared, but I have no idea if my mug shot and fingerprints are still on file today for "uttering."

I'm cold. I will lay down for a while.

To be continued.

(I finished the Christmas cards on time and have since seen several, beautifully framed, in homes.)

(I'm warm and rested.)

Often B and I would be without a penny, but we trusted that the Lord would provide.

There was a cheap Chinese hangout for five-minute hookers, drug addicts, and petty thieves on the corner of Elizabeth and Dundas. The wide and usually deserted lane beside the gallery was often used for "up against the wall quickies" picked up in this café.

One night, B and I were in bed when a violent argument and fight started between two men down in the alley. I leaned out the window, lowered my voice an octave or two, and yelled, "Fuck off. Get lost." They scurried away and B said, "Let's go down, they may have dropped some coins in the fighting." We went, flashlight in hand, and recovered over three bucks. We quickly got dressed up and went to Lindy's for a steak. Those were the days, my friend.

That summer was the summer I met Morrisseau. Paul Bennett, who had hired me to teach up north, decided he would like to try *la vie bohème*, and rented the second floor of the gallery. B and I moved to the third.

Well, Paul (later to be director of the Stratford Gallery, then the Ontario Craft Gallery, and now God knows what) loved the colours violet and blue, loved coloured glass and Victoriana, and loved organs (the musical kind). He was also the total opposite of B and I, in that he was fastidious to the point of obsession.

The gallery building was old, creaking, and dust-filled. His vacuum was on most of the time, and he quickly got tired of the happenstance, hand-to-mouth existence that was the old village. He moved out, and on to bigger and better organs. B and I were relieved when the vacuum finally stopped.

The village was losing its never-ending battle with City Hall. We had thousands of signatures on our petition – those of people from the area, from Toronto, all of Canada, and tourists from most countries of the world – so we prepared a march on City Hall on the day they were voting on our demise. Over a hundred people carrying pots of geraniums walked from my gallery to the council chamber. Bill and Betsy Kilbourn, quite a few aldermen and many establishment figures, joined with the artists and shopkeepers. I gave a speech, if you could call it that, but we knew we were doomed. The old saying, "You can't fight City Hall," proved correct, and our days were numbered.

I look back on it now and realize that it was probably the first time in Toronto's history that citizens became a voice – a force – demanding the right to have a say in the city's development. The public and the press alike were forced to take sides. Most of the press (and, my God, there was a lot) was for us, the underdog, the spirited and Bohemian community that wouldn't say die.

A year or two later the battle to save Yorkville village from high-rise development was in full swing, and I believe if we had not been there before, Yorkville would probably not have survived (if "survived" is the word, now that pseudo-façades and chic white-painting has taken away the true character of the gracious old neighbourhood.)

This is when Ed Mirvish came into my life. I was doomed and desperate. Anne, Ed's wife, and little David used to visit my gallery often, and had purchased works by Morrisseau and by a young man named Martin Berkowitz. Martin was something else. Young (eighteen, I believe), Jewish and full of anti-family, anti-society, anti- anti- anger, he drew strange and wondrous man-animal forms with acid lines at once alive and vitriolic. His exhibition (a sell-out) and Morrisseau's had put me on the map as a dealer. The fight for the village gave me the spotlight I have never been able to resist. The press, radio, television, I was there for them, always mouthing off (I hope with some sense, but I am not sure).

Ed Mirvish approached me soon after City Hall's decision and asked me if I could "create" a village. He was, and is, highly approving of talent but his taste built Honest Ed's. Do I have to say more?

Anyway, I asked what part of Toronto he had in mind. He said Markham Street at Bathurst and Bloor. I nearly shit.

We went over, and on the way he explained that the city had made him provide a parking lot because of the traffic jams caused by Honest Ed's success. He had bought up the entire east side of Markham Street, from Honest Ed's south to Lennox Avenue, and had levelled the backyards for parking. His wife, Anne, always a firey and creative lady, had given up acting and opera singing, and was deep into sculpture. He had created a superb studio for her in one of the houses. He had then proceeded to paint each building a raw and blatant tone of pink, green, yellow, blue.

I viewed this strange technicolour madness, and my heart sank. But I had no alternative. I had no money and soon I would have no gallery. So I suggested that if I could choose which house I wanted, and if his workmen would remodel it to my specifications, I would attempt to assemble a village. He agreed. David Horne, husband of Mercédés Horne, a painter I was showing, did the architectural work. I bought an old barn, and (it was a new idea then) faced the building in barn board. The floors inside were painted a putty green; one wall was made from the same barn board and all the other walls and the ceiling were painted white. The Markham Street Gallery opened to great raves.

B was blossoming as an ideas man. He had a flair for antiques and the then very popular boutique-style of women's fashion. He, as always, wanted grandeur, and he opened Tiffany's next door to my gallery. His opening, "Breakfast at Tiffany's," was a raging success, as the sidewalk was filled with tables, a fashion show wandered through the crowds, and Debbie Alter, a dear friend, came in old pajamas, a tattered housecoat, and huge rollers in her hair.

Two shops do not a village make. Gaston opened his famous bistro, Brian Dodge and Tom Keeling opened antique shops, Jessica Roff, my first-ever secretary (on Elizabeth) opened a bookstore. (Jessie and I talked in the old village. She asked what kind of shop she could possibly open? I said, "You read don't you? Open a bookstore." She did.)

I talked my mother and sister into opening a children's wear shop, The Little Princess, which soon turned into the Village Café, as mother's heart was in feeding the starving artists who began renting studios above the shops.

I've run out of paper. I wonder if it all really happened, and realize I'm still only showing you the tip of the iceberg of my life (apologies to the AGO exhibition).

Dear M.

It's true – I never was a businessman. I didn't go into the gallery business to make money. I was never interested in having a solid stable of artists whom I would represent into perpetuity, even their estates; but that is the way you make money in the gallery business today. I was interested in discovering new artists and in teaching buyers about contemporary art, not in making great wealth. I guess that's partly why I'm here, not back in Toronto planning another opening.

I was always looking for the new, the young, the different, the exciting, because my chief joy, and really the purpose of the gallery, lay in discovery. This had its price, of course. I would introduce new artists and sell their paintings for fifty, one hundred, maybe as much as two hundred dollars, and, just as their prices started to go up, they would move along to another gallery! They always went with my blessing. I wasn't being robbed. I always needed the extra space for another new talent and was glad these artists I had launched were well on their way.

In the early 1960s, the second floor of my gallery on Markham Street was called the Young Collector's Gallery, and nothing I showed there was ever over a hundred dollars, because I wanted to encourage young people to buy art as much as I wanted to show young talent. Every Christmas I held a miniatures art show, where nothing cost more than fifty dollars. All my artists–and many others–did small paintings just for the show. I would decorate the gallery with cedar boughs all around the ceiling and hang wide ribbons from them on which I'd hang at least 150 pictures–all framed and priced at fifteen, twenty-five, fifty dollars.

Those were the days when we had joy and fun, and the gallery business was not just business. Openings were extraordinarily festive – and crazy. I had an opening once of Erté's original art deco designs and watercolours. Everyone had to come in period costume. I brought in a piano for the day, and Tom Kneebone and Dinah Christie came and sang Cole Porter songs. Very special.

When I held an exhibition of Genevieve Klaisse's circles (she does circles much like Josef Albers does squares), I had plastic pendants of one of her circles made, which went out with the invitations. For a show called Paris Today, which brought together many artists from the Denise René gallery in Paris (Claude Yvel and Vasarely, among others), I made plastic models of one of Vasarely's Op art pieces to give away. I rented the billboard at the corner of Yonge and Bloor and put up a poster that said, "What is Op? Who is Denise René? Where is Paris at? . . . The Pollock Gallery." Dorothy Post came to the opening and sang Piaf for us. That was fun. But galleries can't afford those kinds of openings any more.

No one can afford to run a gallery of discovery any more, either. The discovery galleries now are largely government supported. In Toronto, for young artists today, there's A Space, YYZ, and the Mercer Union, but none of them have to support themselves from sales alone. As a result, they all tend to show quite extreme art, very little of it saleable. They go for conceptual art, performance art, and video–you can't hang any of it on your walls. It's all important work and has to be shown, but still I'm sorry that there's practically no place in Toronto now that shows paintings, drawings, and sculptures by unknown artists. There's a good reason why there is no such place – financially, it's almost impossible to do.

Between 1960 and 1966, I showed only the work of young Canadians, except for my very first show. For that I rented a van and drove with a friend to New York, and I brought back a show called the 10th Street Scene by young, undiscovered New York artists. But my focus in those years was on Canadian artists – Fournier, Berkowitz, Morrisseau, Thelma Van Alstyne, who was and still is one of the finest abstract colourists that Canada has ever produced.

The Markham Street gallery, which I opened after the

village was destroyed in 1963, was another scene. I had been several times to London, Ontario, which had become the centre of the Canadian *avant-garde*. Jack Chambers came from there, so did Ron Martin, who did outrageous black finger-paintings. I held his first show of collages, which used stamps and cigar bands. They were charming. In London I also met David Rabinovitch, who was doing large outdoor sculptures in sheet metal, rolled like cornucopia – quite exotic and quite beautiful. I arranged to hold an exhibition. The morning before the show was to open, no sculpture had arrived. There was a horrible blizzard that evening, and at midnight – still no sculpture. Finally, about one in the morning, David arrived in a half-ton pick-up truck filled with flat sheets of metal. During the night, he actually created the sculptures right in the gallery, twisting the sheet metal and nailing it to the floor. Not at all what I wanted! But it was a stunning show.

Carole Condé and Karl Beveridge were two quite radical artists I discovered. Karl was doing very simple, linear wooden constructions; Carole was creating intricate geometric designs constructed on the wall of the gallery. She would stick pins in the wall and then stretch grosgrain ribbons around the pins. If you bought the work, what you got was a roll of ribbon, a box of pins, and a diagram of how to put it all together. In those days, this was quite inventive and was, I think, the beginning of conceptual art. Today they're collaborating on photomontages that are politically quite radical.

It was an exciting time in Canadian art. Painters Eleven were on their way out; they had split up. William Ronald had gone to New York, Harold Town was becoming more of a verbal than a visual artist, the others had gone their own ways. Jack Bush was a great talent of that earlier era. A gentle, but tough man. He was a Sunday painter all his life – he held down a job until he was over sixty and put his three sons through college. It was because of the job that he could paint what he damned well pleased – he didn't have to sell anything. The Group of Seven were all Sunday painters, too, and *they* painted what they wanted, not what they thought they could sell. They paid a price for that freedom – the price of having to work for a living.

Freedom *is* expensive. Today, many young artists feel they have a right to be kept while they create, and now we have Canada Council grants to support them. I'm not so sure I approve of artists getting Canada Council grants before they've produced a good body of work. I've seen artists get grants and then freeze; they get painter's block, they can't paint, they're so terrified of having to produce. I think it's a bit like welfare, and that doesn't produce the right conditions in which to create anything. Too often, also, it's the squeaky wheel that gets the oil, the grant – artists who can talk a great deal about their work and innovative trends in the world of art, verbalizing about something that doesn't quite exist and, a great deal of the time, at the taxpayers' expense.

Yes, I miss it; but I'm still glad I'm not in the thick of it.

February 25, 1986

Dear M.

Thank God for your letter (you being God in this instance). I have been slowly (or not so slowly) disintegrating and keep wondering if I'll make it. Your words stimulate thoughts and memories, some good, some painful – but all real. Your life and loves, past and present, are, for me, pieces of a jigsaw puzzle. Do you realize how much we are alike in many ways? It's your common-sense that keeps you on track, and my lack of it that keeps me on the edge. You seem to have accepted much within you and have emerged with self-respect. This must help you in your professional support of "the young in need." My life is strewn with attempts at giving support, but, as in the case of the hero (?) in *The Immoralist,* I choose the thief, the cheat, or in the instance of Little J, a true psychopath.

I have never felt myself worthy of fame, and when I did achieve it (in material terms) didn't know how to handle it. I suppose it's much like the whore and the pimp – she must have someone lower than herself.

I think it was 1978 when I heard Morrisseau was selling pictures to an antique dealer. It began because of Norval's insane interest in elegant objects. This time a silver samovar.

Well, the shop was a front for a family of The Families. A son, (whom I never met) had just come back from the West Coast where daddy and the boys had set him up with a shop. The shop had folded, whether due to lack of business sense or due to a desire to lose money, I don't know. However, the son was at loose ends and opened a gallery in downtown Toronto, specializing in native art, including Morrisseau's. As Morrisseau had never been "faithful," I just figured it to be another passing phase of his. It wasn't. One day, while I was working in my warehouse on Richmond Street West, two men arrived and asked if I was Jack Pollock. They then produced I.D. cards and informed me they were undercover agents in the vice squad. Jake Mol was the name of the key man. I can't recall the name of the other.

They asked if I knew Norval Morrisseau, if I realized he was in Toronto, staying at the Sheraton Centre, and if I knew who had paid for the tickets from Thunder Bay for Norval and his two "young friends." They then informed me that the family's man in Thunder Bay had paid for the tickets (in cash) and that, as of that moment, I was under what they described as "loose" police protection. They had taped conversations in which it was stated that Jack Pollock must be eliminated as the major dealer of Morrisseau. They also stated that, as I was a public figure, they did not expect physical violence, but were sure that financial pressures would be exerted. I was given a card with a private phone number on it to call in case of problems. For more than two years, I lived with Jake Mol's card in my pocket.

We met several times, usually by appointment on a street corner, as we both casually walked by. He said he felt my phones were probably tapped, and I should try, if possible, to warn Morrisseau. I told Norval who he was dealing with. He

171

refused to believe me, and as they were paying for materials and supplying him with drugs and young boys, and a large house in the country, I had no way of convincing him of the danger. They amassed a huge collection of original paintings (very uneven, as I was the only one who could, and did, guide the erratic genius of his talent). They then moved to larger quarters farther east.

Prints were big then, and so they began producing "limited" editions of mechanically produced silk screens and would bribe Norval with dollars, dicks, and dope to sign them.

Morrisseau is an amoral genius. He also knew no fear, and finally he started defying them. They had several more series of prints printed, but Norval wouldn't sign them. Michel Abaziou, a publisher from Montreal, had contracted with Methuen, who had published the book in English, to produce the French edition of the book on Morrisseau. I had a contract with Abaziou for a percentage of both the special edition and the trade edition. He decided to produce the portfolio of prints, which was to accompany the French special edition, with the family. Why – I don't know to this day. I do know I received several telephone calls from them because Morrisseau had asked that I choose the works for the prints, and also because they knew I was the only real authority on his work.

I contacted Jake Mol. He said go to the gallery, but under no circumstances to commit myself. He said if I wanted to act as consultant and be paid in a legitimate fashion, it could not be construed as illegal. I went to a meeting, saw about twenty pictures, told them which ones I thought the best – and left. I refused to do business.

When the French edition was launched, together with a major show of Morrisseau's work, I never went near it.

Back to Morrisseau. He was becoming a royal pain in the ass to the family. They had the huge collection of originals, they had hundreds of signed prints, but they also had hundreds of unsigned prints. Norval came to my gallery one day and said they had been to his house. They had brought pieces of wood and tools and had demanded Norval carve his signature into the wood so they could block-sign prints. I suggested Norval go away for a while as rumours were that the family was tired of his "prima donna" ways.

Morrisseau managed somehow to get free, but then he tied himself up with another crook (the name escapes me). I gave up. Without the Morrisseau sales, my gallery was financially deprived. Soon afterwards I started on my personal path to hell. I often wonder if the first young hustler type to offer me cocaine was working for the family. I don't like to dwell on that shit, but it's not impossible.

Morrisseau finally became frightened and fled to the bush in Northern Ontario. It seemed that the family had succeeded: the Pollock Gallery collapsed, and here I am.

February 26, 1986

Dear M.

All this delving into the past has brought back memories of one of my favourite people, Pearl McCarthy.

Pearl McCarthy established the *Globe and Mail's* art page and reigned for many years as undisputed queen of the fast-changing art world. I consider myself privileged to have known her, and her early support of me inspired me to grow and to take on challenges.

An Oxford scholar (no mean feat in her day), she never wrote for other writers, nor did she use a pat and private language, a style already becoming popular with the intelligentsia. She looked at art through her own eyes and attempted to bridge gaps of understanding by writing what she saw. She did not build her reputation by demolishing others, rather, she constructively criticized their art. She was also a champion of the new, somewhat raw, talents of the day.

I have known very few women in my life who have earned and deserved the title "Lady." Pearl McCarthy Sabeston was, and is, at the top of my short list.

She covered the very first exhibition in my gallery, the 10th Street Scene, a collection of young contemporary New York artists, and our meeting kindled a spark that I will never forget.

She would often call me in the evening (those days that the Bell and I were talking) and invite me to her apartment for a nightcap. When I arrived, she would be all woman, wearing hostess gown and slippers, and we would sip brandy and talk until the wee hours of the morning. Colin, her husband of many years, had died, and she lived in circumstances of frugal elegance. Few knew, as I did, that she was selling off the family silver and crystal in order to live.

We talked of her early life with a mother who rejected her and told her constantly that she was ugly. She was, in truth and according to photographs, plain. Her father's solution to the problem was a practical one, at least to him: dress well and in the finest possible manner. So Pearl developed the art of costume. Her clothes became creations. Draped, folded, sometimes hung severely, her dress was always at one with her being.

She wore hats – big hats, floppy hats, black velvet hats with a dash of mystery and intrigue – and, very essential, proper walking shoes. Pearl walked more on her weekly rounds of galleries than many *sportif* types today. Ah yes, and the cane. Always a cane. I recall her sweeping into the gallery wrapped in a splendid Irish tweed cape, wearing a version of a deer stalker's hat. That was class!

Her sense of what was proper led to an interesting pre-Christmas decision. For several years she and Colin had commissioned Dora de Pedery-Hunt to create their holiday cards, and once I visited a few days before they were to be mailed. She showed me one of them, just back from the printer, and I thought it handsome, as indeed it was. Pearl stated there would be no cards sent that year. "My name is larger than that of Christ," she exclaimed, "and that just won't do!" So, hundreds of cards were paid for, and destroyed.

When "Honest Ed" Mirvish purchased and refurbished the Royal Alexandra Theatre, I was given two seats to the *première* of the first play. My first thought was to ask Pearl to be my date, even though she was not too well. When I arrived with a white orchid in my hand to take her for an early dinner at Winston's before the show, I found her pale and exquisite in a floor-length gown of rich black silk complemented by a rope of pearls. I remarked on her dress, and she replied, "Balenciaga—Mother had two of them, she was buried in the other!"

We arrived, along with the Who's Who of the social world, amidst flashing lights and took our seats in the fifteenth row, centre. As the curtain rose, she leaned over, and beaming, said it was a dream and, to top it, did I know we were two rows in front of Lady Eaton!

The play, *Never Too Late*, was not good. The star, William Bendix, projected nothing, but the event was a special moment in my life because I shared it with the greatest Lady of them all – Pearl.

She was ever-conscious of death in her later years, yet continued her love of acquiring knowledge. When her body was found one morning, she was propped in bed wearing an elegant bed jacket, and beside her was a textbook on the Greek language.

A postscript: A year after her death I organized a memorial exhibition and sale to establish a Pearl McCarthy scholarship fund at St. Hilda's College, University of Toronto. Artists, dealers, and collectors contributed and Dora de Pedery-Hunt struck a fine portrait medal. I have never heard of anyone receiving this scholarship, but trust it is given to those thought deserving.

While sitting in the gallery during that exhibition, I recalled conversations with Pearl about "the girls" (Frances Loring and Florence Wyle). She had known them well, and was appalled that no gallery, including the Art Gallery of Toronto, showed any interest in exhibiting their work. Born in America, they had spent over fifty years in Canada, and were responsible for some of the finest figurative commissions for public sites. Pearl had suggested I call them, but I'd felt young, wet behind the ears in comparison to their stature, and I'd hesitated.

Loring and Wyle both sent pieces to the memorial exhibition, and that gave me the courage to pick up the phone and call them. A deep, rich voice answered and I explained who I was. Neither Frances Loring nor Florence Wyle knew anything of the new gallery scene, but they courteously invited me to visit their studio, a splendid old church that they had moved from north of Toronto to its present site on Glenrose Avenue, just east of Mount Pleasant. I was told that Frances liked whisky and that Florence drank only ginger ale, so I arrived with a bunch of tulips, a bottle of V.O. and a large bottle of Canada Dry. The studio was awesome, though dusty, and Frances sat, majestically, rather like my image of Gertrude Stein. She was large, handsome, with eyes of deep and probing penetration. Florence, in bunched-together men's trousers, men's shirt with rolled sleeves, was already slightly fey, and insisted on diluting her ginger ale with water, as it was much too strong.

We talked of Pearl, the art world, and I timidly suggested I would be honoured to do an exhibition of their work. To my amazement, they agreed, and I think the prospect of a show was a lift for both of them. Frances Gage, a former student of theirs, and already a fine sculptor in her own right, took on the enormous task of selecting, with me, the works for the show. Several maquettes were discovered and small editions were cast from the clay originals. Other larger works had a patina that made the plaster take on the look of bronze. I produced a modest catalogue, bought many tree-size plants, and painted one of the galleries black for the occasion. The earliest works were portraits each had done of the other in the early part of the century. Bronze figures of war workers during the First World War were borrowed from the National Gallery, and Frances Loring's monumental work *The Goal Keeper* dominated the main gallery. A serene and beautiful life-size three-quarters nude girl in soft grey plaster by Wyle was the highlight in the blackened gallery. Busts of A.Y. Jackson, Vincent Massey, and Frederick Varley were juxtapositioned with narrative works like *Chicago*, *The Hound of Heaven*, and Wyle's powerful Carrara marble, *Sea and Shore*.

The day of the opening drew near, and I don't recall before, or since, ever feeling such a powerful sense of history in my gallery.

As Frances was large, and not too steady on her feet, we had arranged a wheelchair at the door. Alan Jarvis, a staunch supporter and dear friend, had written a brief tribute in the catalogue, and he was officially to open the exhibition.

It was a sunny Sunday afternoon. We waited, and waited, and finally Frances Gage arrived with Florence Wyle. Loring had had a stroke that morning and had been taken to the Women's College Hospital, where she stayed, mostly in a coma, until her death almost six months later.

Florence, fortunately, was not aware that had happened and spent several hours in a child-like kind of trance, one moment recognizing guests, the next perplexed and not able to grasp the occasion fully. A.Y. Jackson arrived on time, but Varley was an hour and a half late, as he had to find the tie the girls had given him almost twenty years before. It was a bittersweet afternoon, but I knew Pearl was smiling in the wings and saying, "Well done." I can still see the wheelchair, empty and waiting, and if I have any regret, it is that I did not act sooner on Pearl's advice.

Their work sold relatively well, and I felt as though a great gift had been bestowed on me. Florence also went into hospital within the week, and they died within three weeks of each other, each not knowing of the other's presence in the hospital.

Shortly after their death, a memorial service was held in the studio, and as A.Y. was beyond reading publicly, it was my great honour to read from Florence Wyle's published book of poems.

I have recently received a letter from the AGO stating they

now own all works left in the estate. I trust they will be exhibited regularly, as Loring and Wyle are major figures in our country's artistic history development.

They founded the Canadian Sculpture Society and were avid supporters of young, aspiring talent. Why, when the Group of Seven (their friends whom they supported and often fed) were accepted, no support was given to them remains a mystery to me. Their work varied greatly, with Loring presenting a strong and powerful use of clay, rugged and externally aggressive. Wyle, on the other hand, was accused of soft and pretty pieces, but *Mother of the Race*, and *Sea and Shore*, and the young girl all had a fineness that came from inward, sinewy strength. Her almost overworked surfaces belied the dynamics of her form.

I knew them little, but I feel I knew them well. They were proud, hurt, and justifiably annoyed by the lack of interest in their work. I, with Pearl's guidance, helped to right a few wrongs, and give the public a chance to pay homage to two great Canadian sculptors – the girls.

I tried to interest Harold Ballard to buy *The Goal Keeper* for the Maple Leaf Gardens, but with no success. I still dream of it, cast in bronze, standing nine feet tall – *the* symbol of our great Canadian sport.

February 27, 1986

Dear M.

My memories of Morrisseau open many old wounds. I have tried, for years, to document the nightmare of 1973-74, which involved Norval, a government agent named Bob Fox, and me. It began when filmmaker Henning Jacobsen, who had been commissioned to do a National Film Board film on Morrisseau, came to me for an introduction to Norval.

I knew that Norval was in the Kenora jail. He had been there for over four months. On more than one occasion, I had bailed him out of jail. But this time the Kenora police chief refused bail, stating that if Morrisseau was to survive, he would have to dry out completely. Reluctantly, I allowed him to remain imprisoned.

Two months later, I visited him in the jail and found that he was well and being treated like a prince. He had one cell in which to sleep and another one he used as a studio. Some of his finest pictures were painted during that period. I bought several, leaving cheques totalling $6,000 with the warden.

Before going back to Kenora a couple of months later, this time with Henning Jacobsen, I phoned the jail and found out that Norval was being released on the following Monday. I suggested that we and the camera crew, the director, and various assistants arrive on the Sunday night, so we could be sure of his sobriety the next day. We talked to the prison officials and Morrisseau; everything was arranged.

On the plane I met Bob Fox, who worked for the Ontario government's Indian Affairs Department. He told me Morrisseau was well and that the cheques I had left for him had been used as a down payment on a house in Kenora. I was pleased.

We arrived at the Kenora Holiday Inn and, after dinner and drinks, went to bed, having left requests for early wake-up calls. When we got to the prison in the morning, I was informed that Mr. Fox – are you ready for this? – had released Morrisseau the night before. The hunt started and we found him after a while, totally drunk and incoherent.

Camera crews cost thousands of dollars a day, and Henning didn't want to waste their time, so he asked if I could possibly try to sober Norval up. I sent one of the assistants to buy six bottles of Baby Duck, six bottles of soda water, and a large bottle of grape juice. We poured out the Baby Duck and refilled the bottles with a mixture of soda water and grape juice. I invited Norval to my room, where we sat around for four or five hours drinking that shit. In the end, he seemed slightly less pissed.

Meanwhile, Henning had tracked down the large roll of paintings that Morrisseau had done while in jail. I told the hotel manager that we wanted to rent their ballroom. I then got a tranquillizer from the script assistant, gave it to Norval, and he went to sleep.

Back in the so-called ballroom, I stapled all the pictures to the walls of one section to simulate a kind of studio, and also got an easel, paints, and so on. Then I went out and bought some clothes for Norval as he had messed up his own.

Finally, at about ten that evening, Norval woke up. Although not sober, he was willing to be interviewed. We filmed all that evening, then gave him another pill and told him we would start early the next morning to shoot an outdoor sequence.

Norval's wife, Harriet, and two small children of theirs came to the hotel. We all set out for the lake shore, carrying picnic lunches and toys for the kids. Once there, Norval kept going into the bushes, to piss, he said. Finally, we discovered he had hidden a bottle of whisky there. How he had got hold of it, I'll never know. Then things went from bad to worse and most of the shooting had to be postponed.

The paintings we had used the night before were still at the hotel. Norval told me to take them to Toronto and sell them. Before I took the paintings, I made a list of all of them, signed it, and left it at the hotel desk to be picked up by the lawyer Fox had mentioned was looking after the purchase of the house.

The day after I got back to Toronto, Fox came to my gallery, accusing me of theft and demanding Morrisseau's paintings. As I neither liked nor trusted the man and, fortunately, had left the pictures rolled up at my apartment, I refused to give them to him unless I received permission to do so from a sober Morrisseau. Fox left, threatening to sue. I immediately took the paintings to my lawyer, who had them placed in a vault.

I contacted the lawyer in Kenora, who denied any knowledge of having received my receipt. He told me the house had been bought in Fox's name, as the owner would not sell to an Indian. As a government agent, Fox was forbidden by law to use or abuse his privilege by profiting from any dealings with Morrisseau, from the purchase of the house to the sale of his paintings. Refusing to sell to an Indian, if the money is there, also is against the law.

About a month later, I received a court writ. I was charged with theft. I panicked and phoned Jim Fleck, who was Premier William Davis's chief adviser, and told him the whole story. The next news I heard was that Fox had been relieved of his job and had moved to Mexico.

Yet another writ came and then a call from Davis's office, informing me that the charges would be dropped. I refused to let that happen, as it seemed to me that if they were dropped, there would forever remain an element of doubt. I couldn't live with that. So, in March 1974, I flew to Kenora with Richard Baker, a young assistant lawyer, taking along my gallery files, letters, and accounts. The government paid to fly Fox back from Mexico and set him up in a hotel – the same fucking Holiday Inn.

I was in the prisoner's box for three days. Richard was nervous, I was past feeling. On the third day, Morrisseau arrived. Looking filthy and sporting two black eyes, he took the witness stand. He said he had only one agent – Jack Pollock, his friend.

The court adjourned and we had to wait until the next morning for the judge's decision. Enclosed are his remarks. I have never sobbed so hard or shaken as much in my life as when he exonerated me. Fox immediately flew back to Mexico. God knows what happened to the house; Morrisseau certainly did not get it. I was over five thousand dollars out of pocket.

On the way home, the young lawyer, Richard, confessed this had been his first court case!

You can't make it up!

An interesting side note: Two of the people who had been witnesses throughout the entire filming were Tom Hill, an Indian who worked for the government, and Elizabeth McLuhan, Marshall's daughter. Neither of them would offer statements or testify on my behalf.

P.S. The name of the film is *The Paradox of Norval Morrisseau*. It has been on television dozens of times. If you get a chance to see it, you will recognize his drunken condition.

I thought it was interesting that although the court case was briefly mentioned in the Kenora papers, nothing appeared in Toronto. I am sure there would have been headlines had I been found guilty. When I returned, I asked Kay Kritzwiser at the *Globe and Mail* to write it up, as I felt the story should be told, but I guess innocent verdicts don't make news!

Also, when the AGO did their abortive Native Art Show about Morrisseau and his followers, who were the curators? Tom Hill and Elizabeth McLuhan.

Tom Hill, then working for the Federal Department of Indian Affairs, would see paintings at my gallery, talk to Morrisseau, and offer to buy them for less. The Art Bank, whose mandate is to buy pictures from the artist's dealer or, when there is no dealer, from the artists themselves, bought a large collection of Morrisseau paintings from a private collector. Arturo Swartz (Dr.), the collector, was a buddy of Trudeau's, and Luke Rombout was the head of the Art Bank. Neither Morrisseau nor I, his dealer, benefitted from the transaction. So on it goes.

Maybe you are beginning to get a sense of what the art world is like: scheming, manipulative and, quite often, downright fraudulent.

IN THE DISTRICT COURT JUDGE'S CRIMINAL COURT
FOR THE DISTRICT OF KENORA
B E T W E E N :
HER MAJESTY THE QUEEN
- and -
JACK POLLOCK
PROCEEDINGS, Monday, MARCH 11th, 1974 at the Court
House, Kenora, Ontario.
BEFORE: His Honour Judge L.A. McLennan
JUDGMENT, VERDICT and REMARKS

JUDGMENT

HIS HONOUR:

This has been a trial of a very serious nature, partly because the offence of Theft is a serious criminal offence, as pointed out by counsel, and partly because the Accused is an individual who is very prominent in the business world and in the artistic world of this we have heard in the course of the evidence and that the matters involved here are of very serious consequence to him. . . .

Before I proceed to comment to some small degree on the evidence, I think that I should deal with the matter of credibility because credibility has been stated to be an issue in this case. To an extent it is, although I may say that on the whole of the evidence there is a marked similarity between the evidence of the Crown witnesses and of the accused as to the events with which we are concerned. There are, however, some points where they differ and one or two of those points have some importance as to the conclusions I reach on this case. . . .

I may say, therefore, that on the question of credibility, where there is a conflict between the evidence of Mr. Fox and the evidence of Mr. Pollock as to what was said or done, I prefer and accept the evidence of the accused, Mr. Pollock. . . . I base my conclusion on my impression of Mr. Pollock in the witness box and my impression of Mr. Fox. I will go this far that Mr. Pollock impressed me as being clear-cut, decisive and honest in the giving of his evidence without the slightest attempt at any time to evade or to parry a question. He met everything face to face and in following him through some hours of evidence one had to be impressed I think by the deep sincerity from which he seemed to speak.

With respect to Mr. Fox I was not always so satisfied. There were times when I could not escape the conviction that he was evading a direct answer to the question asked. There were repeatedly times when he was uncertain as to just what was said or done and he would frequently revert back to the phrase "it was my understanding that this was so." I was not so concerned with his understanding as I was with what the other person should or could have understood from what happened. . . .

I am satisfied on the evidence that Mr. Pollock when he took the paintings honestly believed that the pictures he took were Morrisseau paintings and that he had authority to take them from the owner, Morrisseau. That belief was based on his dealings with Morrisseau over the three or four days that all these events occurred in, and also based on their mutually satisfactory dealings which involved, and I believe him on the part of Mr. Pollock certainly, and I think also from what he said, on the part of Mr. Morrisseau, not only a business relationship but friendship.

I am satisfied that Mr. Pollock was not aware when he took the paintings that Fox had possessed the paintings as an agent of Morrisseau, if he was an agent, because Mr. Pollock was never told. Indeed, whether Fox was an agent or whether he was not, was academic. I am satisfied that Mr. Pollock was never told that Fox had any specific interest in the paintings other than that of being the immediate custodian of them, bearing in mind that Norval Morrisseau had just been released from custody.

I am satisfied that Mr. Pollock made no agreement with Fox to return the paintings to him nor was he ever called upon to accept or refuse any such undertaking. I am satisfied that fraudulent intent is negatived by the manner in which Mr. Pollock immediately safeguarded the paintings when he learned of the controversy. I am satisfied that he was justified in not returning them immediately on the demand of Fox. Having regard to all the circumstances which I am not going to go back over and re-hash; having regard to everything that he had learned while he was up in Kenora in May, I am satisfied that it was a reasonable position for him to take and that he had reasonable grounds to feel that these paintings should be safeguarded until proper assurances were given him of the authenticity of the claim being advanced by Mr.

Fox. So, while there may or may not have been a taking from Mr. Fox of the paintings, it is clear and I so find that it was accompanied by no fraudulent intent but on the contrary with a very definite colour of right. At the material times Mr. Pollock had no knowledge whatsoever of a special interest of Mr. Fox in these particular paintings.

It is apparent also that while there may have been something in the nature of a taking, there was never at any time any attempt to convert the paintings to Mr. Pollock's own use, or to the use of anyone else. They never appeared in Pollock's Gallery but were immediately placed in safekeeping until returned.

I think it is unnecessary for me to make any further comments on the evidence.

Mr. Pollock, would you please stand up.

Jack Pollock, I find you NOT GUILTY of the charge which has been brought against you.

It is seldom that I add anything further in discharging an accused person but in this case I would like to do so.

I am well aware as we all are, of your position and it must indeed as your counsel has stated have been a very traumatic experience for you to be faced with this trial.

I think it is to your credit and I say so, that you chose to enter the witness box and to expose yourself to cross-examination even though it may very well have been that there might not have been a case at the close of the Crown's evidence. That may be of little comfort to you, but I again say I find in this evidence no suggestion of any fraud or misconduct on your part.

It may be a matter of argument whether this prosecution was justified, or having been started that it was pursued. However, that is of small solace to you, but perhaps there might be some additional comfort to you because it occurs to me that the trial may have done some good by focusing public attention on the serious and tragic social problem involving the life and potential of Norval Morrisseau. Any one who heard this man give evidence and read the letters filed as exhibits would have to feel that this is an extraordinary man capable of deep sincerity and powerful expression. Indeed you, yourself, while in the witness box eloquently described him as a great Canadian artist bordering on genius and you stated, and with your experience I think it was a professional statement, that he has a potential as a great International artist.

This man has clearly been exploited over the years, not by you that I can see, but by his own people and by other Canadians, perhaps even by people in authority and there is a danger that this unfortunate situation will continue. In that respect this trial may have done some good. You may sit down. You are discharged.

February 27, 1986

Dear M.

The plot thickens. As I sit here, dog turds are glowering at me from the crypt. The only pair of shoes I own, other than my ancient black boots, are chewed to rags, and I pray for a miracle. Tomorrow, the 28th, Joanne Kates (food critic for the *Globe*), her "man," and their six-month-old baby arrive for lunch. Tomorrow, the 28th, the electricity will be cut off. Tomorrow, the 28th, unless the monies come through from Canada, I will have exactly eighteen francs in my pocket (about four bucks).

I'm pondering faking illness so I can cancel Joanne's visit. I may just lock the doors and retreat to the "upper room" (that was the title of the United Church monthly I was weaned on). If the electric people can't get in, they can't cut the power. It is cold and damp again, and if there's no power, there's no heat.

It all makes for a hilarious story, if it weren't so fucking real.

What do I serve Joanne Kates? Dog food casserole?

The house is a disaster area. I haven't painted for over two weeks, I haven't even jerked off! That tells you how bad it is!

I am in bed about twelve to sixteen hours a day, get up to feed Damian (so he can shit) and occasionally feed myself.

I will at least pick up the turds, wash the floors with Javex, and try to air the place a bit. The butcher in the village is closed for two weeks, so no meat on credit. The Co-op will allow me groceries, so I shall have to come up with some kind of meal based on what I can get.

I have never met Ms. Kates, but have heard she is a tough, strongminded bitch. Her writings can certainly be devastating. Who knows? Maybe the great food critic will die of food poisoning in the ancient crypt of Lou Paradou!

Decision – Damian is going to the Humane Society to find a good home.

Decision – Scrub the floors. Get rid of the piss and shit scent, and try to find some flowers.

Decision – Start painting again, even if no one wants the fucking things!

It's now three in the afternoon. I am in the middle of scrubbing the crypt. Next, the *premier étage*, then a week's dirty dishes in the sink. At least I'm mobile, for a change. I'm still trying to figure out what to serve Her Majesty tomorrow. They arrive at noon. If I get most of the housework done, and if the money happens to come tomorrow morning, I could perhaps manage to get to Cavaillon and back before noon and start buying the food. Who knows? Only the Shadow! I'm now waiting for someone to take Damian to the pound. It's the only fair solution to *that* problem.

The local grocer sells candles so I may do a romantic number – candlelight and wine.

Fuck – you can't make it up!

I am taking a breather – the old heart and body are not used to physical labour. The crypt is clean. Smelling like Mr. Clean (in France he is Monsieur Propre).

The *premier étage* should be a little easier, as no saltpetre falls from the walls to create mud. Poor Damian, I have shut him outside and he is crying and jumping at the door. I am a sucker, I guess. I should have told Michel to ask God for the right home for him. If I don't get rid of him today, I don't know what to do–Joanne Kates has a dog, too. I presume he is at least house broken.

I still think a soap opera of my daily existence would be hilarious. Trouble is, no one would believe it–a cross between "I Love Lucy" and "Deep Throat." I find it hard to believe that anyone can fuck up as often and as ridiculously as me.

Hair shirts are itchy
and racks are true twisters.
So, stick to the grindstone
you'll only get blisters!

I have blisters on my hands now from the fucking mop. Where are slaves when you really need them?

I'm going to tackle the kitchen now, leave the *premier étage* for later tonight. Dishes don't demand as much physical effort.

Dishpan hands and an aching back – this housewife shit is for the birds. Oh, for a bathtub to soak in. I have to finish cleaning tonight, as there'll be no hot water if the electricity goes.

Cinderella had a fairy godmother. I'd gladly settle for an old queen with a mop and a bucket right now.

I'm going to go to the Cercle and have a Scotch – double – on the tab. If nothing else, I can still get pissed and pay later.

February 28, 1986

Dear M.

Well, I made it. Jean-Michel arrived this morning and took Damian away. I went to the Co-op and bought provisions for a six-course meal.

Joanne Kates and Leon are charming. What a pleasant surprise! They both adore the baby, and are totally equal in the sharing and caring of her. Joanne said it was one of the rare times she is ever invited to anyone's home for dinner.

She also said the food was superb (and she ate seconds of just about everything).

Although I now owe the grocer three hundred francs, I feel more like a human being (that fucking phrase again!).

The electric people didn't arrive – I don't think they work on the weekend, so I have electricity until Monday. No money – no mail – no news. But I will paint tomorrow.

Goodnight sweet prince. I shall survive!

March–June 1986

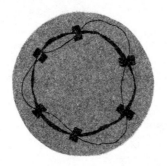

Dear M.

The weather is truly beautiful. For over two weeks now there has been sunshine, and temperatures often reach seventy degrees. The almond trees are in full and glorious bloom, looking like brides of Christ – veiled and yielding. My saucy little peach tree has just begun her hot pink tease. Who the hell am I to bitch and complain when all around me is a celebration?

I have to get my ass in gear, as my show in Saint-Rémy opens Friday, and I have three largish canvases half-finished.

In reviewing (in my head) a lot of what I have written to you since 1984, I begin to worry my letters might sound bitter. I cannot allow this, and truly I don't believe, to be my natural disposition.

It seems to me that if vengeance is to fuel our motivations and lives, we must have a feeling of some superiority to fire our cannons from. That I lack. Although I give "lip service" (thank you, dear Freud!) to projecting a feeling of warmth, I think it a feeble way to keep me going. But I suppose keeping going is all there is.

Your not-too-gentle kick in the nuts about my immortality was greatly appreciated. Spankings can be meted out in different manners. Your way hit home.

Who am I? A devious, darkened, self-deceiver (poetic, eh what?). A minor key trying desperately to be major. And, often, a tired and used body, ready for release.

Whom would I like to be? A hybrid—you, Mother Theresa, and a song-and-dance man with a straw hat, a cane, and a spotlight. In other words, an intelligent, caring, exhibitionist!

Seriously, I cannot think of anyone with whom I would trade lives. There are many others who have qualities I admire, but perfection is, as we know, dear M, made impossible by the powers that be so that we all have a chance at attempting an approximation of it.

We are all born with handicaps; we live with deceit and selfishness, we are too often weaned on rejection and guilt. But we are also nourished by touch, blessed by caring, and, if fortunate, loved.

I would like to be a self-believer. I would like to be strong enough to give support to others, with a reserve sufficient to sustain myself. I would like to have, what I try so hard to give others, a sense of purpose. And I would like to think, as Mahalia Jackson used to wail, "My living has not been in vain!" My feelings of deficiency are based in the habitual practice of justifying my erratic and often self-destructive ways. I have been good—I deserve to be bad; I have been nice —I have earned the right to be naughty!

What you and I seem to be dealing with is a fifty-six-year-old adolescent, who through niceness and charm has gotten away with murder. The murder of his true spirit and being.

I don't know who I am. I don't know who I would like to be. And the puzzle of life arrived without instructions!

I do know that the more negative vibrations I get from others about my "hobby time" in France the more determined I am to prove them wrong. Whether that comes more from stubbornness than common sense, at the moment, I am not sure.

The past few weeks have been difficult, as memories of the needle, the hit, the rush, the world of escape, haunt my sleepless nights. I suppose it is good to be here, alone, somewhat protected, to face these demons.

One of my major fears in returning to what others describe as "the real world" is returning to the cocaine so available in that world. I am not Sampson (long or short hair). I am not a saint. And I fear my weak and self-defeating self would not resist temptation for long. No one who has not experienced a serious addiction problem can, I suppose, be expected to understand the shadow that is always there, the beckoning door waiting to be opened.

I want to survive for my allotted time, but I often feel pressured to go out with a bang. Would they, who have a false belief in my strength, want me to return and face a devil I am not sure I can conquer? Would "real work" for a short time be more socially acceptable than this tired old fart, pushing a brush around for maybe a few years?

We all want others to fit our image of them. I have tried, and often succeeded in filling that image, that role, for others. Of course, skill in role-playing creates a thick and all-too-believable façade. But, dear M, I can't change the mirror image I know to be there. It is that reality that scares me. Leather doesn't make me strong; *Lacoste* doesn't make me sadistic. I am, too often, a frightened boy who still catches himself wanting Mommy. To me, these days, weakness seems the ultimate sin, and often I stand guilty.

You talk about the Church, but for me it gives no answer. The discipline necessary for true faith is awe-inspiring. The positive achievements of those truly committed to religious belief are to be admired. But, for me, responsibility belongs to the individual. Religion can give the base, but each unique being interprets and gives value and true meaning to that base. Just as positive belief can create miracles, so can misguided foundations provide the platform for genocide, famine, and destruction.

Shut up, Pollock, you're in over your head!

March 22, 1986

Dear M.

I have just arrived home from a long, exhausting and exhila-
rating day. It began at nine-thirty this morning, when two
Canadian couples (Picton and Peterborough) arrived to take
me and the last of my pictures to Saint-Rémy, on the way to
my appointment with the cardiologist in Tarascon. I finished
installing the show, with titles and prices, then went to the
doctor's for my two o'clock appointment. Gerry Conrath met
me there, as I needed someone to translate the jargon of a
doctor. Good news. My valve is fine. Not so good news, my
heart is racing far beyond its capacity. I recall your observation
after my brief Toronto visit – "your motor is mad!" Well, that
madness makes me very vulnerable, physically, to heart failure. So, the doctor changed the medication (again) and tomorrow I will take the prescriptions to the pharmacy.

After seeing the doctor, we returned to Saint-Rémy, and I
put tags on the pictures, arranged flowers and finished the
last details. At six o'clock, the *vernissage* (the opening). The
tables were laden with food – potato and herring salad, with
a homemade mayonnaise, *lots* of garlic, tons of smoked ham,
wonderful cold omelette (a provençal specialty) and barrels
of the wonderful wine Terre Blanche. Over a hundred and
fifty people came from Apt, Avignon, Cavaillon, Gordes, Bon-
nieux, and Ménerbes. Gerry Conrath played the piano for a
while (sentimental forties tunes) and then a jazz band arrived,
and I sang and carried on. Seven small pictures were sold (for
a total of just over three thousand francs) and the photographer from the local paper arrived, as did its critic.

Then out of nowhere, a tall, attractive young man
appeared, introduced himself as one Roger Morier, a Toronto
writer, living and writing in France. He said he'd seen my
poster in Aix-en-Provence, knew of me and the gallery, and
had decided to come. He is a friend of Joanne Kates and said
she raved about me, my house, and my cooking! He couldn't
believe the support I had at the opening and has decided to
write a feature article on me for the *Globe and Mail* (apparently

he writes for them quite often). I think it would be rather strange, and in a slightly perverse way, enjoyable, for people like Kay Kritzwiser to see an article on me.

The exhibition is fine, but not quite as good as I would like it to be. However, I am painting and the France-Canada Association have, apparently, scheduled another exhibition in Lyon and one later in Cannes.

I continue to be a pimp for my "Blue Boy" in Toronto, as I sold one *Piece of M*, and another collage titled *3022*. I hope you enjoy the vicarious pleasure!

Another plus is that a strange *femme d'un certain âge* arrived, and asked me to do a one-hour interview on Radio France – in French. She feels my "charming" approach to the language would be a welcome relief. So, on April 2nd, I do the interview. Jean-Michel will tape it, so maybe we can all have a laugh!

Living here gives one a perspective on daily news. The elections here were, to me, frightening, as Le Pen and the Fascist right won over thirty-five seats. Then, yesterday in the *Herald Tribune*, that asshole Buckley wrote an article (enclosed) demanding all AIDS persons be tattooed on the arm and the ass!

AIDS is a problem we cannot ignore. It is ugly, murderous, and spreading. I feel you and your brothers in the psychiatric profession will have a special role to play as the tragedy unfolds.

Ignoring AIDS' horrific presence will not make it go away. The promiscuity of much of the gay world is being challenged and, probably, rightly so. A society that, on the one hand, has condemned, and on the other, has permitted places such as baths and the dark rooms of bars to exist for purely sexual purposes is in deep trouble. No such condoned places for sexual relief exist in the heterosexual world. We cannot have our cake and eat it too, so to speak. I say all this as a product, a result, of the two-faced social dilemma, and the world of twilight lust and passion. I probably have never felt the singular love and caring of another to any great depth because of my continued appetite for the fantasy of the physical. I can't imagine what it must be like to "come out" now, not only with society against gays, but with prejudice fuelled by the fear of disease, death and despair. I fear for the young. The right-wing Moral Majority has a wonderful cache of ammunition for their on-going battle of prejudice.

Maybe out of it all will come a sense of commitment and an empathy, which as we are well aware has been lacking. My past was doubly dangerous, as intravenous drug use and sexual promiscuity are both major vehicles of the plague. It is also strange that the "passive" partner is more prone. "The meek shall inherit the earth"? – well, so much for that.

My little peach tree is almost vulgar in its horny pink display. The mistral blows today, but I feel like I might survive.

I have decided, who needs another Pollock? Pollock does!

April 8, 1986

Dear M.

Well, this was the week that was! Falling from grace can be a painful and exhausting experience. Why do I *need* so badly that at times all logic and common sense dissolves, and I tumble into a pit of meaningless attempts at touching and caring? Such was the case with Pascal, a beautiful young man (twenty-six), architect and would-be painter. We had a few drinks together, went to his home (part of an old *mas*), and then hashish and some kind of strange tea, which I suppose was laced with acid or LSD. Time warp – blackness, almost three days of empty logic, and now, eight days later, I have returned to the real world. I had to mend fences with Jean-Michel (not so difficult), Françoise (much more difficult), Gerry, and Jeannette at the Café des Variétés in Saint-Rémy.

Stupidity! This all started the night before I was to do a radio interview in French in Saint-Rémy. I did do it. Jean-Michel and Françoise took me. Apparently, after the interview I wanted to lie down, and Jeannette showed me a room above the café, where I passed out. When I came to I took off in a bus for Cavaillon. How I got to Cavaillon, and then back here to Gordes, I don't recall. The interview, apparently, went well but the woman who interviewed me thought I was tired. Tired? I was comatose!

I came to somewhat the next day, phoned Gerry, who told me the horrible truth, and then I had to go back to Saint-Rémy to apologize to Jeannette. Gerry drove me, and to my relief, Jeannette was truly sympathetic. I suppose she has seen it all. Camus was in that café the night he drove madly and killed himself. Nicolas de Staël was there the day he committed suicide (or fell) to his death in a drunken stupor.

I phoned Jean-Michel from Jeannette's and he said he and Françoise would pass by the house later that afternoon. Thank God, they accepted me, and tried to understand.

Last night, I prepared the dinner I had planned for Jeannette, Jean-Michel, Françoise, Marc (my doctor in Saint-Rémy), his girlfriend, Gerry, and the young Canadian journalist Roger Morier.

I bust my ass and prepared eight courses. The menu included the first asparagus of the season, fresh *moules* in *pastis*, grilled *chèvre*, curried cream of celery soup, *gigot*, pears, Roquefort, salad, and bananas *flambées*.

We were at the table from eight until two in the morning. The meal was a smashing success, and all my excesses of the past week seem forgotten, but I still feel sordid, shitty, and totally exhausted.

In retrospect, too bad it wasn't cocaine. At least you don't black out and you still have some control over your behaviour. But cocaine would have been worse in other respects, I suppose. At least there were no needles, and I have no desire for a repeat performance. I think masturbation is probably my life mate. I jerked off six times the day before yesterday, hoping to have a heart attack and die. All I got was a slightly tired prick, and a very tired hand!

David Pelletier's exhibition at Moos you described in your letter brings up a constant battle I have with that genre of contemporary art: totally figurative, sadistic, and indulgent. The martyrdom of Mark Prent over the charges laid against him of obscenity during his show at Isaacs is ample justification for exhibits such as this. Prent also is highly masturbatory, and my great problem with this "school" of art is that after the initial shock, after the first confrontation, all that is left is skill and craftsmanship. The truly haunting and oft-times horrific art of the world (mostly religious – Picasso's *Guernica* and the *Grotesques* by Goya and a few others) continues to disturb, drawing us again and again into its clutches. Most contemporary exponents of this form of art seem to me to be applied, rather than felt. A kind of playing the organ (pardon the pun) with all the stops out. Disguised as Fine Art, many artists' works become accepted by the "in" people.

Some have pulled it off. I truly admire Keinholtz. For me he is a true believer and his work continues to haunt my vision. The almost faceless, yet highly figurative plaster images of Segal are ghost-like spectres, I find them unforgettable. The power in figurative art, for me, comes from the real made more real. Muscle beach and baskets for days are turned out for jerking off. The disturbing and powerful factor in a Hockney male is that the figure is just that – a male.

When I first exhibited the *Cavafy Suite* in the Markham Street gallery, many people were outraged. Why? Because Hockney had managed to create images so ordinarily male that they could be of your brother, your husband, and you. If they could be categorized as gay they would immediately lose their threat, placed in the safe world of boxed thinking. (Those Hockney etchings were ninety dollars framed, and I sold very few. I had to sell them off cheap later to pay my bills. God knows what they are worth today!)

The young sculptor, Pelletier, has his job cut out for him. Continuous shocking dulls the senses, and craft can carry you only so far.

A friend sent me a note recently with reviews from all three Toronto papers on Scott Symons' new book, *Helmet of Flesh*. I remember once when he and his wife arrived at the

AGO for a costume ball – his father-in-law was president at the time – he wore an enormous cod piece and not much else, and she was bare-breasted. The whole event was horribly embarrassing.

I would like to read his novel. From the reviews it sounds highly self-indulgent and masturbatory. It might serve as a warning for any literary attempts I might make at describing my life.

April 11, 1986

Dear M.

Openings, openings, and more openings. Yes, they are quite dull affairs nowadays.

One of the strangest openings I ever held was for an exhibition of Eric Rutherford's paintings. Eric was a British painter whom I'd previously shown in group exhibition. I had sold a few of his paintings and we were planning a joint show of his work and the sculptures of Jack Culiner. One day, I was in the gallery, working with Jack on the wording of the invitation, when the phone rang. It was Eric, calling from someplace in the States where he was teaching. He said, "Jack, darling. I have a problem. Maybe you won't want to exhibit me, after all." I couldn't imagine what he was talking about, then he pronounced, "Jack. I am a woman!"

Now, Eric was a grandfather. He'd been married four times and had a twelve-year-old daughter with Gail, his current wife. He was fifty-four years old and over six feet tall. And here he was, telling me he was a woman.

He said he'd understand if I cancelled the show. I gulped and said, "Eric –" "Erica," he corrected me. "Erica," I said, "I am showing your paintings. I am not showing you. And I believe in your paintings. But I do have a problem in that several people have bought paintings by Eric Rutherford and several other people, including Mrs. Signy Eaton, among others, are interested in coming to see this exhibition. I think it's going to be tricky for Erica to arrive instead of Eric. So I suggest that we should do an article in the press before you come." He said, "Do what you want. It's public knowledge that I am a woman."

I phoned Kay Kritzwiser and, for the first time in my career, asked for a favour. (Kay had dined with Eric and Gail when they had visited Toronto a year or two before, and she had liked them very much.) I told her the story, and she nearly collapsed. She did talk to Eric/Erica and wrote a very tasteful column along with two photographs, one of Eric in his army uniform and one of Erica in her tweeds. The headline read (as you know, newspaper headlines are never written by the columnist or reporter, but always by someone else): "What a difference an A makes."

The show went on, and Erica arrived. She knew she would have a terrible time getting through immigration at the airport because her papers were still in the name "Eric," but she was furious that she had had to go in drag–as a man–to get across the border. A lot of strange people came to that show, which did relatively well.

Erica has continued to produce good paintings and very beautiful serigraphs. Doris Pascal represented• her with the prints – figurative images done in stunning colours. She's a consummate artist and a very fine teacher. She lives in Canada now.

That was quite the opening.

April 25, 1986

Dear M.

This morning the mail brought a note from Joanne Kates (as you know, she is living near Cannes, and was here for lunch). Well, she is on radio CHFI daily, and she sent me the following text of one of her one- or two-minute spots to be aired the week of April 28th.

"I heard there was a wacky Toronto artist named Jack Pollock living in a village called Gordes, so I looked him up the other week. He has no phone because they cut it off after he called Toronto too many times and forgot to pay, so we corresponded by mail, and he invited me for lunch.

"This guy used to be the owner of the Pollock Gallery in Toronto, he was a businessman, but take a look at how he's changed.

"We arrived for lunch just after noon. He was in the kitchen of the 800-year-old house where he lives, which used to be a monastery.

"Soon we sat down. He wouldn't let anybody help. There were six at the table.

"First came a curried cream of celery soup, with a fine, rich stock. Then came avocado in a honey and ginger sauce. Then came a lot of fresh mussels in a very wicked sauce with a serious amount of butter and brandy. (Let's not talk about cholesterol.) And after that—no, I am not kidding—there were two fresh guinea hens served with a casserole of baked pears with Roquefort cheese. For dessert, there was a pistachio ice-cream cake brought by one of the other guests.

"After coffee, I looked at my watch. It was six p.m.! See how people can change. Some people, including me, would call that getting civilized.

"I'm Joanne Kates, restaurant critic, *Globe and Mail*."

So much for Julia Child!

Today, I got a postcard from Nadine de Montmollin in Geneva which was sent to the Gallery Kruger, where she works, from Gallery Moos. It is a reproduction of Charlie Pachter's rendition of the supreme court judges, badly painted, and cleverly titled *The Supremes*. Cleverness is the enemy of art, and I find the commercial slickness such as Charlie Pachter's sickening. On Markham Street, I had Charlie's first show (graphics he had done at Cranbrooke, on a beautiful hand-made paper). His early work showed he had great talent. But he, like many, finds business and hustling more important than art. The "Canadian" bit, with moose, beavers, and so on, that both he and Joyce Wieland have milked, is embarrassing. Any image can be art, if only it is approached with a personal vision and a committment.

Jasper John's *American Flags* and his targets are superb examples of the everyday transcending the mundane. The flat and vulgar surfaces of Warhol's early work are powerful statements of social conditions. The work of Claes Oldenburg and Jim Dine is also very effective. But cream rises to the top, dear M, and the hustlers, such as Pachter, will find their level. I, at least, march to my own drummer, create my own images, and am seriously involved in picture-making.

The weather has been up and down like a toilet seat – one day glorious sun, the next grey, damp and raining.

This morning is sunny. So am I.

May 6, 1986

Dear M.

Your letter of April 20 arrived yesterday. I, like you, decided to re-read all your letters since Christmas. A few words – your remarks on the value of monastery life – gave me a key to your furtive searchings for a meaning and *raison d'être* for life. So did your distinctions between real and fabricated, or commercialized, faith.

I remember when Marshall McLuhan converted at a mature age to Roman Catholicism. I was puzzled. But it's true that many great thinkers and writers are capable of both profound thought and a true belief. How I envy them! I have great respect for those who have worshipped, loved, and believed. My crypt, which did put you off, is not at all what you felt – or let yourself *not* feel. Practically each object has been discovered in the flea market – dirty, discarded, and abused. In my vaulted room they can at last be at rest. I often sit alone, candles burning, and study the kindly, accepting face of the unknown cardinal. The large wrought-iron cross – rusted, yet majestic – was once, I am sure, guardian of a roadside shrine. These objects, the crypt, and the village itself make me aware of the power for good (and, I am afraid, evil) in the Church of the past.

More than one person, at my show in Saint-Rémy and at the house, has remarked on the use of the cross in many of my compositions. Also, I'm aware that the step from crown of thorns to barbed wire is not that great.

When I ponder the death of Frisé and Alain's physical and mental damage, I am left with one simple truth. I am here for a reason. That truth, in quiet moments like this, supports my attempts at creativity. My work is at least *mine*. It looks like no one else's. That does not make it good or bad, but it does suggest an attempt at personal communication. What more can I do?

Then the destructive forces within me insist on being heard. Who earned the reputation of a "retarded child"? Who perpetuates continually that image by deed and action? Who, in most instances, shuns true caring, feeling not worthy and unclean? Who often physically exhibits his feelings of uncleanness, unworthiness? No one else but, as the saying goes, me, myself, and I.

You, dear M, have your private hells. I have inklings to them now and then, although our survival methods are almost opposites. My completeness is curtailed by my preferences, be they genetic, environment, or social impositions. My love of children only testifies to that incomplete link in my chain of life.

Your perfectionist approach to life would be almost impossible for anyone to measure up to, just as much of my slovenly, don't-give-a-damn approach makes me an unlikely life partner for anyone.

So, we each have ourselves; small and somewhat frightened at the core, child-like and vulnerable, yet wearing armours of different hues to achieve the same, non-natural goals of isolation, aloneness, and sadly, often only public acceptance.

Would that a forgiving God could touch me and instill some sense of true worth!

Would that your God could ease the tightness of your being!

May 20, 1986

Dear M.

I am just back from Montluçon, where I "represented" Canada at an international art show. I was treated like royalty – given a dinner with champagne, Charolais fillets, escargots with fresh *foie gras*, a wonderful Beaujolais. My picture was in the papers (again) and I've been told that I won a prize. I know I am not among the top three winners, so I shall probably get a certificate of some sort and a handshake. I have to go back this Friday when the Minister of Culture gives out the awards.

Now for the other side of the show: The exhibition is dreadful – a kind of international version of the Toronto Outdoor Show but with less exciting young talent. To win a prize in such a show is no great feat. Of the five judges, three were commercially oriented women who represented artists in the show and the two others were men – limp dicks, wimpish, and totally benign.

I did, of course, dry fuck the world, wearing black leather, my bear-claw necklace, and so on, and arriving mysteriously out of the night.

If any of this translates into sales, then the trip will have been worthwhile. All my expenses were paid for by the committee (or the Consulate, I'm unsure which). Every other artist, if you can call them that, had to pay eighty francs per painting just to get them hung, plus expenses if they wanted to attend.

I took nine paintings. I was allowed ten, all the others were allowed only five. I ended up hanging only seven, as the committee felt my barbed-wire constructions were too political. (Remember, this area was all once part of Vichy France during World War II.)

One amusing moment was my arrival at the *vernissage*. I had been driven to Montluçon by my friend Marilyn, and we were both booked into one hotel for the first night and were to be moved to another for the second. It wasn't worth unpacking, so all our clothes and belongings were in the back of her car. Since I was robbed two years ago, I have no suitcase, so all my clothes, complete with a new costume of pure white and very tight pants, pure white shirt with a stand-up collar, black boots, and black leather vest, were in the large straw basket I normally use for shopping. I had nowhere to change before the opening, and the director of the show suggested I use the public john. So I went in, stripped, and once naked found my change of clothes was still in the car, having fallen out of the basket during the journey!

Soon there was a line-up outside the john, banging on the door, and I had to redress, carry my basket out to the car, retrieve my "purity" look, return, wait for the john, and then do my caterpillar-butterfly number.

Lots of laughs.

May 26, 1986

Dear M.

I telephoned Gerry Conrath in Aix today. She was very upset for me, as Eva phoned her last night, telling her the house is rented for a month, beginning June 15 (about three weeks from now). Why she didn't write me directly, I have no idea.

Thought: The Outdoor Art Show is the first week in July. I am kicked out of here June 15.

Decision: Somehow I will come to Canada for that period of time (maybe, as before, only three weeks).

I realize, in retrospect, that my last visit was artificially inseminated and truly theatrical. The closest I came to being me was that brief moment in your kitchen, when I touched your shoulder. I don't mean that as anything more than the simple contact of friendship it was, but it was, for a split second, everything.

The incongruity of the image I project and the real me is overwhelming. I am not an artist, I am not a writer – I am a sham, a hollow being, screaming silently for a reason for being. I play the fool well and feel closest to being alive when others laugh at my predicaments – at least they recognize me.

But, too often, I flash, I shine with all the artificial beauty and brilliance of a rhinestone – fake, false, and only momentarily attractive. The flipside of this is my persona as the melancholy Dane – dark, brooding, demanding some kind of understanding.

But, dearest M, none of them are real. I am not a Charlie Chaplin. I am not a diamond. Nor am I Hamlet. I run, I hop, I skip, I jump – anything to escape the cavernous hole I sense is me.

Do most people spend their lives trying to escape what they feel is *not* there? Fuck! I'm wallowing, but the truth is I do feel totally void. I don't want to come to Toronto. I don't want to face that reality. I don't want confrontation. I don't – I don't – I don't. (Temper tantrum time, like being on the floor, stomping my feet and vigorously yelling No! No! No!)

At fifty-six, immaturity is a piss-off, childishness is boring, and attention-getting behaviour embarrassing. No wonder people become less close to me. I scare them with the negatives I project at myself. If I don't care, who should?

This piece of theatre called life has had too many acts. My so-called intermissions are less and less frequent. Why the fuck doesn't the curtain fall?

Shit! Shit! Shit!

May 28, 1986

Dear M.

The news of your cottage and its progress warms me. I'm glad you have your own "Lou Paradou" to escape to from city life. We all need such escapes from time to time. We all develop patterns to survive, and a period in the country is healthy – and healing. Of course, other patterns are anti-nature, anti-desire, and anti-human. My problem pattern seems to be my attraction to the unobtainable, or the *almost* unattainable.

I have often been attracted to the young through the superior-teacher-knowing part I feel is in me. Innocence is the greatest of turn-ons, yet to some extent I remain innocent. I can be shocked. I can be "not amused" by crudeness and vulgarity. Yet I can be aware of danger and be highly charged by the power evil possesses.

What is my fascination for the opposite? Black-white, pure-evil – all relative, of course, but nonetheless present? But good, bad, right or wrong, I have not, in my adult life, pretended to be other than I am. Perhaps, for that reason I have never been called a faggot, fruit (to my face that is. God knows what has been said privately), and have never been in any way assaulted personally. I respect others and because of that I can demand some respect for my differences.

Here in Provence, we live a quiet and almost unknowing life of "under the skin" sensuality. The horror of AIDS is almost impossible for me to comprehend. But facts are facts, realities have to be faced. You are absolutely right when you state some kind of moral restraints are necessary in a world of so-called freedom. Freedom is very expensive and few of us have the resources to afford it. Safe sex, as I understand it, returns to what I have found satisfying, masturbation. Though lacking the touch, the taste of another, at least it gives a release. I loathe "safes" and was never into (if you'll pardon the pun) anal sex to any great degree, either as fucker or fuckee.

In my new celibate state, I've come to realize that the actual act of sex itself was rarely satisfying. It gave me pleasure, yes; it let me build empires of sexual power, yes; but that one-to-one, caring completeness that many may have achieved has escaped me. Everything has a price, dear M, and I believe most of life is, as you said, lonely.

I also believe I react to an inner voice that seems to vary each encounter from total emptiness to supreme authority. God! how often I am bored by pedants! Also, not as often, they make me aware of my lack of scholarship and intellectual pursuits. These poles, and the degrees between them, form my behaviour. It is easier to look down than up!

Back to moral restraints and AIDS. One of my major fears

for society (gay and otherwise) is the lack of caring for others that can come from the despair of being diseased.

Syphilis, before the discovery of penicillin, was knowingly, even viciously, given to others. It killed. It maimed. The unborn were affected. It touched, tainted and terminated lives at all levels. Moral social justice blamed it on whoredom and promiscuity.

We come to the word "vengeance" again. This must never be mistaken for victory, for vengeance is not victory, it's the act of the desperate, the uncaring. Victory for me would be to win the battle of self-respect and caring. In this pursuit, vengeance has no role.

My other fear is that, through ignorance and fear, family and friends will desert and build a wall of alienation around those who, tragically, have become infected with AIDS. The disease alone is terrible to bear without adding the horror of rejection to the tragedy.

My heart goes out to those young men, some just boys, who not only have to fight the battle of public stigma and rejection because of their homosexuality, but no longer can have the freedom of sharing with another without the nightmare of death shadowing their love.

The pack (and I do mean pack) of letters arriving your way soon talk of some things that suggest a sort of telepathic contact. They were all written before your letter arrived today, yet much of what I wrote is, I think, highly relevant to your concerns right now.

Most of those notes are from steerage, and I await another first-class moment.

June 9, 1986

Dear M.

I have no idea where I will be a week today. I've had absolutely no word from Eva directly, but she has phoned Gerry twice, to pass on the information that I must be out of the house by next Sunday. I'm in a slightly comotose state, not believing the whole thing and trying to grow cobwebs. Eva gave Gerry the names and dates of the people arriving, and *so* hopes, "Jack will be there in the area, he is such a wonderful guide!"

It now seems almost certain that the electric and water will be cut off. I have no money to pay the bills. The walls are blooming with the powdered residue of saltpetre. The shower still leaks, and now pours into the main room by the window.

Sure, it's warm (the mistral lasted nine days this time and nearly drove me mad--madder?) But, there is no outside table for the tiny terrace (public property) nor *chaise longue* for sunning.

Yes, I will clean the house the best I can. Yes, I will have the laundry done (all the sheets are about twelve years old and wearing thin). But I cannot pay the electric and water. I cannot have a plumber fix the shower (an estimate was four or five thousand francs, as the floor has to be ripped up).

I've decided I'm not going to play guide. I shall not be near the house for that period. Where I will be, God knows, but I will do what I can, and leave. I am tempted to stay, refuse the people who arrive, and continue my work; however, they are innocent.

Eva and David don't have a legal leg to stand on as they have not informed me ever. The mail works, so do telegrams.

I have been informed that I may be having an exhibition in Lyon and another in Cannes. (The Montluçon award was a silver medal and certificate.) I was prepared to work all summer, as you suggested, open the door and put up a sign, "Atelier Pollock," and somehow survive.

Now, I don't know what the fuck to do.

June 16, 1986

Dear M.
I wish you were here to see Lou Paradou really decked out in her finest. I have scrubbed, cleaned, vacuumed every square

211

inch. My bedroom is clean and crisp. Every sheet, towel, and dishcloth is freshly laundered.

They (the first of three groups, this one consisting of five people, names and sexes unknown) were due to arrive yesterday. Louis, the manager at the Hostellerie provençale, has said I can stay there for two weeks, but each night in a different room, as they have to rent what they can. Last night I had two huge double beds, wall-to-wall carpet, and the first bathtub I've used in France for years. The rooms were just renovated, and are decorated with Laura Ashley prints. The john is marble! That was room one. Tonight I hear I have room seven, and so it will go each day.

The pisser is that no one has arrived. I am very happy to have been forced to get my act together and clean Lou Paradou, but I don't want to go back there and dirty sheets, and who knows, they may arrive late at night.

My clothes, paints, and so on, are in two plastic sacks and my suitcase. They rest near the door, as does a roll of my recent canvases. I have written a note of welcome to the "mysterious five." I've put fresh roses from my little terrace and cards from ten or twelve restaurants in the area on the table. I also said I would be at the Hostellerie provençale for about a week, and they can contact me there. I will come down every day to change clothes and check the mail.

Your message rang loud and clear on the phone, so I didn't call Eva; I sent a telegram instead: "Electric and water may be cut off. I will not be here. Your problem." That was five days ago, and no reply. So, tough titty!

The reason I have a room in the Hostellerie for only two weeks is that Louis, the manager-cum-owner, is in some kind of deep shit with the gendarmes and the government. He said he is leaving the end of the month and going to Germany. I have to take my paintings off the walls before he leaves.

I am working with the young pianist at La Renaissance on a requiem-type composition for Frisé, who burned to death last summer. I have the words and I sing into a cassette the repeated, chant-like notes, then he will piece it together. It should be completed this summer.

Just another normal day in Jack's life in a small village in Provence!

June 23, 1986

Dear M.

This past week has been one of the heaviest since I arrived at Lou Paradou. With two francs in my pocket, I have been living in a luxury room with breakfast, lunch (wine), dinner (more wine). Louis, the manager of the hotel, is close to a saint for me. There are only eight rooms, yet he allows me, in fact insists I stay until I have some logical plan.

I called the embassy in Marseille in desperation and they will repatriate me (that is a one-way ticket borrowed against my passport, which cannot be used again until the debt is paid). I don't know what to do. I spent today in bed, not wanting to see anyone or even paint.

The "famous five," who have finally arrived, had heard of the Joanne Kates broadcast and asked if I would prepare dinner, if they paid for the shopping. So last night I made a dinner, nine courses. It was strange, cooking in my own kitchen, and then leaving to sleep in the hotel.

My nerves are very bad, and I shake a lot these days. The unknown is fearful, the promise or surmised promise unfulfilled. The "five" have gone to the Riviera for three days. (They are all professionals and can well afford it.) But I cannot bring myself to go into Lou Paradou. I go to the mailbox (nothing for over ten days) and return to my room to read, paint, and try to find some sales to enable me to come to Canada with dignity. I may arrive, paid by the government, as a repatriated and embarrassed citizen, if it seems the only solution to the problem. Surely I will sell enough in Canada at least to pay back the government, have my passport reinstated, and return with a small sum to keep me going.

I can see me, standing at the opening of the twenty-fifth anniversary of the Outdoor Show with Koffler, Silcox, the dignitaries, the mayor, and me, without a valid passport, being introduced as the executive director and co-founder of the show. You really can't make it up, dear M!

P.S. Things do happen in bunches. This evening I went down to the terrace for dinner. As I sat sipping my Côtes du Luberon, a young man walked carefully across the square. He was wearing a T-shirt with "Toronto, Canada" on it. I recognized him and began to shake. It was Alain. One year ago today was the hateful accident, and he is here visiting La Mayanelle where he used to work. We embraced, and he sat and talked, very slowly. He has one more year of therapy (he said) but, although not retarded (to me), he is very slow and still handicapped. He asked about the evening of the accident, what had happened, where it happened. I had to relive the experience, and I am now in a state of shock. My sense of guilt (remember, he gave me his helmet) cannot be erased, and I feel terrible. Tears flowed when I saw him, and, although I was pleased to find him functioning, I found his limited and slow comprehension horribly sad. I had bought him the T-shirt in Canada in November and sent it to him via his family. He will come back tomorrow for lunch. His beauty (and he is mannishly beautiful) has been softened by a strange emptiness.

I cannot write more.

July – September 1986

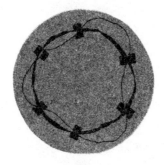

July 16, 1986
Gardiner Road, Toronto

Dear M.

What a strange and wondrous sharing we have developed! This visit, as forced and farcical as it started out, has proven so far much more rewarding for me than my last visit (and I am learning it's *me* who counts).

I have, this trip, a grip on real issues as well as on fantasy, and I have confronted and won a few battles. I have the paper in my hand that gives me the legal right to my half of Lou Paradou. I have (as if I need them) over a thousand copies of a strange little book, *We All Are All*, written by some nutcase in 1980. Plus ten copies of the special edition complete with three original silk screens each.

Liam Lacey of the *Globe and Mail* has interviewed me over the phone and presumably will do a small item in a column called "Briefly." Morley of the Marianne Friedland gallery arrives tomorrow morning, and Chris Hume of the *Toronto Star* will be here for lunch on Friday.

Yesterday began with sun and ended with sorrow – it was Nicholas's funeral.

Young Nicholas was twenty when I met him in the Clarke Institute. He was attending Queen's University in Kingston, going to be an engineer (like his father) when he had the first of his schizophrenic episodes. I had just walked out of the townhouse on Seaton Street, leaving it and its contents to B. I lived for two months in the Waldorf Astoria on Charles Street.

Nicholas was diagnosed, began lithium treatment, and was released. He arrived at my "suite" one early summer afternoon, wanting to talk. We talked, went out for dinner, and saw *Barry Lyndon* (one of the most beautiful films I have ever seen). I said good night on the sidewalk and went to bed. This pattern was repeated for over six months. By then I had a one-bedroom apartment on Maitland. One evening, as we sat and talked, he said he had to go to the john (down the hall from the living-dining area). Twenty minutes or so later he called me, and I went in to find him naked on my bed. His intimacy was overwhelming. His love and lust for his father frightening.

For several months Nicholas and I (playing daddy) had a series of ritualistic encounters. I knew his family, they were suspicious of me at the beginning, but then, as they discovered their inability to cope, were pleased by my support of their son. Then, as I expected, Nicholas went off his medication and disappeared. Later, a letter arrived from Vancouver. He was pan-handling, had grown long hair and a beard, and said his name was Nick. He said Nick was a bad boy, and stole sometimes (as he did from me once, on his return). The family and the shrink at the Clarke (I can't recall his name) worked out a kind of necessary human blackmail. He would be given a cheque once a month (from his father) *after* his injection. It was a slow-release dose, one shot would be effective for the whole thirty-day period. He struggled with this problem, saw me occasionally (mostly as Nicholas, but as I said, once or twice as Nick).

When Nick phoned, I sensed the change in his voice, and soon realized the totally different perspective of this other being. The real shock for me came one evening when the phone rang and a soft, seductive voice said it was Nicole. He arrived, his long blond hair tied back with a ribbon, his face shaven, and under the soiled, torn jeans and workshirt, black lace panties and brassiere. He later told me he went into the laundry room of an apartment building and stole them.

I saw Nicole two or three times, Nick slightly more, and then he disappeared again. This pattern was repeated for over ten years – a letter, a card, a visit.

As Nicholas, he once referred to Nicole and Nick as his playmates. He said he was tired of them. When his mother died of cancer, he felt little sense of loss. The father remarried, and then, yesterday, the news. Nicholas, Nick, and Nicole had walked down the centre of the highway and into a transport truck.

The service was led by a blond, handsome, gay priest in his mid-thirties. I, in cream linen rather than black leather, with white carnations rather than red roses, re-enacted the Requiem for Frisé. This time for Nicholas.

P.S. Nicholas's father just phoned, and I am having lunch with him tomorrow. He wishes to buy a painting, and to say thank you. I would like to lend him any support I can.

July 17, 1986
Gardiner Road

Dear M.

Nicholas's father arrived at noon. He liked my pictures (he said) and took four home to peruse. We went to lunch, shared sorrow and loss. He looked weary, but well. He has belonged to AA for several years, learned to control his rages (it seems), and has remarried. He said that about three weeks ago (I was still in France) he visited Eva and found out I was financially "unstable." He asked for my address, to forward some financial assistance, and Eva said she didn't know where I lived these days. He thanked me for being what he couldn't be for Nicholas.

I arrived home an hour ago (it's after midnight) and found an envelope on the stairs. It is from Nicholas's father with a beautiful note and a cheque for $2,500. He is buying three pictures and the cheque was "on account." I now have the money to retrieve my passport. I am pleased that he did not offer me money as payment for my caring. I would, as you know, have refused. He said the pictures are for him, one each for the remaining children, and will be permanent reminders of what love and true friendship was about.

I signed one of my prints "In Memory of Nicholas," and his father is having it framed for the Clarke Institute.

Chris Hume phoned (or rather, his secretary) and cancelled lunch. He phoned a few minutes ago and said he will call Monday. Nothing from the *Globe* – ups and downs, like the toilet seat!

Gardiner Road

Dear M.

How do I begin? First, I went to see the play *Nunsense*, a wonderfully funny send-up of the Catholic Church, loving and naughty, irreligious and irresistible. Second, Nicholas's tragic death, and then today a wedding in a Roman Catholic High Mass.

I was looking forward to the wedding. Bruce (the young man who shared my loft for two years) was best man for his brother Eric; Ken and Michael, his other brothers, were ushers.

His mom and dad care for me and visited Gordes last year. They did a video of me in the crypt, and spoke of how much I helped them understand and accept the complications of "the other way."

The wedding invitation arrived in Gordes in early May and I hesitated to refuse. The day I arrived, I phoned; they were delighted.

It was a *grand* affair. There were six bridesmaids, a flower girl, a cute seven-year-old ring bearer, and the stunning beauty of the three brothers and three friends, all in their twenties, all bedecked in tails, bow-ties, acting as ushers.

I was first invited to the parents' home for breakfast – bacon, eggs, toast, coffee, the works – the first full breakfast I have had in a long while. The bridesmaids had made over one hundred Kleenex puffs and we proceeded to tape them to three cars. We drove to the bride's home to decorate two more cars there. On the way we (Bruce and two brothers and I) passed a garage sale. I suggested we stop to buy the tackiest thing we could find for a surprise present, and we did. (I had taken a print.) The object of our affection turned out to be a truly horrendous shield, almost three feet high, of oak-stained wood one inch thick. On it was a bastard coat of arms against a background of red velvet, and two candelabra, each holding two candles. This was in base metal, trying to assume the aura of pewter. After buying it (I paid ten dollars) we bought four candles and told no one until it was presented, aflame, at the reception. Good fun.

About the church service: I was prepared for (and wanted) a sense of ritual and spirit. I was not prepared for the pseudo-Scandinavian architecture of the church's interior. I welcomed the candles, incense, and altar boys. I did not welcome two young ladies in tasteless white (not quite white) shifts, one with a pony tail, the other a dutch-boy cut. I wanted elevation from the father; I did not want a spiritless, aging eunuch who got lost at least five times in the course of the ceremony. Bells rang (brass from India, I believe, modern and clumsy). Candles burned in brass sticks pretending to be gold.

It was over one hour of rhetoric that did not touch me, with the exception of the Beatitudes read by a maiden aunt of the bride's. The priest droned on about two becoming one, the absolutes of marriage, and the non-existence of divorce in God's eyes. How I wish he could have been believable!

Christ had charisma. His servants, if they truly believe, should be able to share their inner experience and joy, even fear! But this patched inner-tube of a priest, robed in a soiled, ill-fitting robe (again pretending to be white), showed scuffed shoes, ankles, and white sport socks. Charismatic he was not.

What Church do you suggest I try for a taste of spirit? You

have said I have Calvin in my closet. I believe that I am much too generous of spirit to entertain his cold and calculating ways. I do not, however, accept false mumblings and impoverished posture in the guise of faith. What you will make of this observation, I cannot guess. But I feel, and I mean *feel*, that I have a cross that needs the lift and support that only simple faith can give.

After the reception, I asked the valet at the Old Mill to call me a cab. The third cab was mine. I always sit in the front and play verbal games with cab drivers. What was I doing at the Old Mill? Attending a wedding. Where was I heading? Bay and Dundas, because I was just here from France (snob!) and wanted a little action. What do you do in France? I paint. I used to own an art gallery. What's your name? Pollock.

The brakes went on, he visibly paled, and said he had been a dear friend of my brother's. He felt guilty he did not visit him in hospital because he was going through personal problems at the time and he couldn't face my brother's death.

I began to feel cold and damp, reached out and touched his shoulder. We both had tears in our eyes and lumps in our throats.

"You remember when you were a kid, and Bob brought you out to the Eastwood beer parlour and you sang 'Danny Boy'?"

I remembered.

"He always said you were the smart one of the family."

I nodded.

Bob, as you may recall, was ten years older than me and until I was twelve or thirteen, we were at war. But, as teenagers, we became much closer. He married, "deserted" me, divorced, remarried, then died. He was an alcoholic, but as tender as only one with deep love and sadness can be.

I told the cab driver I had written a poem for Bob. Then I realized that the baths were the last place I should go. I redirected him to Gardiner Road. When we arrived, he asked if I would be offended if he refused the fare. I said yes, I would be, and gave him a twenty dollar bill, telling him to have a drink to Bob and me. He handed it back and asked me to sign it and said he would always treasure it. I suggested he come in and I gave him a print, let him read the poem. He held my shoulders, thanked me, and left. The twenty dollar bill was on the piano. I cried.

Dear M.

You said before I left that you were proud of me. I suppose I am proud of myself for my brief moments of control and concentration. But back here in Provence with again, yet, or still no money, no canvas, and with the winter approaching, I feel I am a madman who can, and does, have moments, even brief periods of clarity and purpose. My cycles, circles, seem to be fast becoming a whirlpool, the undertow growing stronger after each brief surfacing for air.

I was feeling a bit better about my work while in Toronto, and sensed a "hanging together" of the different imagery I've been painting. However, here, now, it all seems a stale and hollow attempt at self discovery. No news of further commerce, no review. God! rejection is a pisser!

The world around me here has become a fiery hell these past two days as forest fires rage, swept along by the mistral, dry and unrelenting. Yesterday, Jean-Michel, Françoise, Sophie (Eric Warot's sister) and I went to the Conrath's for dinner. Gerry, David, and number-three son, John, are "camping out" as their modern showplace of a house will not be ready for occupancy until the end of October. The highways past Aix-en-Provence were barricaded, detours everywhere, and large charcoal clouds loomed over the mountain ridges. We finally arrived at Rousset (chez Conraths) about eight o'clock and had drinks in their hedge-enclosed garden. An hour or so later, we went out for a stroll and were horror-struck and awed by the crimson glow and leaping orange tongues of flame everywhere. The air smelled of charred life, the smoke choked, and a fallout of grey ash rained down around us. Through stinging eyes we viewed la montagne Sainte-Victoire, that regal presence made immortal by Cézanne, now surrounded and looking as if it was perched on a funeral pyre. For miles on either side the forest was scarlet enclosed and aflame. The area reverberated with sirens, wailing their unashamed sorrow, and I saw five Canadian aircraft swooping low to dump their loads of water into the inferno. Eerily illuminated, the undulating lower hills were backed by the dense charcoal black of billowing and ever-swirling smoke. Above this the clear night sky was dotted with the glamorous, glorious stars of Heaven.

Is the devil beautiful?

God yes! Awesome, filled with the power of destruction, and at the same moment giving a spectacle not possible to imagine, or recreate. I felt the pulse of Turner's masterpieces of London aflame.

I thought of Frisé, love child of Gordes. Hundreds like him are out there giving their best. (A radio news bulletin just gave the news of three volunteers dead, one just seventeen years old).

We returned to the protected enclosure and David began the ritual of the barbecue. I sat dazed as I watched this man deliberately create fire, my guts twisting and my eyes running, not just from smoke, but from a deep sadness.

There has been no rain for over three months. The mistral blows dry and uncompromising. The earth is parched, arid, cracked, and scaly. Crops are less and less productive and the vineyards, the soul of Provence, are threatening to dissolve into a kind of parchment past. And now comes fire, destruction, murder.

We ate brochettes, cold salads, cheese, fruit. We drank wine from the vintages of *les années passées*. At midnight we left and drove through what should have been quiet, tranquil darkness, but now transformed into a nightmare of bloody hills, twisted and charred ruins, and a cavalcade of over forty fire engines, shredding the silence with their screams.

Engines new and modern, engines at least forty years old, tired and puffing, but giving. As we approached Salon on the autoroute, the mirage disappeared, and we were once again in starlit, tranquil Provence. But our eyes still stung, our bodies smelled of the death of ashes, and the grey film was everywhere.

I talked with Gerry today. La montagne Sainte-Victoire stands silent, surrounded by the grey of death and mourning, but victorious.

The fires are now raging throughout the hills above Cannes and Nice. Still the mistral insists on assisting destruction. Still the heavens have no tears. Still God is deaf to wails and pleadings.

And I sit, stunned, wrapped in a stupid kind of self-pity, and weep.

August 30, 1986

Dear M.

I have been thinking of Nicholas's death. Chemical imbalances such as his are difficult for me to comprehend. I do know his personality changes were almost total. We who rely on a world of fantasy as a support system seem capable of compartmentalizing reality and dreams, most times. I have had, as most people have I suppose, those moments when the real has felt truly unreal, and fantasy has become fact. What is it that brings us back? What forces a return to a world that is, most times, disappointing by comparison?

Your profession has, I am sure, brought you into contact with many whom we call mad. Do those who seem to be unfeeling really feel? Do the captives know the prisons they are in? Please God, no, because I believe that for Nicholas this knowledge was too great a burden to handle.

My mind goes back to Little J, the boarder of my Rosedale penthouse. He was a psychopath. But I felt in him, even after the mess of the fire and destruction, a saddened and empty soul. He seemed to feel no guilt, he acted as though possessed by the Devil, yet there was a part of him that was a frightened and abused child.

My lack of education, intellectual knowledge, has often been expensive, in both material and emotional senses. However, I know enough to realize I would still rather believe in others than live a life of walled-up protection and fear. I blame no one for my mistakes, but often wish others would understand my motives.

Your remarks, both in November and during this past visit, are indelibly printed in my mind. "If you choose to live a life that to most of society is alien, then you cannot demand the support of said society" (or words to that effect). I wonder if it is a conscious choice on my part? If it is (and in all probability you are right) then why do I put myself through such shit again and again and again?

Weak, self-centred, immature. But, please God, kind and caring.

Strong, aggressive, a survivor, yet I seek the perverse, the pain.

If ever there was a multiple personality, *c'est moi!*

One would think if someone knew as much about himself, he could conquer his fears and faults. Wrong. Why? I don't know.

You once said I was an inspiration. In this light, at this time, I find that hard to accept, but I hope slowly to become a bit of an inspiration to myself. (If that happens it would be quite a shock.)

A quiet, unassuming expatriate Canadian gentleman, living and painting amidst the calm and beauty of Provence. Host and former *bon vivant*, now graciously accepting age and a small but growing reputation. Wild-oats past, oatmeal present. (What a crock of shit!)

The challenge for this morning is to attempt to exorcise the devils of the forest fire image.

Helen Boyd's son Peter is staying here in the tower room. He is a joy, and although only a house guest, has been contributing more than his share towards food, wine, and cigarettes.

Later: Dusk has arrived. Peter is playing his lonesome and sadly beautiful guitar in the tower. I have worked on the fire images all day, about a dozen smallish works on paper. I found the monoprint, pressing technique a fine way to suggest the gaseous, almost ethereal movement between flame and smoke. Midnight blue, grey, grey-white, black, and scarlet. I'm attempting to catch the tossing and swirling of mistral-blown colour and form. Abstract they insist on being, as abstract they were. The problem is they don't give the sense of terror, the awfulness of the scene.

Daily household fiascos happen sometimes quickly and unexpectedly. All I wanted to do was wash the dishes. Suddenly the drains in the kitchen back up. The floor is afloat with suds and water. I mop it up, open the window in the light well and the front door. The draught slams the window shut, knocking over two pots and smashing a casserole. I reach for the window and slash my thumb on the fridge door, and it is a bloody mess. All in less than five minutes.

Nothing like a little distraction to break the monotony!

September 4, 1986

Dear M.
It's been a tough day. I started by deciding to do a landscape, a monoprint landscape. I did several, kept four out of ten, then was bored.

So, I set myself formal problems. Shape, form, negative, positive. Black, rusted barbed wire (that goddamn barbed wire), and greyed greens-blues. The shapes create points of tension, and I am exhausted, but pleased. It seems the beauty (landscapes) and the beast (barbed wire) go hand in hand. The average was better for the black pictures and I will keep six out of eight. The landscapes are pleasing, I suppose. Their colour and form satisfy me, but they seem to be a little "limp dick."

Henry Moore's death the other day was sad, though expected. I wonder if all the so-called modernists who have put him down for years (Roald Nasgaard for one) will have the decency to reassess the man and his work.

An interesting tale about Moore is that Ben Nicholson and he were sparring for the hand of Barbara Hepworth at one point in their lives. Ben won (or lost as the case may be). The hole, which both Hepworth and Moore explored so deeply, was ever-present in modified and shallow form in most of Nicholson's abstract works. Of the three, I think Barbara was the lesser artist. She was damned good, but for me, not great.

Moore gives his best work the simple strength of a labourer's vision. I admire his lack of pretention, just as I admire the fine intelligence of Nicholson, who has a superb and refined sense of taste. Hepworth, on the other hand, often ran hot and cold. Taste and tack are often close. (Who the fuck am I to talk?)

September 6, 1986

Dear M.

I am heavy. I am just going through the motions of creating. I was probably right thirty years ago when I realized that I can, at best, be mediocre.

I just tried to tidy up a bit and counted over one hundred works on paper. There are at least as many in Canada, plus canvases.

People *like* me, or are intrigued by what they think is an interesting character, but I don't believe many think my work at all valid.

Why do I continue to beat a dead horse? What's the point in kidding myself that my work is worth the effort. I suppose it does (or has, up until now) get me from yesterday to today to tomorrow. But shit, that's just not good enough.

The sins of the fathers – no, I can't blame my drunken, bitter dad for my fuck-ups, except maybe for my "addictive personality," as the Donwood loves to call it.

Excess as a true malady makes sense. Obsessions with sex, cocaine, and now a strange, forced celibacy. Sure seems twisted to me!

At this moment, I want to destroy. It isn't anger – it's keeping the lid on rage.

I remember so many times going through fine shops with tables fitted with crystal, clenching my fists to hold back the temptation to destroy.

Destruction – that's what it seems to be about. Setting out with a strange kind of perverse system to cut off, terminate, and run afoul. I have, and still do, often cut off others from a fear of contaminating their sense of goodness. I feel often evil, and wonder about the Devil and his beauty.

Why haven't the ravages of time and self-abuse revealed themselves in a logical, physical disintegration? Why the fuck do I still go on? God, in his infinite wisdom, must have many more likely and deserving candidates for survival. Is He perverse also?

Most times I must admit He tips the scales with some strange temporary salvation, but how long can He hold the balance of power? And why should He bother?

The whole business of power is at the base of it all. Your choice of profession, my "master" role and "star" effect. Your calculated grey-blue trust, belonging; my leather, de Sade-like image, *pas très, trop*. Both types of roles are exhausting. Somewhere, in the middle, is truth. Please God we find it before it finds us out.

I start out this letter complaining about my mediocrity. When we realize that 99.9 per cent (as Ivory says about its purity) of us are in the scheme of things, mediocre, I suppose it's highly presumptuous for me to demand more.

I just wish I was in some way communicating more than I seem to be. In teaching, I feel I did. In your profession I *know* you do.

The solitude of painting and writing is a forced deprivation, and yet, without the decision to be alone here, I probably would not be around to bitch.

So, the squirrel continues in the cage, round and round and round again.

I feel quite stupid, as I have written all this crap and answered myself, but it doesn't seem to lighten the weight. I can help most others, but I'm trapped in my own very personal indulgences and traits.

I suppose we all create many varied reasons for our unreasonable behaviour. That, too, appears to be part of the survival mechanism. Can you teach an old dog new tricks? (Are there any tricks left?) Please God!

P.S. I just smiled to myself. Things must be a little better.

September 9, 1986

Dear M.

Well, as you have said in the past, it's always darkest before the dawn.

Yesterday's joy goes a long way in helping to restore some sense of worth.

Klaus and Ruth, a middle-aged German couple, no children, came to visit. They liked my work, spoke English so I could communicate a little easier, and bought a forest-fire picture (that series is not bad) and a small still-life.

It's strange, but it has taken me fifteen years (three years here full-time) to look and feel the landscape in any real personal way. The *Luberon* series are really monotypes, using horizontal composition and broad swaths of mixed colours. They sing, and I feel more people will relate to them. More "attractive" to most because of the tie with nature, nevertheless they are not corny. They seem, as most work I am satisfied with, to come through me. I breathe heavy, work at a furious pace, then collapse, quite exhausted and content.

It feels good to give back some of the wondrous beauty I have been surrounded with here nestled in the Luberon mountains.

What I will do with them I don't know, but I shall continue to explore the landscape. I have a sense that it's a kind of breakthrough. They are energetic, yet seem effortless. Clouds float, hills loom and recede, the red clay of Roussillon jostles with the grey-greens of the fields. They work, goddamn it!

It is strange that I should return to the monoprint process after all these years. The two works of mine in the National Gallery collection, the pictures Kathleen Fennick chose for the Canadian Pavillion at Expo '67, are all monoprints.

I used glass and oil paints then and controlled the image and the structure with blackout, and repeated printing. With acrylic, it's a one-shot deal, more than half are trashed, but those that work, sing. I explode colour on the paper, then pull off and adjust the results. Speed is essential, as acrylic dries very quickly, and my knowledge of colour and form sure come in handy. Wow! It's good to think and write about something positive and not self-damning.

They look as though I absorbed Impressionism and then gave it a contemporary run for its money. Monet comes to mind, but with a madness that is, of course, yours truly. Blues, lavenders, ochres, siennas, greens in every hue, not much red.

Shut up Pollock, just keep working!

P.S. Today, at breakfast (oatmeal, not wild oats) a letter arrived from the Centre Culturel Canadien in Paris, and I am to be part of a group show opening the end of January.

September 22, 1986

Dear M.
It has been a productive two days. I just finished the second in a series of large works on paper. They are still-life, but

fragmented and slightly cubist, as were my drawings last year.

I paint the entire surface black, draw and re-draw with paint, then begin the journey of selecting colours, mostly semi-opaque. Much of the surface is left velvety black, with blues, greens, violets, greys accentuating plants, bottles, boats, and the ever-present *épis* – the bars on my windows.

Peter has arrived back at Lou Paradou. God, it's nice to share, and yet have privacy and freedom. Peter has claimed the table by the fireplace and writes endlessly. I sit here below and paint. We enjoy and share meals and evening chats, but we are both motivated to produce. He feels he will stay the winter, and I say *amen!*

Now, if we manage three thousand francs extra, we will buy an old wreck of a car (four wheels and a motor that moves) and we could at least do laundry and shopping. I feel this winter will not be the black despair of yesteryear (please God!).

I'm glad you enjoyed the new collection of stories by Alice Munro. She has been a favourite Canadian writer of mine for quite awhile. Her stories are, as you say, beautifully crafted and she seems to "sum it up" so nicely.

For the past twenty years or so, I think most of the more important Canadian literature has been by women. Some I like (Alice Munro, Margaret Laurence, Marian Engel); some I don't like (Margaret Atwood); but many more female than male voices seem to be heard and read. Robertson Davies and Mordecai Richler are exceptions. Have you read *What's Bred in the Bone*? I think I mentioned it in letters earlier. Davies' pompous sense of British word and deed is cut of a different cloth from most Canadian literature.

And thanks for the latest news from the Toronto art world. A more unlikely trio could not exist than Walter Moos, Simon Dresdnere, and Evelyn Amis. Obviously they have an inventory problem, but would not, as I did, just have a sale. I rented the St. Lawrence Market, sold works by Hockney, Albers,

Nicholson, and Vasarely for half-price. But, of course, that's not done in the "holy" world of art.

The marketplace of the international art world has, for many years, relied on the auction houses to establish prices by the supply-demand process. The value of paintings by the Group of Seven and other "hysterical" (historical) painters has been determined this way, but no auction has been successful in defining the merit, quality, and value of our contemporary scene. Towns, Bloores, Coughtries, Rayners, even Danbys have made miserable showings, and I recall twice going to Sothebys to bail out Morrisseau and Fournier, to try and protect their value.

The opposite was happening in New York City. A consortium of dealers bid up and bought the Warhol *Campbell Soup Can* for $75,000. All these dealers had stock-piled Warhols, and his price more than tripled overnight. Not much to do with art. This happens regularly, and there have been occasions when Canadian dealers have used unusual circumstance to make money for themselves and for the artists involved.

I recall when Jack Chambers was diagnosed as having leukemia. Nancy Poole let the press know about his illness. Prices zoomed, Chambers went into remission for over six years, and continued to produce quality, if not, in my opinion, great art.

Barker Fairley's marketing is another example of good solid business practice, but it has little to do with art.

But the rumours of my death and demise didn't do dick-all for my market. So, I guess I know where I stand. Fuck them all. I'll just "do my own thing." Christ, shut up, Pollock, you sound like a bitter old fart. (I have been doing my own thing for a long time now. It's become the "in" thing to do your "own thing.")

Really, dear M, what kind of God could have created this impossible mayhem called life? If He did intend to give us freedom, a sense of independence, and choice, then He should have toilet-trained us, set examples, and shown a path.

If, as I suspect, there is perversity in Paradise, then He must be getting his rocks off regularly these days.

If Jesus, his "son," was sent to show the way, why don't we record his human frailties? His sexuality? Did he burp, fart, void, laugh? Where were his "unwholesome thoughts," his anti-social, fuck-fight attitudes? What about the evil thoughts all mankind is saddled with? Use, abuse, power, abound, with or without Christ.

No one can hope to measure up to the perfection of Christ, so the stage is set for sin, guilt and, of course, the ultimate power trip, the absolution of past so-called sins and indiscretions. Forgiveness, confession, and your groping profession all attempt to cope with the rat's nest of our often irrational and chaotic thought processes.

But we all are all – priests and sinners, pimps and whores, doctors and patients, black and white. None of us escapes fleeting thoughts of violence, aggression, and control of others. No one can totally control the strange, perverse, and oft-times destructive ideas that flash momentarily through our consciousness.

Some act upon them, others deny their existence, and chastise those who admit to them, and others try to come to grips with the thought and the deed, settling, please God, for a kind of magic, safe world. A world of the games of children, of the garden of earthly delights, of fantasy, controlled, yet experienced through sharing in the theatre of the senses.

"Heavy trip" was the hippy response.

I'll second the motion.

September 26, 1986

Dear M.

Life is good. (That's a switch, eh what?) This past week has been grey, inside and out. Rain for three days. Both Peter and I have colds and are coughing.

It was good to go through a week of shitty feelings with someone. It helped both of us, I think. We have a similar sense of humour (a bit scatological and vulgar) and we feed off each other's putdowns. Good fun and great company.

Tonight Denis, his wife Chris, and a friend of theirs (Parisian, gay) arrive for dinner. Thank God we have money and can produce a mini feast. Carrot and orange soup, *chèvre grillé*, avocado with honey and fresh ginger, *poulet* with garlic and lemon, *haricots verts*, *fromage*, *salade verte*, and Peter will make a special dessert. Not bad for life at the poverty-line!

Peter never ceases to be amazed at my good fortune. I told him of my horseshoe theory, but added that the true secret is to care, and give, without strings attached. If we do that (and I believe I do) somehow our needs are met.

These last-minute miracles have become such a logical pattern for me, that I believe I understand the jealousy and envy of others.

Not many will take the chance. Not many will let themselves gain pleasure just from the giving. Not many will *trust* that their needs will be met.

Sure, my valleys are deep, and many days and nights are heavy and grey, but my blind faith somehow sees me through. As I say, life is good.

Francesca, a young lady (Italian-born, lived in London for ten years, speaks five languages), has a crush on Peter. He is playing it cool, but maybe something will develop. She is thirty-one, pretty, boyish, and has been having an affair with a twenty-one-year-old, ex-shepherd who works for the Moulin here (a program for handicapped people set up by Canada's own Jean Vanier). He chose to work with the disabled, as an alternate to military service. Luc is his name, and he is sweet and innocent.

Francesca had to seduce him (that's about a year ago) and now he is like a puppy dog, and she, I think, being animal, is bored. I'll keep you posted on the bed-springs of Provence!

It seems hard to believe that we are only animal, vegetable, mineral, mostly water, and nothing else. Why the chill of fear? Why the pure moments of pleasure? Why the sense of evil, the struggle to achieve? Where does my feeling for you come from? Where have the feelings of my family gone? Did the taxi-driver friend of my brother's fulfill a mission? Why am I blessed?

The structured dogma of religion attempts to give support, and through that support, a way of life supposedly based on love of mankind and caring. The problem I find is that most faiths are like a suit of clothes off the rack. You have to accept the ill-fitting jacket, the low crotch, the short pant legs, because they weren't made for you. When those in the service of God (priests and theologians) attempt to alter and adjust the costume for the unique measurements of the individual, the "ready-to-wear" boss (the Pope) gets angry. It cuts down on efficiency and profits.

So, many of us buy the package, take it home, and busy ourselves with private alterations. But most times we feel inept, as we are not professional tailors, and we wonder about the final result. If we can *believe* it to be successful, then the image created for ourselves and others will have a sense of rightness and comfort. If our doubts about craftmanship and ability weigh us down, we are awkward, uncomfortable, and doubting.

I am learning to sew, to adjust, to alter these days, and I feel content with most of the results (with you as an inspector and instructor it has been, and continues to be, a goal-oriented quest: a quest for balance between extremes).

Comfort does come from doing something well. Fear of the final result cannot ever be completely eliminated, but if each nip and tuck, each stitch, attempts to better the last, then at least we strive for growth, and maybe prepare for the "fashion show in the sky."

I believe you sew very well. You also assist many in the alterations of life. You are important to many, and precious to me. I *am* blessed.

P.S. Horseshoes are clunky costume jewellery, but they help me make it through the night! In conversation with Peter, I keep recalling many, many incidents from my past. To write them as letters now seems pretentious, so I will wait. But I have a backlog of bedtime stories for you in the future.

October – December 1986

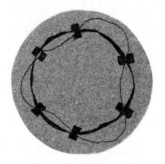

Dear M.

Today has been a laid-back, slightly hung-over day for both Peter and me.

My beliefs continue to be proven. Yesterday, Peter and I had about forty francs between us. The mailman arrived with a letter from Wendy Penfield, who'd included a bunch of wonderful stamps and two hundred and fifty francs, the last cash Eric and she had left in French currency. Nadine de Montmollin had arrived in Gordes the previous day, and I and others of her friends had planned to visit her. Now I had cash, I phoned her up and suggested she not rush about and shop, but rather I would make a soup, buy stuff for a picnic, and we could all eat on her terrace.

Well, the orange-carrot curry soup, pâté, ham, a huge salad, cheese, a lemon torte, and two bottles of wine cost a hundred and fifty francs of our sole fortune, and Peter wondered at my sanity.

Lunch went splendidly, and as we were leaving, Nadine's cousin pressed an envelope in my pocket and said she had planned to take Nadine for lunch but this was so much more pleasant. There were two hundred francs in the envelope. We had fifty francs more than when I decided to prepare lunch!

Peter just shakes his head in wonderment. I try to explain that true love and caring is a circle, and giving is the golden thread that holds it all together.

We relaxed for a few hours after lunch and then friends from neighbouring Cheval Blanc, arrived to take us to a fête in their garden. About twenty people and a huge paella (the pan was about four feet in diameter). Chicken, rabbit, shrimps, *moules*, rice, *haricots verts*, lots of *pastis*, wine, and whisky. So, today we, being slightly fragile, are taking it easy.

I leave on Thursday morning to hitch-hike to Cannes. The Etobicoke Art Group are having a banquet in my honour, and then I shall teach for a few days. I will take a small portfolio of recent paper works. I might sell a few. Hitch-hiking to a grand banquet in a château in Cannes is vintage Pollock. I remember hitching a ride to Barrie to be a guest on TV and hitching home again. The producers never knew!

Our poor village square has been turned into a mini CNE with rides, fish ponds, a carousel, noise from farting rifles, breaking balloons, scratchy records of oom-pa-pa, and so on. It is the annual village *fête votive*, which lasts for four days. I suffer through it and do enjoy seeing the kids having fun.

The Hostellerie has a new dishwasher, dark, handsome, about twenty-nine or thirty. He is a "working priest." You must know of this hybrid, which financial constraint within the church has produced. I knew one here a few years ago who was a plumber-priest. This one seems interesting and wants to visit Lou Paradou to see the crypt. He has heard of it and is fascinated. I'll keep you posted.

November 15, 1986

Dear M.

It has been over a month since I wrote pages of garbage, and decided to destroy them, rather than bore you again, yet, and still, with my seeming monstrous heavies.

Peter, Gabrielle de Montmollin and I share Lou Paradou now, and Gabrielle will stay until the new year; Peter probably until spring. They are good people, and I find depression much more difficult to indulge with them here. We all love to cook, share the clean-ups without question, and, thank God, neither of them are squeaky clean proper.

The problem with finances is more difficult for me to accept with others around. Peter has had difficulty getting money owed from Canada, so he is washing dishes in Le Provençal on the weekends. Gabrielle has budgeted for her sabbatical and has a small financial base.

Me – you know me. Unlike other times, right now there is not a single dollar that I can expect to earn. As a giver, it was much easier wallowing in self-pity alone. Now, I feel embarrassed at not being able to contribute at least my share. Certainly, Lou Paradou is a roof over their heads; sure, the village is a good place to be; but me, I need to feel the joy of contributing. Oh well! It's another new experience. The house is active (one guitar, two electric typewriters).

This week I seem to be coming out of my funk, and have started painting some small works on paper (*again*).

Colours are low, paper is scarce, but I feel a little more like riding over the black and grey of my past month's immobility.

December 1, 1986

Dear M.

Your observations about the timing of my idea for a "book of revelations" and the AIDS crisis are interesting, but I feel all the more inclined to think that the ability to seek safe alternatives (a *true* one-to-one relationship with another), together with an open and caring acceptance of that other person's world of fantasy and experimentation, which allows sharing and role playing, are perhaps the keys to establishing some sanity among the chaos.

The other alternative (for which it seems I have opted) is self-imposed (and self-indulgent) abstinence. The dry fuck, the cock tease, the innuendo, the innocent, but not-so-innocent, playing with words and phrases, the stimulus of not-completed physical arousal, they all seem healthy and, along with the essential sense of humour, food for survival.

I don't believe any revelation of my excesses, given the period (mostly before 1982), would vary much from what people presume existed in the sub-culture world of dark and whetted nights. It may be news to some that with all that seeking, searching, and demanding, the actual physical act was rarely the issue. A perverse power play was the name of the game.

Family table talk here has opened strange and forgotten memories.

My early Cub and Scout days, singing and entertaining soldiers, the Kiwanis Club, and old folks' homes, with Robert Harvey, Tommy Common (who went on to his own television show, drugs, booze, and death) and Harold Johnson, fat Harold, on the piano. I suppose I was eleven or so. We were at Harold's practising when his mother, a huge woman, came into the "parlour," sat in a large chair, and beckoned her plump two-year-old son to her knee. With one swoop, she caught him up, unbared an enormous swollen breast, and he started sucking. I panicked, pissed my shorts, and ran.

From the age of five I was friends with a boy named Henry. He lived across the street on Perth Avenue, and his father was a Communist. The party leader at that time was Tim Buck. Because of that, my father, in drunken rage, forbade me to associate with Henry.

When I was six, he stood on the sidewalk as I walked out of our house flanking my baby sister's casket. We went through Perth Avenue Public School together, with Miss Fenton (a wonderful bird-like creature and a member of the Perth Avenue United Church Women's Group, along with my mother. It was called the Sunshine Group and they baked, made church dinners, quilted and gossipped). We also had Miss Abbott, a stout "old maid" with terrible body odour and a bristly moustache, who was constantly garbed in stained, uniform-like dresses.

Henry's life and mine took different turns as he found the High Anglican Church (St. Martin's in the Field) and went to Humberside Collegiate. I found God in the name of some strange roaming evangelists called "Youth for Christ" and was saved (are you ready for this?) by none other than Charles Templeton. (No wonder my life of grace was short-lived!)

Henry and I drifted apart and then he got married, had two daughters, and his wife died tragically when diving into the lake at her parents' cottage. The two girls went to live with the maternal grandparents, and somehow or other Henry and I decided to share an apartment. I get confused with dates, but I believe it was 1957. I had returned from England, was working for Bruce Dougall (Glidden Paints) and Henry was working as a salesman. We rented a one-bedroom apartment on north Yonge Street. I painted the entire kitchen-dining area black and every cupboard door a different pure colour – red, orange, turquoise, yellow, blue. I recall it working in its vulgar way. We slept together – no sex – and we had a sign (a small lamp in the window) which meant one of us was "entertaining." The other would stay out for at least an hour, then telephone. It worked. He met a beautiful woman who was separated, with two daughters. We found out her husband was a strange semi-closet case, living in, I believe, Kitchener, and was refusing her a divorce.

Like kids in some strange "Our Gang" comedy, we planned and executed a piece of theatre that resulted in C's divorce, and her and Henry's subsequent marriage.

Henry hired a private detective, who found "the husband," as we always referred to him, frequented a quasi-gay bar in Kitchener on the ground floor of a slightly seedy hotel. We went there, rented two rooms with adjoining doors through a common john. I went to the bar, quite easily got "the husband" warmed up, and retired to my room. Our sixty-nine position was captured for posterity by Henry's flash camera; the evidence provided the lever for securing the divorce; and I was best man at the wedding.

So, on it goes. Henry "got the call," so to speak, and

became an Anglican priest. As the husband of a divorced woman, he could not be assigned a church in Canada, so he accepted a parish in Minnesota. Many years (and four more daughters later) he visited B and I in Toronto. He had just returned from a cure-retreat for alcoholics, and looked well.

I had purchased a superb black moiré chasuble embroidered with silver threads in a large cross emblem on the back and gave it to him. I found it in the flea market in Avignon. Henry was delighted and later wrote to tell me he wears it each Good Friday for the special Easter Mass.

I don't know, or care, what happened to the candid camera photo, nor do I know the fate of "the husband."

I have no address for Henry these days, but would like to touch base.

I am glancing through *Tatler*, a very chic publication that Gabrielle brought back from London. In a review of a book on Rodin, the writer, in passing, refers to Diaghilev's fury when he discovered Nijinski in bed with Rodin! We all are all!

That same year, 1957, I went to Provincetown and met several people who figured in my life for several years. One, Raoul Pen Du Bois, a brilliant gay set and costume designer from New York, and his assistant Waldo Angelo, son of the leading Italian undertaking establishment in New York. Du Bois had accepted the task of creating the sets and costumes for an ill-fated attempt at reviving the Zeigfeld Follies. I was hired to assist Waldo, and I had fun briefly with feathers, sequins, tits, and ass.

My brief moment of glory came when I designed an ostrich-feather curtain, thousands of plumes strung on nylon chords in *ombré* shades from palest pink to fuschia. I also worked on headpieces for the gals, chandeliers with twinkling bulbs, lit by tiny battery packs in their hair. Also tits encased in cocktail glasses, tipped with cherries or olives for nipples.

The obvious became obvious after three disastrous performances when the chandeliers tangled with the plumes, and moulting ostriches abounded.

As I learned later, the show was being backed by laundered money and was not supposed to succeed.

Kaye Ballard, a great, warm, wonderful talent, was the star. Several nights we sat in the small space of our black and primary dining area, while Kaye made lasagna, all getting pissed. Those were the days!

In the parcel of letters you have now received is a short item clipped from the *Herald Tribune* on the "vengeance aspect" of some AIDS victims, especially young hustler types whose reason for sexual encounter had at its base warped and twisted attitudes. No one, dear M, wants to think about the horrors of the disease, nor the tremendous waves of fear, hatred, and rejection that are being felt, but about two weeks ago, in the magazine rack at the Provençal, I counted six major French publications, the *Time, Newsweek* type, with full-colour cover stories on the subject. It won't go away if we ignore it. It will almost certainly get worse before getting better. We have to accept the facts as they are placed before us. Most cases are homosexuals and/or drug abusers. Rectal passing of the disease is by far the most proven method of transference, along with main-line blood contact through needles.

I hope St. Mary's Drugs on Yonge Street continues to supply syringes to those who ask. They have been actively trying to help stop the spread of disease for many years, and have fought court battles to legalize the selling of syringes, or as users call them, fits, machines, cranks.

I trust that if gay movement activists are truly caring they are striving to educate and to allay some of the fears the nightmare is stirring.

As I stated in letters a couple of years ago, the major role I see for your profession is the solid support and advice given to the young, the neophyte, the bewildered, and the damned. Sexual "preference," I believe, goes well beyond a simple preference and choice. Decisions are made, patterns are established, and perhaps chemistry plays a role, as yet unknown to its fullest, in the day-to-day development of that personal sexuality which sets some of us apart.

How often I have wished I were "normal." How often I have prayed to be less complex and more accepting of the *status quo* of the heterosexual majority. But I know I touch a chord in almost all men that has its base in sensuality. I do believe we all are all. I believe the absolute straight queer-basher is akin to the woman-hating faggot queen. Both are incomplete as human beings and both are emotional cripples.

The AIDS war will, as all wars, bring out the best and worst in society. The Hitlers, the Goerings, the Churchills, the spy, the counter-spy, the victor, and the victim. Florence Nightingales will flourish, martyrs will be blessed, but, dear M, what lessons will be learned?

The Catholic Church, because of the fallability of man and the doctrine of the forgiveness of sins, for centuries has been able to condemn so-called deviant behaviour and still accept its existence within its own ranks. As disciples of God, Christ, Mary, whatever, priests have been ordained with the magic power to pronounce "naughty boy, you have sinned, but you are forgiven, try not to sin again."

Simple minds believe this to be possible. Continuing the sin has a price, but it is not too difficult to pay. A few well-chosen words, some tangible proof of repentence, and off we go again. I don't believe the Church, or any of us, can have cake and eat it, too.

The insistence on celibacy in priesthood is an anti-human flaw that stains the very fabric of the institution. Warped ideas and, historically speaking, unspeakable acts, have been the result of this barbaric attempt at total domination of the human spirit.

Yes, there have been, and continue to be, those who can sublimate their natural desires to the point of inaction. Yes, there are those who have and continue to repent honestly and humbly for their moments of falling from grace, but there are also thousands who find in the institution itself a protection for the very sins and misdeeds it, as the Church of God, condemns.

I tire of Pope John Paul's total rejection of birth control while also crying out on behalf of needy, illiterate followers who cannot be fed. I am angered by his Holier than Thou attitude (mind you, the Church says he *is* Holier than Thou) toward his own bishops and theologians who have moved into the twentieth century and strive to cope with a tapestry of social and sexual threads that doesn't quite hold together.

My awe and wonderment is reserved for Mother Theresa. She, unlike a lot of others, puts her money where her mouth is. She believes, loves, and cares without judgement. If the Church exists only to produce such a wondrous example of human caring, then I suppose it plays a positive role. But now is a time for all good men to come to the aid of the party.

The party's over, the war has begun. Please God, the powers that be, Church, State, and the true "spirit," keep a lid on sanity and do battle with prejudice and ignorance. That's our only hope.

December 2, 1986

Dear M.

I have been thinking a lot recently of my early years in the gallery – the exciting years, when I was high on discovering new artists, not on that bitch mistress, cocaine, and other artifically inseminated pleasures.

A high point for me in those early years was my return to England in 1966, when I first saw the graphics of David Hockney and Richard Hamilton. There were very few innovative printmakers in Canada in those days. Doris Pascal had championed a few people who were doing etchings and prints. Vera Frenkel was an exciting, if cerebral, printmaker, who has since gone on to do videos. I had shown Jo Rothfels's work. But, really, there were very few graphic artists.

Before I left for England, I had read of the graphic art being done in London, Paris, all over Europe, but I'd never *seen* it. I was amazed at what I saw in London, particularly at the Whitechapel Gallery. The work was superb–and inexpensive. It was already being called "Pop" art. Everyone always thinks of Pop art as being American, but the term was coined by a British critic after seeing the collages of Richard Hamilton, particularly one collage of a muscle man holding a lollipop, or popsicle. He dubbed it "Pop" art, and the name stuck. So, Hamilton is really the father of this genre, not Warhol, not Lichenstein.

I realized that a show of this work in Canada could have a tremendous impression, not just on buyers, but on artists. I thought they would do very well to be able to see, absorb, really look at this inspiring new work. And they did – they learned a great deal.

I brought a selection of work back with me, and the show got rave reviews. I showed Peter Sedgley, David Hockney, Richard Hamilton (of course), and Bridget Riley. Bridget was the queen of Op art. Vasarely was its king in Paris, but Bridget was queen in London. Her work was enough to give me vertigo. You could hardly look at it; it would never stand still. Hockney had been to California by this time, and he had done the stunning prints called the *Hollywood Collection*. I brought them over as part of that first show.

I showed Allen Jones, who had a foot fetish, I think. He did a series about marriage, where the figures were andro-gynous–half-female, half-male, each emerging from the other. He did a piece called *Shoebox*, which was a box containing several black and white photos of shoes with stiletto heels, and a beautiful cast-aluminum shoemaker's last. Quite S and M, but very striking. He went on to do hyper-realistic females in terribly subservient, sexist positions–for instance, a coffee table of a woman lying on her back, supporting a sheet of glass. Talk about male rage!

None of the artists themselves came for the show, because I didn't know them well at that point, but, subsequently, in

1967 or 1968, Richard Hamilton arrived as a result of working with Marcel Duchamp on sections of Duchamp's large glass piece, *The Bride Stripped Bear by Her Bachelors, Even*. The glass was cracked at one point, and Richard was rebuilding it, with Duchamp's assistance and support, because there was going to be a major Duchamp retrospective. In the process, they did two multiples – two pieces of glass with images between them. I had these pieces, and Richard and Marcel both came to the gallery for the opening.

Av Isaacs and, I think, Michael Snow were responsible for bringing Marcel and John Cage together (John Cage was an extraordinary musician and composer of electronic music – the "wet fart" school of music, I used to call it) for a game of chess in the auditorium at Ryerson. It was a great artistic event. There were Marcel Duchamp and John Cage playing chess on an electronically wired board, so that, every time a move was made, there was a pattern of strange noises. I left at around four in the afternoon; I couldn't take it any more. You waited so damn long for one of them to make a move, there was no continuity between the noises. But it was a spectacle. It was really performance art long before there was such a thing as Performance art. In the sixties, we called them "happenings."

Jim Dine once did a wonderful "happening." A friend of his had been killed in a car accident, I believe, and the happening was titled *Accident*. It involved red crosses, bandages, police sirens, ambulance sirens. It was very moving; horribly real.

I have a hard time thinking of the performance art of today as being connected with the visual arts – painting, drawing, and sculpture. I think that it has its place, but I think it's theatre. I remember lecturing at the Ontario College of Art to some final-year students on how to present their work to galleries. I told them not to include in their portfolios everything they had ever done, but a body of work that looks like it's going in a clear direction and that gives a sense of personal identity. One wonderful punk girl – orange and purple hair, tight leather skirt – stood up and said, "Mr Pollock, I don't have a portfolio. I am a performance artist." So I said, "Well, I suggest you build a repertoire!"

I am digressing. My brain is spinning with thoughts and memories of my past work. It's hard to grasp just one and write it down. Anyway, that exhibition in 1966 led to single exhibitions of several of the artists involved. I held a major retrospective of Richard Hamilton's prints—everything he had ever done – and I had a major exhibition of David Hockney. Hamilton did not come to his retrospective; he came when Duchamp was here. But David came over for his show – and that's quite a story, too.

David had just published *Grimms' Fairy Tales* with, I believe, seventy original etchings. Petersburg Press published it. It was just magnificent. For David's show, I had his early prints, including some that he had done while at the Royal College of Art. I had the complete *Cavafy Suite*.

Dear friends of mine, Kay and Hunter Thompson, who were avid collectors and very strong supporters of the gallery, had said that they would throw a cocktail party/reception for David at their house after the opening. David was to arrive by plane, come directly to the gallery, and after an hour or two go to the reception.

The opening opened; David didn't arrive. The opening closed; David hadn't arrived. Kay and Hunter went back to their house to receive all the guests they had invited, and I sat in the gallery, waiting and worrying. Finally, David walked in. I couldn't be angry with him, but I did discover later that Gary Michael Dalt, the art critic, had caught David as he was getting out of the taxi in front of the gallery and had whisked him away to the Park Plaza Hotel and had surreptitiously recorded an interview with him via a hidden microphone. Poor David thought I had okayed this meeting. I was furious when I found out what had happened. David was totally innocent.

He is an amazingly simple man; dyed yellow hair (not blond, yellow straw), big round hornrimmed glasses, pudgy, and charming. He is one of the greatest living artists, as far as I am concerned.

Henry Geldzahler was the curator of modern art at the Metropolitan Museum in New York. Later I worked with him on the television film on Albers, and I was also responsible for Henry coming to Toronto to give a couple of lectures. Henry and David had been good friends for many years, and David has done many portaits – drawings and etchings – of Henry. David was also doing etchings of Moe and his wife, Celia, who is David's most famous model.

When David was living in California, he met and fell in love with a student, Peter. He did one large etching of Peter, nude, from the strange perspective of looking up. It was marvellous, but no one would buy it: a frontal nude of a man just standing there – it wasn't at all erotic.

I had a great deal of difficulty selling Hockney's work, and I think it was because of what they were. There was no pretention. Those early etchings were drawn with a kind of acid truth, but they were not highly realistic; they had an element of slight crudeness. His subjects became Everyman and Everywoman. Flawless.

December 3, 1986

Pollock Galleries
One – 205 Elizabeth Street, 1960-1961
Two – 201 Elizabeth Street, 1961-1963
Three – 599 Markham Street, 1963-1971
Four – Phase II, Portland Street, 1966-1968
Five – Dundas Street West, 1972-1975
Six – Toronto Dominion Centre, 1972-1973
Seven – Scollard Street, 1975-1982
Eight – 209 Adelaide Street East, 1980-1983

Christ, dear M, I was all over the map! What held it all together was the tremendous support that others gave me, the idea man, the dreamer, the snotty-nosed kid from Perth Avenue who decided to be somebody.

Heading the list of people who gave (and received) support are B and Eva: blind love and blind faith. I relied heavily on others to do the tidying up, the pulling together; I just created situation after situation of stimulus and excitement. As my star started to rise, I became obsessed with the public image I was building, the sense of daring, outrage, controversy. I recall getting a headline that "Pollock states Riopelles were falling off the canvas!" Riopelle was then painting extremely thick impasto-knife pictures, and the surface of the oil would, logically, dry first, creating a crust, then the inner paint dried, shrank, and created a space which quite often caused cracking and flaking. But, of course, who the fuck was I to blast off about Riopelle, the then Canadian darling of Paris?

My outspoken opinions were, because of their blatancy, shocking and adored. I quickly became the product of my own world of power. I remember the terror I felt at the idea of my first lecture. Along the line I must have learned a bit of grammar, as I didn't, and don't use "dees" and "dos" and "them kids" or "youse." But the idea of standing in front of an auditorium filled with unknown faces, most of whom I was sure had university educations behind them, was scary.

I got my public feet wet in the battle to save the Gerrard Street Village. That fight and my "discovery" of Morrisseau were both national news items. I got a taste of lights, mikes, and recognition. I found that common sense is not a common commodity. I discovered that people complicate almost all decisions with cloudy and usually indecisive thinking. I just "called it as I saw it." Intuition, gut feeling, is at the base of much of my observations. Also this strange and potent cord I seem to have with the sensual in almost everyone and everything.

I would encourage my students to believe that all of us have a right to personal taste, in life, in love, in art. Appreciation was different, as some base of comparison, some gleaned knowledge, is essential for value judgement and assessment. Life, art; art, life, emotions, intellect, technique – it all made, and it still makes, sense to me. A successful attempt to balance these areas made life, art, boring and predictably dull. One element too aggressive, too overpowering, and everything fell apart. Each work of art must be viewed with a simple yardstick of sensibilities, which most people have developed just from living.

So much for communication. As my public ego (I suppose that's the word) began to overwhelm my personal doubts, my time was filled with people–not close friends, not the deserving B or Eva–but crowds, bolstering, supporting, and feeding the outrageous persona I had to keep alive.This public being went on the stock exchange of sex, and bidding for a while was healthy, if kept secret from B and most of the sun-lit followers. Bigger became better, more became more, and by 1979, 1980, no one, including me, could keep up to my pace. Buying major art in bulk (I bought a complete Vasarely edition once), robbing Peter to pay Paul, diversifying my energies between the wonderful young Canadian artists I truly cared most for and the "biggies" of international renown all proved too much, even for me.

Debts, doubts, and dope all seemed to fall in at once. Debts, because of my total neglect of any financial responsibilities; doubts, as the more I learned, the more I realized the little I knew (and still know); dope, cocaine, that wonderful white bitch mistress of fantasy, because it offered false power and escape.

I avoided correspondence, commitment; I ran from financial crisis, and I rarely spent any time alone with B. I was giving five classes or lectures a week, attending one or two dinner parties, galas, fêtes, and all with casts of thousands. B wanted, needed, and deserved some kind of partnership, some sense of caring. I gave – oh yes, I gave – but gold, gifts, and galas are not the stuff to base a relationship on. Trust, sharing, some quiet and tranquil moments, these I denied.

All bombs have a fuse, all relationships a breaking point. B loved the glamour, drank up the elegance and the social whirl of our existence, but he, unlike me, remained faithful and was ravaged constantly by jealousy. I, in an attempt to keep peace at any cost, became deceitful and devious.

His succession of business ventures were all attempts at building his self-image and developing the individual man. But he bored quickly, did not enjoy routine, so his shops were closed half the time. He was rude to people who could help, and each venture finally fell apart. No wonder–he was always "Jack's friend," and who needs that shit constantly?

He has taste, he loves and hates passionately, and sees most things in a black and white way. Quick to make decisions, almost never admits he's wrong. God! how we ever survived fifteen years is a mystery!

I thought his dedication and loyalty too good for me. He deserved someone who could be a constant. He saw me as I was – self-centred, promiscuous, and determined. Oil and water. Neither of us was totally right, neither totally wrong. He worked much harder at the relationship than I did. I took it for granted.

Then he met R. It was the first (and last) threat for me. I could accept and justify my whorish behaviour because I loved (what a word) only B. There had never been, and has not been since, another to whom I felt as close. I probably could have accepted an anonymous fling for B also. (As you are aware, most gay relationships that have survived are "open" to a large extent.) But I couldn't accept the emotional and binding relationship that developed between B and R. The gallery was in tatters. Moving it to Dundas Street had proved to be my grand folly. I couldn't stand being in the gallery. I couldn't stand being at home. The gallery was ready to explode; all advised bankruptcy.

I walked along Gerrard Street past Allan Gardens. I knew B would be home, showering and preparing to see R. I stopped at the corner of Sherbourne. Traffic was racing by. I felt compelled to throw myself into it. Instead, I stopped a police cruiser and asked to be taken to the Clarke. I was interviewed and admitted. B came daily. I had a meeting with good and kind people from the art community (Arthur Gelber among them, along with my accountants, and Eva). I refused bankruptcy and took it upon myself to liquidate as much as possible (over a million dollars of inventory in international graphics had accumulated).

After about two weeks in the Clarke, B arrived one morning, shocked, dishevelled, and shaking. He always drank more than I did, and one of our problems had always been my inability to accept drunken, and aggressive, behaviour. Well, he had drunk a great deal the night before, went to bed, having dropped a cigarette on the couch in the library-den. Luckily he escaped with no burns, but almost half the house was gutted, many works of art were destroyed, most of my art library was burned, and the entire house was water-soaked and wasted.

God! I felt anger, pity, rage, but made an attempt to support him. Everything crowded my head. I insisted on seeing the damage for myself and, accompanied by a nurse, visited the ruin – Victorian chairs, charred and sprung, were thrown about the lawn, windows smashed, the dank, putrid smell of smoke and destruction was everywhere. I climbed the stairs, the carpet soaked and black, and saw the charred ruins. I broke down and returned to the safety of the Clarke.

B's guilt was horrific. I justified his actions, but realized neither of us could go on like this. He moved into the small Four Seasons Hotel on Jarvis, while the insurance company tried to clean up the mess.

I never returned to Seaton Street. I left the Clarke after about a month and moved into the Waldorf Astoria on Charles Street. I lived there for several months, striving to patch the gaping holes in my professional credibility. I found new quarters for the gallery on Scollard Street, but realized that things could not get worse.

A telephone message from Florida was left at the hotel for me. Al Latner of Greenwin had heard of my situation. He said he had talked to his real estate manager, and I was to contact him as he had a one-bedroom apartment for me free for a year, while I got back on my feet.

Maitland Street. Who would believe that the apartment would be in the same building two stories higher than R's? Each night I would see the car I had bought with B, parked in front. *Quelle histoire!*

B has always been good at making money from adversity. The insurance paid for all restoration, reupholstery, cleaning and reframing pictures, and his hotel stay.

Divorces are terrible for everyone. Small things become viciously large. Petty behaviour abounds on both sides. Rage, destruction, and abortive attempts at being civilized clash in a tumult of emotion. Friends don't really know what to do. I was almost universally more liked, but many understood, and rightly so, B's loyalty to me all those years and my errant and obvious abuse of his trust. Even now, over ten years later, the conflict is not resolved. I fluctuate between negative and positive thoughts. People who saw my not-so-private descent view the episode through discoloured lenses. But there is no right and wrong in the overall. Emotions and behaviour were shitty on both sides.

I sit here, thinking about power, the beginnings of my "shock-wave ascent" and know I wouldn't trade places with B, who now seems comfortably settled. I also know that my letters to you, dear M, are not meant to shock. But I need to write them to exorcize some of the cloudy and murky patterns in my life.

If this doesn't come through, then I'm failing at what I have always wanted to do: communicate.

December 4, 1986

Dear M.

The story continues. The Phase II gallery on Portland Street, which I opened in 1966, was a strange venture. I still had my gallery on Markham Street. Some artists (Paul Fournier, Cathy

Sennett-Harbison, Thelma Van Alstyne, Carole Condé, and Karl Beveridge among them) had begun creating large works. It was difficult to view them in the Markham Street premises. As well, I was already concerned about my relationship with B and so, when Jared Sable (then a cement block salesman and collector) told me of his uncle's warehouse building, I looked, liked, and rented. It was set up as a large gallery for viewing major works, with living space behind, and I intended to attempt the difficult problem of breaking with B (on my terms, at that point).

I painted the whole space white. The living room area at the end was separated by a welded iron wall by Andrew Posa, the sculptor. Tables were made from marble slabs (spinach-green and black) on welded stands. Other furniture included chairs, tables, and so on, painted by Cathy Sennett-Harbison (now famous for her "Wrinkles" stuffed toy). There was a kitchen equipped for serving a cast of hundreds, and the john, as factories would have it, was a space with a urinal and two toilet compartments. I painted the john violet, put black-boards and chalk in the cubicles, had a smashing black-tie opening, and began to try to split myself in two – Phase II and Markham Street. Of course, what I got was lots of publicity, not much action, and many illicit sexual encounters (cabbies, so-called clients). It was, in retrospect, a forerunner to New York's Soho area, but it was also a kind of sex bin, with art thrown in as an extra.

In 1970, I turned forty, looked around, and felt I should be a man of property, with property. Wrong!

However wrong it was, I started thinking about buying rather than renting. I moved quietly, and in 1972 Debbie Alter's mother, an old-hand real estate pro, found two houses on Dundas Street. They could be purchased for forty thousand dollars each. I had no money, but had a stack of works valued at over a million dollars.

B and I devised a scheme to sell "building blocks" for a thousand dollars each, each redeeming itself in fifteen hundred dollars worth of merchandise at retail price. Only two weeks after the initial letter, almost eighty thousand had come in.

Peter Hamilton, a very bright young architect and collector, began the plans for turning the two Dundas Street rooming houses into possibly the finest space that Canada has ever had for a private gallery.

Energy was high, excitement everywhere. I was, as they say, "on a roll."

The renovations were to cost, in the end, much more than the property investment. Mortgages and fly-now-pay-later schemes got me through the ordeal. What a dream! What a nightmare!

In the midst of all this, on a cold day around Christmas, Lister Sinclair came to the gallery on Markham Street with Fay Hanks, his secretary-assistant. They usually did the rounds on the weekends, and we had become friendly. Lister asked, if there was one living artist I would like to do a television show on, who would it be? I said Josef Albers. He said, get him and we have a show.

Now, Albers to me was a god. I showed his superb prints (I bought them through Denise René in Paris, who had published them) but I didn't know him. That night, I telephoned New Haven information and found that Josef Albers was listed and got his number.

The next morning I called. A cool and distant female voice asked who I was, and why I was calling. I explained who I was, what the CBC was, and what our interest was. She said to call again at six that evening, and she would discuss the matter with Mr. Albers. (I thought she was a secretary—it was Anni Albers.)

At six sharp, I called and was informed Mr. Albers would like to meet me to discuss the project. Could I be there the next day at three? I gulped, said, "Of course," and hung up, shaking.

I flew to La Guardia airport, took a limousine to New Haven, a taxi to Orange, Connecticut, and arrived clutching a bouquet of white tulips, as I didn't dare to take colour to the master.

After driving around the area for ten minutes (I was early), I knocked and was received into one of the warmest cool spaces I have ever seen. All was white – walls, furniture, fine venetian blinds – white, clean, and uncluttered. The joy and colour of Albers' squares on the walls radiated light and beauty, transforming the coolness of the decor into something human and loving.

Josef and Anni were gracious and warm, and what was to be a half-hour discussion turned into an afternoon and early evening of conversation on art, life, teaching, and humanity. He was, finally, at eighty, being recognized as the giant figure in the history of colour in painting.

The Metropolitan Museum in New York had just opened his retrospective, the first by a living artist in its history. He was financially secure, probably for the first time in his dedicated life, and had cut off any gallery representation.

We talked, he liked me and my approach to teaching and his art. We discussed the proposed television show, and he graciously accepted the challenge.

Now, I really had to measure up.

Within a week or two I went back to New York, with a camera crew and with Lister Sinclair, the executive producer. We filmed a walking tour with Josef and an interview on a bench in the Met, surrounded by the glory of his squares.

He was simple, direct, stubborn, opinionated, and always had the twinkle of mischief in his eyes.

Why the square, Mr. Albers?

"Because it sits where you put it. It doesn't move or bounce around."

Why the same composition for over twenty years?

"It's just something to hang colours on. I found perfect proportions, then went on with colour." His father had been a house painter. He knew how to paint edge to edge (masking tape was a trick for the amateur).

He disdained his fellow Bauhaus teacher Johannes Itten, and refused to accept his ideas on colour.

"He separates them all with black lines. Colour should interact. You know my book, *The Interaction of Colour?*"

Yes, I knew the book. I also knew that more than any other artist, Albers had made me *feel* colour, feel the vibration, the merging, and the union.

"Colour should marry and multiply. No divorce is allowed. Expressionism is excess. You keep your pants done up when you paint!"

Then, like a little boy, he stood in front of a panel (he always used masonite, never canvas) and pointed out, "You see that blue, you see that green, you see the red they make?"

Warm, cool, light, shade – within the geometric box of the square, all nature seemed to abound, pulsating and alive. Henry Geldzhaler, the curator of Modern Art at the Met in those days, had organized the exhibition and had given us the privilege of filming when the gallery was closed to the public. The Met's awesome vaulted spaces were made somehow intimate by the colour of Albers.

As he worked on masonite, and mostly in square format, the largest paintings were four feet by four feet. The exhibition was beautifully installed, and a smaller gallery contained his early representational drawings and woodcuts, including a fine and sensitive self-portrait, as well as aggressive, simple brush drawings of owls. Nicholas Fox Weber has since written a fine book on the drawings of Albers.

Much of the filming was done in Josef's basement studio – a spotless, super-organized space, again with venetian blinds. He used controlled artificial light and worked flat. Many coats of special gesso were applied to the rough surface of the masonite. He would then apply the paint directly from the tube with a palette knife. All colours were pre-mixed, manufactured, and each would be identified on the reverse side of the work by manufacturer's name and brand. First the description and number of coats of flat white undercoat, then: Grumbacher – Cadmium Red Light; Windsor Newton – Scar-

let; Grumbacher – Crimson, and so on, then the type of varnish. Everything was documented.

I wondered and asked about forgeries.

" 'They' didn't do it first," was his reply.

Josef loved to talk about his little *Schvindels,* the "round
squares" he created, in which the colour softened and fused
edges, and tones and values floated. His supremely elegant
black and white drawings were also *Schvindels.* What appeared
solid block-like forms one moment became hollow and negative the next.

There is very little of the theatre of Vasarely in the work
of Albers. There is, in the place of visual gymnastics, a pure,
sure intelligence, which imparts the joy of self-discovery.

Josef adored projects, and during this time was in the final
stages of producing the giant, two-volume masterpiece *For-
mulation-Articulation* at the Ives Sillman workshop. Both Nor-
man Ives and Cy Sillman were past students of Albers, and
the printshop had published many original Albers serigraphs.
This project was an enormous undertaking, and included new
images created from early Bauhaus glass painting designs, as
well as squares and a fresh, exciting series of abstract compositions based on early pictures and using the image of the
treble clef. This series is one of the first examples of serial
painting in abstract art. I was reminded of Monet's haystacks
and his stunning variations on Rheim's cathedral.

Anni was a Berliner, born Anni Fleischman, from a well-
known family in publishing. Josef, the son of a carpenter-
house painter, was born in Bottrop. They met and fell in love
at the Bauhaus. Anni was in textiles and Josef was exploring
the possibilities of glass painting.

In 1933, Hitler came into power, the Bauhaus was closed,
and the Albers, through the recommendation of Alfred Barr
at the Museum of Modern Art, arrived in the United States
to teach at a revolutionary new school, Black Mountain.

Anni's dedication to weaving, which, until recently, was
dismissed as a craft, laid a solid foundation for what we now
call Fibre Arts. After years of battling the stigma against craft,

in 1956 she gave away her looms, and to this day concentrates on drawing and print-making.

The filming finished, I returned to Toronto, but subsequently enjoyed and was enriched by monthly visits to Anni and Josef.

Anni, tall, aristocratic, proud, was at once a mature artist and a romantic schoolgirl. I remember her telling of her youthful fantasy of being Mae West, with a gun on her hip! Josef was not large, but was compact, and full of latent energy. Fast, fastidious, and impassioned, he never vacillated. He was definite, sure, and while I did not always agree with him, I always admired him.

His white hair was carefully combed, his complexion, apple-pink and shining, and those eyes, sparkling, darting, daring, the gleam of love and adventure always there.

Well, I am dry at the moment – I can't think straight.

P.S. I'm enclosing a short piece I wrote on Albers a few years back.

Josef Albers

Much has been written of Josef Albers, his tenacity and his precise, judgemental approach to the visual experience of the twentieth century. No man before in the history of art had limited his compositional horizons within such rigid and formal confines. With Albers, the idea of serial imagery became, not a restriction, but rather an open window for our perceptions. Through the discipline of highly selective and often obstinate opinions, he liberated the passion and the personality of interactive colour and form.

His ambiguity and the subtle, constant activity of his images have little to do with the obvious optical exercises of others, such as Victor Vasarely and Bridget Riley.

Reduction, simplification, and beauty raise the simplest of forms – the square – to an unforgettable personal icon. For over thirty years, Albers adhered to this seemingly rigid composition, which he had invented. The materials he used were unyielding masonite lovingly surfaced with gesso, and the simplest of tools – a knife. Then the alchemist/child was released to explore the world of colour, not as with others in the past within the context of imagery and narrative, but colour for colour's sake, each nuance continuing a romance that ended only with his death. His relationship with colour was as demanding and ever-changing as life itself. Colour melded, fused, and actively created blends and tonal perceptions of vision. It is as if he re-invented the rainbow.

Albers – Bauhaus master, revered teacher, and brilliant mind – was a paradox, a creator of miracles, and an ever-wondering child, a sorcerer's apprentice who excelled his master. His greatest gifts, and his heritage to us, were not mechanical or mathematical. His vision was not in the geometry or physics he employed. The greatness of Albers was in his non-knowing knowing – his constant search for harmony and accord.

Precise, opinionated, direct, and honest, he recognized the boundless energy of the visual experience and obsessively sought answers through questions. The child in Josef was constantly amazed at his own discoveries, which, as a teacher, he loved to share. Inventive, inquisitive, he was blessed with a generous spirit that laid firm foundations for the continuing dialogue of visual and rational approaches to colour.

Ever the explorer, the perceptive eye and questioning mind of Albers charted courses, which he documented and recorded. There were no guarded secrets, no mystery of trick or technique; the simple truth was the focus of his searching.

His pragmatism is illustrated well in a story Josef told me about him and Piet Mondrian. One morning, in Piet's studio, Albers watched as Piet painfully and patiently painted over a black line in the pure white of the background. He said nothing but a few days later returned with a roll of black electrician's tape. "Piet, when your canvas is white, place the tape in different positions until you feel the composition is correct, then paint." Piet listened, sighed, and returned the tape to Albers. "I have to make the mistake," he replied.

Josef Albers was born on March 19, 1888 in Bottrop, Westphalia. Before entering the Bauhaus in 1920 he had already attended the Royal Art School in Berlin, the School of Applied Arts in Essen, and the Munich Academy of Art. In 1923 he became professor of the preliminary course, taking over from George Muche and Johannes Itten. Anni Albers recalls this moment fondly, as it allowed Josef to ask her family for her hand in marriage.

Together, yet in uniquely separate ways, the Albers constantly challenged and assisted in new and exciting avenues of visual exploration. The same restless probing that resulted in the *Homage to the Square* masterpieces, is made visible in Albers' early black and white drawings. A shape, solid, block-like one moment, is transformed into a receding negative form, then returns to solid mass, all within a glance. The facts of geometric proportion and design can be described and accounted for.

The magic of this visionary remains the wonderment of its creator.

December 13, 1986

Dear M.

Today is busy. As the fifteenth is a Monday, we (Gabrielle, Peter, and I) decided tonight would be best for a fête to celebrate the fifth anniversary of my open-heart surgery and my pig's heart valve. I have not had a cent in my pocket for about a month, but I have been counting on something turning up. Yesterday, with a Christmas card came a cheque for twenty-five U.S. dollars from Anne de Boismaison-White. So today I bought pasta (lots of pasta) and I will make a sauce. Gerry Conrath will make a large salad, Pauline and Gabrielle

Levy, my dear friends from the other side of the Luberon, will bring *saucisson* and bread. Nadine brought olives; Alain and Denise, Nadine's cousins from Monaco, brought twenty-four bottles of wine; Gabrielle has made oatmeal cookies (one large one in the shape of a heart); Peter cooks the sauce. We expect thirty to fifty people.

We have done a number on Lou Paradou. The crypt glows with eighteen candles, and hollyhocks and pansies adorn the table.

Dear M, I am truly blessed.

The house looks wonderful: I've hung over forty pictures, and all the corners are swept and clean. (We do have a pet water beetle in the upstairs john. He has been part of the family now for over three months. Charlie, good little fellow, minds his own business, doesn't seem to have a mate. Sound familiar?)

I have decided I have a green thumb, as I've grown geraniums, begonias, and a very healthy African violet plant, along with spider plants. Even my oleander, which was just dried sticks when I returned from Canada, is lush and healthy.

We now get *Time* magazine (a week late) as Nadine sends it on from Geneva. God! The world's a mess. Reagan, Oliver North, Iran, the Contras, AIDS, the Pope, condoms, Paris, the students, riots, police brutality. How the earth survives is a wonder. We seem to do all in our powers as tenants of this planet to destroy her goodness and gifts. We exploit natural resources and turn them into unnatural weapons. We treat our fellow man as despicable. In the name of God, or gods, we ravage, pillage, and condone genocide and contamination. The generous spirit, which I believe is God, seems to be suffocating in self-indulgent power struggles.

Happy New Year!

Gerry Conrath sent to Boston for a T-shirt for me. It arrived yesterday emblazoned with "Have you hugged a pig today?" Also, a black and white checked shirt and a red V-neck pullover arrived from Barbara, Ron, and my sister. I have just showered and shaved, and I am wearing the T-shirt under the open checked shirt, black corduroy pants tucked into the strange black suede boots (fringed) that I bought in Paris. A bit of a costume, fitting for a *fête de cochon*.

At dinner last night we talked about good and bad. It started with music (Peter is highly intolerant of most) and, of course, it turned to art and photography (Gabrielle works hard at photos these days). I felt old, and tried to defend differences. My catholic (notice the small letter) taste comes from years of teaching and trying to pry out what was unique in each student. I would never demonstrate, and often saw in mere beginners things I wish I had done. I said so. The problem with doing something once is the chance, the accident, the mistake which turns out well. With series pictures, such as my damned and loved still-lifes, formal problems demand formal solutions.

The monoprint stamp collages and landscapes use the planned accident, the intentional mistake, the sureness of the unsure. The basic fundamentals of technique I learned and forgot, I still use. Composition has never been much of a problem for me – corners (the bitch of many painters) seem to integrate naturally with the picture plane. Colour is my real challenge. Playing it safe becomes boring, so risks have to be taken.

It is that risk I like to see in others. In music I enjoy melody and find comfort in the variations of simple tunes such as those by Bach and many modern composers. Peter is a snob in many ways, wonderfully full of gesture, phrase, and put-downs. His vocabulary is astonishing. He loves the blues. Not the pseudo-blues – the real thing. He is not tolerant of most classics, and loathes sentimental torch-type songs (you probably do, too). I can, and do, wallow in the B-movie beat of a Linda Ronstadt, or the tacky syrup of a Streisand. But then, what has my life been but a series of Joan Crawford-Tyrone Power mini epics?

I can cry when a boy loses his dog. I can laugh when a phony butler trips. I allow myself involvement with the cornball and the common. But then again, I am common; a weed not a flower.

So much for this crap – I'll continue this saga tomorrow after the fête.

P.S. I just read my mini assessment on the state of the world and realize that nature retaliates with her own weapons: disease, drought, and the ultimate denial, death. Tit for tat. Which came first, good or evil? Natural laws become unnatural acts. Shut up Pollock! Go away!

December 14, 1986

Dear M.
The fête was an enormous success. About forty people came in total, the core being twenty-five very special friends. Food was good, wine flowed, and the last guests left at two in the morning.

This morning I, being more together than the others, got up, cleaned up, washed the dishes and realized we are ten bottles of wine richer (two vintage, none plonk), and discovered in the fridge two bottles of sparkling Blanc de Blancs and a fine bottle of champagne!

We drank to you last night, I made a speech in my fucked-up French, and we all partook of the large cookie heart Gabrielle had made. She decorated it with a chocolate pig, squiggly tail all around the edge.

Most of us don't have second chances. The talk last night was about the new Jack, the less frenetic Jack, the working Jack.

What a joy for all, if the kid from Perth Avenue makes good!

December 23, 1986

Dear M.
The air here is brilliant, crisp, much like a day in Ontario or Quebec when fields are covered with weighty blankets of

white. But here, unlike the rolling hills of the Eastern Township, our low mountains, guardians of the valley, are still mostly green, and the incredible, indelible sense of lavender, violet, is ever present. We passed la montagne Sainte-Victoire yesterday—the grey ashes of mourning still encase her slopes, reminders of the ever-vulnerable and fragile balance of elements. She was crowned with a halo of snow, majestic and haughty, and in the valley all around, the lilac, lavender, mauve tints deepen into the earthy and exotic violets of ploughed field shadows, their ridges, bright and dense sienna, weaving and twisting in creative earth works that sing to the harmony of man and his environment.

Christmas is a day away. I have no idea what Christmas Day holds, but I am sure that it will be filled with more Christian spirit here at Lou Paradou than in most holly-decked and tinselled homes.

My gifts to the kids (aside from *another* Pollock picture) are the use of this place to rest, and a support that I give without strings or demands. Their gifts to me, rare and cherished, are love, caring, and respect. The Lord does provide!

I trust you are well, and am sure you will be doing the rounds of holiday festivities. I miss the frantic, seasonal insanity of lighted trees, shopping, cooking, drinking, all in excess, as though the birth of Christ gives licence to indulge.

I hope others are giving to the Salvation Army, Fred Victor Mission, and Sick Kids' Hospital. (Those were my choices for charity.) I wonder if Sunday schools still have a "white gift" service, where children take tins of food, boxes of cookies, and so on, all wrapped the same, place them at the altar of the church, and assist the ladies groups (my mother was a member of the Sunshine Club) to make baskets for the poor.

Christmas Eve, we would help distribute the baskets together with toys (the young people's group would rebuild and paint wagons and such like). There was always a turkey (butchers and the wealthier church-goers donated) and always hard candy and candy canes. Somehow, no matter how poor we might have thought ourselves, we still gave to others.

My rich cousins would get electric trains, but I got a train, mother made sure. Yes, you wound it up, but it still had tracks and a gate house, and I made much better mountains than my cousins. Our stockings were always filled. Christmas baking scented the air for weeks before. The magic of the tree, lights, carols, pudding—and a tired, frazzled mother, attempting to spread love on the troubled waters of my father's alcoholic, destructive behaviour. No, I do not remember a Christmas without tears. No, I do not remember my father ever buying a gift for anyone. Yes, I remember smashed dishes, screaming and violence, but these days, in Lou Paradou, I only wish to remember the joys, the ups, the positives. The tragic consequences of my father's self-loathing have become, with time and experience, lessons well-learned, not to be repeated.

But the lack of self-worth, the inner secret feelings of inferiority, the dark shadows of self-doubt, they continue to exist. The basic problems that drove my father to alcoholic self-destruction, although couched in kindness (*j'espère!*) and tolerance, are the same at base as those responsible for my drug-ridden and hurtful past. I shun violence, confrontation, and vengeance, yet I readily violated the gift of my body. I have constantly confronted my invincibility and have taken awesome revenge on my God-given health.

The miracle of my survival here is the greatest of gifts. Yes, I still think of cocaine; yes, I still am haunted by bath-house blues, but these days I seem to keep those demons where they belong. I try, I try, and it gets easier.

January–March 1987

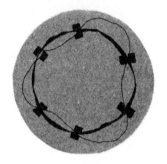

January 2, 1987

Dear M.

The New Year entered with warmth and much loving and sharing at Nadine's. But yesterday, things fell apart. I have no idea what happened to my sanity, balance, and usual tolerance, but I went into a rage, an anger I have rarely felt. Today, I ache. I am exhausted and truly embarrassed about my behaviour.

I suppose caring should be marked "Caution – use at your own risk."

All was well at first. I got up, made my usual porridge and hot chocolate. Gabrielle, Peter, and I shared some time together, and Peter went off to his job as chamber maid at Le Provençal.

I had bought veal, and was preparing the first meal I have paid for in over six weeks. (Francesca, Louis, and Jean-Pierre were coming for dinner.) Anyway, about five or so, Peter came back looking spaced and sounding incoherent. He attempted to joke, poached some apples, then retired to his chamber. So far so good. Then Francesca arrived with pinpoint pupils (as Peter's were earlier) and I started to be agitated. Francesca was, as always, charming, but I began to tense. I worked in the kitchen, both Gabrielle and Francesca attempted to rouse Peter, but to no avail, and my heart began racing.

I was furious, livid, and in the best Calvinist tradition,

outraged. Dinner was ready, Peter had passed out, and I grew more and more neurotic as the minutes passed. Our guests arrived, I busied myself in the kitchen, and finally Peter came down. The meal went well, without a hitch, as I controlled my emotions in front of others. (*Dieu merci!*) But when Louis and Jean-Pierre left, I let out such torrents of pent-up anger and emotion that even I was frightened. I had been shaking in the kitchen, preparing dinner, I could not hold a knife to cut the onions. I was a mess.

I insisted Francesca stay, lashed out at "smoking up" and not being at all responsible for others, and went on and on. I had the good sense to say that I was suspicious of my own emotions, but it was an intense and almost nasty confrontation. Peter adamantly denied, and still denies having smoked anything. I still believe he was stoned, but none of that can, or should, excuse my anger and rage.

Who the fuck am I to criticize? I felt, through the storm of my emotions, a heavy feeling – I was identifying too closely with Peter. He has had, like me, drug problems. I do not condemn, or try not to, the use of grass for relaxation, but my mind just bent, it twisted. I went to bed, took *two* Halcion (read, knocked myself out), and cried myself to sleep, shaking. I did say before I went to bed that I just had to say how I felt, and also said it was out and over.

This morning, I came down and apologized for my extraordinary behaviour, and we all have survived. But, a gut fear of going mad, of the passion of my uncontrolled anger, haunts me. Why? Did I, too, want to get high, to escape, to concentrate on pity and negatives? Was I jealous? Am I jealous? That is an emotional pitfall I think I have avoided most of my life. But now? Here? What a fuck-up. Parents must go through hell and back.

Certainly nothing Peter or Gabrielle have done has been to test me. It was me and my warped perceptions that triggered the shit. But why? Maybe it was a reaction to over six weeks of me taking from them, depending on them for food, drink, and cigarettes. Maybe my sense of using them became too much for me. Perhaps I am not meant to be content. I don't know, but I felt fear and a loss of control that I equate with madness.

Childish over-reacting, temper-tantrum-like behaviour (like the time I threw the jelly beans when I was in the Clarke) and this last episode tell me I know very little about how to handle internal unrest. I do not recognize it building, until it is too late to stop the dam from bursting. Christ, will I ever grow up?

But, dear M, I survived. Thank God Gabrielle, Peter, and Francesca (whom I haven't seen since) also survived. The sun continues to shine, and I ask only for continued health and caring within this very loving family at Lou Paradou.

I made a decision today. In Paris, I shall exhibit only the *Lacoste* constructions and some of the new series of sparse black and white drawings.

Since I returned in August, I have had no canvas and few colours, so my output has been restricted to the new landscape images, which are small and on paper. The new drawings are bold, sure, and clean.

The door I have painted is a high point for me, and I feel four or five other constructions with about six black and white drawings matted on black will also be effective. I wish you could see the new drawings. They are much like my drawing, *November's Rose*, which I gave you, but larger, and more free. Come to Paris and see!

I am terrified, and yet today, after looking at the drawings (all executed in the past few days after Gabrielle gave me a new rapidograph and some paper), I feel less tense.

January 5, 1987

Dear M.

Shit, and double shit!

Good news! I sold two black and white drawings for a thousand francs each, paid parts of most bills, and have about a hundred and fifty francs left.

Bad news. My heart is acting up. Blood pressure is high, and the doctor here in Gordes says if it is not lower by Wednesday, I'll have to go to the specialist, again.

I have not felt well for over six weeks, but put it down to depression and tension about the holidays and having no money. The bizarre outburst I had New Year's Day scared me, as it was totally out of character. There are links between such acting out and unrecognized physical ailments, I think, and I worry about the sanity of it all.

The new black and white drawings are good. I wish you could help me select the ones for Paris. I draw daily, and now have about thirty. Thank God, they are loose.

My sense of being mortal these days makes me wonder at my life as a whole, as a kind of unit, and I realize how much time we all seem to fritter away at vain attempts to establish an identity, which often is at odds with reality.

What am I doing here? Trying to leave a mark, a line, a shape? What did I do in Toronto? Become a parody on myself, a funky kind of creature with a bulging crotch and a teasing tongue, climbing my way through social mazes and ending in the bowels of steamy urgency? Why would I, deep down, still love the rush, the Russian roulette of the high, the power of domination, the sense of self-destruction?

I watch Gabrielle and Peter spending days of joy and freedom, and wonder what they will do, where they will go. Neither has a drive in one direction; both have talents and skills.

Peter's absolute joy at monoprinting keeps him occupied, and the results are good. Gabrielle has finally found a darkroom, and today goes to print some contact sheets of photos taken over the past two months.

No paper again today, but I have enough francs left to buy some. The new rapidograph works like a dream, and I enjoy the freedom of the fluid line. I tear up more than half, but that's just natural, as you can't cover a false note in this type of exercise.

The opening in Paris sounds like it may be fun. The Levys from Ansouis are coming, so are Gerry, Peter, Gabrielle, Anne, Bruno, Anne de Boismaison-White, Claude Yvel, Roger Morier (who is with the CBC in Paris now), and other friends.

The Centre Culturel pays for transportation (read gas and tolls) for Bruno and I to transport the pictures. Also they pay enough for a four-day stay in Paris. Not bad!

January 9, 1987

Dear M.

Your letter of December 22 arrived this morning. I have been feeling fragile as my heart flutter is running rather rampant. I go to Avignon Hospital tomorrow and hope Bertrand Vigne, the cardiologist, can rectify it without hospitalizing me.

The revival of the play *Torch Song Trilogy* continues a very successful run in London. *Body Politics* deserves to fold, as it was, for me, embarrassing and self-serving. Years ago its editors asked me to write for them, but I refused. It was run by those gay activists who, I feel, set themselves up as an opposition to the rest of society. I think the kind of anger and aggression they felt created barricades between gay men and the rest of the world. Is that the way attitudes are truly changed? Love cannot exist in a war zone. You have to be a part of society, not apart from it, to educate the ignorant, the prejudiced. Now, more than ever, because of AIDS, we need to educate straight society about homosexuality, or there will be a backlash worse than we've seen so far. Will *Playboy* start covering up pussies because AIDS is now spreading to heterosexuals? That kind of censorship is just plain silly. If there was ever a time for jerk-off material it is now. Safe sex stresses masturbation, so visual aids should be encouraged, not censored.

The chic bisexual attitudes of the early 1980s are sure taking a beating! The path of pornography, the road of relentless relief, leads to power and control. Very little in tenderness or vulnerability was allowed to exist. Perhaps the purge will force us to recognize human needs of acceptance, self-worth, and responsibility to others. The human factor is, and must be, a survival factor. The theatre of sexual excess was, in fact, just that – staged. Costume, lights (or lack thereof), roles explicitly spelled out: they all encouraged power and domination, not true sexual sharing. The fist was no longer in the jaw. In place of sticking your chin out to be punched, well, you know the alternative.

Power is truly frightening. Lieutenant-Colonel North sounds as close to a psychopathic liar to me as anything else, yet he was allowed (encouraged) to abuse trust and power. Signs of the times.

I stand by the small article I wrote for the *Medical Journal,* suggesting if two people care enough for each other, they should trust and share the world of fantasy and folly that the gods have given us the ability to envisage.

If God is love, if the meek shall inherit the earth, if we should constantly turn the other cheek, then we should presume that true power lies in tenderness and that the ultimate pinnacle of that power is peace.

I sit here, blindly believing that I must do something, that I am obligated by the mere fact of living to give. I have learned that those elements of life that seem most important to me cannot be demanded, legislated, or expected. They are the blessings, the bonuses of striving to communicate understanding and concern. Love, respect, self-worth.

Through you, my mirror image seems far less distorted these days. Through Peter and Gabrielle, I am able to practise receiving as well as giving. I continue to be amazed at the potential for growth still in me that only yesterday, it seems, was arrested.

The sun shines, I draw, and hope to be well for Paris.

That's enough for today.

Sex and Fantasy

If the title of this article sounds titillating, a bit licentious, and perhaps bordering on the prurient, then that in itself justifies this look into a very real and ongoing problem. The centre of that problem deals with some of the basic needs of man: trust and fulfillment through sharing.

To a great number of people, the idea of fantasy together with sexual aids and role-playing suggests a breakdown of social conventions, a loss of morality, and the dawning of a new age of decadence. It also suggests promiscuity rather than the desired goal of one-to-one relationships.

It is exactly this sort of reasoning that inhibits the free spirit, and creates in the place of ease and enjoyment, frustration, fear and in some cases violence. And when the fear of rejection deprives us of trust and experimentation, we are prone to seek anonymously what we should rightfully share intimately.

Therein lies the dilemma. Sexual services do not survive and *thrive* unless they fulfill specific needs. When we discover that our piece of plastic currency can be used to buy an orgasm (the so-called ultimate sexual climax), we suddenly realize that there is a great need for intimacy. We are forced to recognize the problems in maintaining close relationships.

Any physical or mental aids that help in the liberation of body and spirit must be viewed with respect and acceptance. But in a society in which a credit card can be used to pay for an erotic telephone conversation (without breaking any laws), it is obvious that we are not doing our homework. To achieve this acceptance, we must break the barriers of superimposed social behaviour with an understanding of our physical and spiritual needs.

Some of the strongest elements in these imposed life patterns are based on interpretations of religious dogma. The missionary position is more than a punch line to a joke. We seldom allow our senses to embroider the act of procreation. Masturbation is tolerated only until the *real thing* comes along. All of this, compounded by the need to belong to a peer group, further alienates the individual from his or her unique qualities as a thinking, feeling human.

The marriage vows – love, honour, and obey – again establish responsibilities that seem, out of respect and trust as interpreted by society, to further inhibit freedom. These inhibitions are intensified by the lack of creativity in most of our work places.

Routine becomes an accepted way of life, and the escape that is necessary for liberation and survival becomes quite remote. Today's emphasis on sex is in many ways disarming. However, it reflects and feeds the needs of a creatively starved society. Because of mass communication the average person is made aware of many things without understanding most.

Programmed role-playing begins with the pink and blue of infancy. Slowly it continues to colour every facet of our behaviour with patterns that inhibit, and in many instances, destroy the creative act of personal character development. We expect children to outgrow their sense of experimentation, their joy of discovery, and their delight in mystery and in the unknown.

Do doctors still play doctor?

In my observations as a lay person, the words "male" and "female" have become obsolete. Feminine and masculine characteristics often seem to be totally interchangeable. I prefer the word *androgynous*. I find that most people whom I consider to be close to complete human beings are, in fact, that mélange: a melding of both the sensitive and the strong.

Toy boxes should not be for children only, and then relegated to the attic after puberty. There can be a definite need for aids in the sexual games people play. Honesty and trust can liberate and allow mystery and discovery to return to our lives. To fight fire with fire, a return to role-playing based on individual needs seems logical. Exploration of the senses is necessary to keep any relationship alive.

Rather than suggesting promiscuity and orgiastic sexuality, which seems to be the tone of much popular literature and of many seemingly scholarly studies, I suggest an education based on mutual trust. This will allow for a deeper and more spiritual relationship.

When people are physically handicapped the medical profession endorses any form of sexual practice and stimulation in the name of rehabilitation of the *complete* individual. Why can't the same advice apply to society at large, which all too frequently seems to suffer from a handicap and paraplegia of the psyche? Perhaps patience, trust, and a willingness to learn will allow us to grow and to understand our needs. Then through sharing, the richness and fullness of the tapestry of our lives can be realized.

University of Toronto, *Medical Journal*, March 1983

January 10, 1987

Dear M.

It was good to hear your voice yesterday. I am pleased that you like the silver box. It was, and is, a favourite object of mine, and that is why you have it.

The hospital news is a bit disturbing. My heart is in flutter, so Bertrand Vigne, the cardiologist, wanted to hospitalize me immediately, and begin digitalin intravenous treatment. With no money and no OHIP, and a bill for over two thousand francs still owing from my last medical sojourn, I asked for an alternative. So, for four days I must not go out. I must, as they say, *reposer*. Each morning I take twenty drops of liquid digitalin (disgusting stuff), and then on Wednesday I return to Avignon. If my heart has not returned to sinus rhythm, then I must be put in hospital, where they will electrically shock it back. I refused electric shock, and so the case rests. Please God, the next few days of rest and medication will do the trick.

As I have said many times, I can afford to die (that's a one-shot deal) but I cannot afford to be ill or dependent.

Now it is Sunday, January 11, and the mistral has arrived with all its force and cleansing vengeance. I awakened about three this morning, after drifting to sleep with the lullaby of softly falling rain, to the beginning noisy whirls of the changing air. The large steel plates that block the chimney were rattling noisily and I knew the mistral was announcing its arrival.

Now, as I eat my porridge, the brilliant sunlight belies the treachery of the wind. The pansies, drenched and showered by yesterday's showers, are shivering and fighting frostbite. I hope they survive.

The gusts and gales make it easier for me to stay indoors. We surely cannot complain, as the fall was absolutely splendid. A few days of brisk, cold air won't do any harm.

I sense you tensing when I, in my off-hand way, discuss the seamy side of life. It is not that these revelations are new, or even unexpected. I feel it's just that those areas of your longing, leaning, or left-behind memories are not part of your survival kit. They are, and attempt to remain, buried – at rest.

My survival kit necessitates the exorcizing of demons almost by the ritual of public hanging. (Well-hung humour, *j'espère!*)

Different strokes for different folks, as they say.

I believe almost everyone has had thoughts, dreams, fantasies that are as explicit, or more so, than those I have written about. They are just taboo – they are just not mentioned, or even acknowledged. I suppose my expressing much of what most others suppress may be a little much. However, if we all admit to the wildness of our unconscious, the depths of our anti-social subterranean passages, maybe a dialogue between acceptable social graces and the strange dark forces of the mind could begin.

Most people find little laughter in the underground. Sobriety and sordidness are more likely companions than silly, senseless excess. But most of the fiascos in my life are ripe with farce. The ability to view the horror or hells of past experience with a smile or a belly laugh is the gift that keeps me going.

Please God, let more people discover this key, and instead of festering, get on with feeling positive and purposeful.

Rituals, which I have often mentioned, are the keys to any attempt at balanced existence. The making of a "fit," the anticipated rush, the testing of one's power of survival, have been replaced by the dangerous road of taking my pen for a clean and uncluttered walk across the whiteness of paper. Will I make it? Will I fuck up? I do often, but the high of completing a drawing, of pulling off a picture, is surely a more positive and lasting ritual than many others.

I have to have ritual (even my morning porridge is a must). I am fortunate that I have been able to exchange negative for positive. But, the demon never disappears. The haunted is always here. To be aware is to be wary.

I work, I sleep, and I impose upon you the scribbles that I need to write to survive.

Thank you.

January 12, 1987

Dear M.

Twenty-seven years ago I was in the old Toronto Psychiatric Hospital, having suffered the first of my crises. I was then, as now, penniless. Because OHIP didn't exist, I was a ward of the city. It was a time of so-called breakthroughs in treatment for the clinically depressed, and all sorts of new medications were being tested. I had been having a series of black-outs, a kind of faint, that made me disorientated and, as they happened to me anywhere, anytime, were dangerous. I was first admitted to the Toronto Western Hospital, and Don Steele (now a well-known urologist in St. Catharines) was a serious and kind senior intern. They (the powers that be) wanted to give me sodium amytal intravenously. Don, God bless him, backed my refusal. I was shipped home to my wonderful loft on Ossington, just north of Queen

Street, and over Friendly Plumbers – yes, the owner's name was Friendly.

They had done all physical tests possible at Western but had found no organic reason for my black-outs. The black-outs continued, and I was soon admitted to the TPH in a depressed and suicidal state. The doctors there talked of trying sodium amytal, electric shock, which I adamantly refused.

Enter one Dr. Ian Bond – young, bright, British – who was specializing in experiments. First, hypnotism. It didn't work. Then he stated there was a new drug on the market, one that, unlike amytal, which caused loss of memory, did the opposite. It made you vitally aware, awesomely alive, and never forgetful.

I liked Ian, trusted him, and so the treatments began. Twice a week, I think, I lay on a couch-like bed and intravenously was fed Methedrine.

My heart pounded, my senses quickened, and I began a stream of consciousness babble. I was light, felt weightless and a sense of power and well-being. We (Ian and I) opened hidden and dark cupboards of my past, aired the holy and unholy thoughts of my mind, and I saw many of my faults, failures, and attempts at success.

My father had thrown me out over twelve years before. I had kept contact with Mother, mostly through my sister and the occasional secret meeting. Under Methedrine, I began to question my feelings about my father. Yes, he was alcoholic. Yes, he was a bigot and a racist, but yes, dear M, I loved him. I didn't, couldn't, and still today, don't respect his weakness, his lack of judgement, his self-debasing artificial power, but I felt deeply for this tragic figure who had parented me.

I wanted to see him.

He was at home alone every day (Mother worked at Canadian General Electric). After one session with Ian, I took a cab to Perth Avenue and knocked on the door. Father opened it. He was shocked, then tearful, and the reunion was very heavy, weepy, and emotion-charged. He asked me, after an hour of talking, to stay until Mother came home from work. I refused as I had not gone to see Mother. If he wanted to tell her I was there, that was his affair. I left.

I returned to the hospital and collapsed.

That hospital visit was not without its humour. In one of our sessions, Ian asked if I had ever screwed a woman. I said yes, and he asked who the last one was. I said it had been Bibi, a gal who was six foot three and weighed over two hundred pounds. I wasn't making it up! When she said fuck, you fucked. She had very strange nipples – almost an inch long. Anyway, in my studio one evening my friend Ted Turner, she, and I had a drink. He went to the store for smokes, and she said "fuck." Ted came back, and I was, as the saying goes, in the saddle. He sat, smoked, and watched. She didn't care, and so that was that. Ian thought I was making the whole thing up until, a few days later, there was a ruckus in the entrance lobby, and it turned out to be Bibi trying to bring a horse up in the elevator. Thwarted, she arrived alone, in jeans and red turtleneck sweater, nipples for days, and huge hoop earrings, carrying a single rose in a bud vase. Ian was at the desk, and as he said later, he looked up, and up, and up. He didn't doubt me after that.

Christmas came, and so did she, into the hospital with presents, one a beautifully wrapped parcel in the shape of a Haig & Haig Pinch whisky box. She left, I opened it, and discovered a frozen dead rat.

Ian was away for the holidays. What the hell was I to do? If I told the nursing staff that a friend had brought me a dead rat for Christmas, I would be locked up for sure. The windows were all sealed, so I couldn't just dump it. I wrapped it in many layers of newspaper and put it into the garbage bin. When Ian returned, I told him and he roared with laughter. I didn't find it that amusing (at the time).

Two or three days after my visit to my father, both Mom and Dad arrived to visit. I was to be released in a few weeks and my father suggested I move home for a while, as the studio had been ransacked and I had been evicted in my absence.

I did go home and started preparing a series of watercolour drawings for an exhibition I was to have in the Ross Widen Gallery in Cleveland, Ohio. I had finished about ten or fifteen, when I came down one morning for breakfast to find them torn to shreds, my father passed out in a chair.

Have you ever considered murder? I have, and did. I had two choices. I chose to run, tears and fury wracking my body. I wandered the streets for a while, then found myself back at the hospital. Somehow I recovered.

Now, I had to find a place to live, but I had no money. The social worker suggested I look for a cheap place and promised he would cover the initial rent and give me a small amount for living.

I walked through the legendary Greenwich Village past Pauline Fedio's studio and found, on Elizabeth Street, the small, one-storey building. So, the Pollock Gallery began.

January 21, 1987

Dear M.

I have had my porridge, hot chocolate, and toast, and I am now waiting for Gerry to take me to the hospital in Avignon. Last week the heart had slowed down, but it was still in serious flutter. Again, the doctor suggested hospitalization. Again, I refused but now I have no choice. If it is not in sinus rhythm, then hospital for four days (he said) and electric shock to stabilize the irregular pattern.

In eight days Bruno, the photographer, is driving me to Paris with my work. Four days of forced bed rest I don't need right now, but I can't leave it any longer. I don't feel too well, I get light-headed and sleep fitfully, not normal for me. I think a lot about life, death, and taxes. All three seem an ongoing mysterious battle. Life – there *is* a lot to be done. Death – the seeming finality of it all. Taxes – well, the bill arrived, along with new water and electric bills.

My latest drawings show my tenseness, my rigid control – they are tight and designy. Thank God this type have been happening only for a few days. The earlier ones were free and sparse – good, I think.

January 22, 1987

Dear M.

Well, I'm back at Lou Paradou. After long and slightly difficult conversation, Bertrand Vigne gave me three options – one, immediate hospitalization and electric shock; two, spend four or five hours there while they attempt a new device, putting a tube down my throat and using mild electric shock to try to return the rhythm; three, continue with the medication until after Paris (February 9-10) and hope it may adjust itself.

My heart rate has slowed down well – it is seventy at the moment. Vigne feels there is no immediate danger, so I decided to opt for medication and Paris. If, after that, it is not in rhythm, then I will stay in hospital for a few days. By that time I may have sold a drawing or two, and the money will be there to pay the four thousand francs it will cost me.

Bertrand said that many people live with a flutter all their lives. He also said that electric shock would not in any way be dangerous to the friendly pig that keeps my heart going.

So, we shall see.

During yesterday's journey to the hospital with Gerry, we talked of art, discipline, and our continued growth in painting. Also, God knows why, I began to pour out family stories that have long been locked away and hidden about my father, his monumental sense of defeat, his total inability to handle the joys and sorrows of his children.

All of us – Bob, Gladys, Audrey, and I – were tossed out several times, usually at moments of despair. Gladys, with three small children under six years old, and pregnant with her fourth, was banished from the house two weeks before she was killed in a car accident. Audrey, mother of Barbara Anne, was forced to live at home for awhile as Harold, her husband, was hospitalized for a year with TB. Father, in his raging self-loathing, tossed Audrey out of the house, with Barbara Anne, a child of two, in her arms.

My exits and entrances have been recorded partially in other notes to you. But yesterday I recalled the horror of arriving at Perth Avenue and being confronted with the parlour sofa and chair slashed to ribbons and my father with a butcher knife in his hands. I was terrified. I telephoned my brother Bob, and as Mother lived alone with Father, we made a painful, but in retrospect, sensible decision. He was committed to Queen Street mental hospital for a period (three to six months, I can't recall the length of time).

I understand the base of Audrey's hatred, but I always sensed (when thinking rationally) that he was a great tragedy as a human being.

To my mother's family, we were the poor relations. Father had no family to speak of, as his grandmother (Grandma Henry), his mother (Grandma Pollock), and his two maiden aunts, Lavinia and Jane, all lived at Perth Avenue with my mother and father, and were all buried from the parlour while I was a child.

I suppose all this has left its marks on me. Marks – scars and marks.

A portrait of *moi*, aged fifty-six:

Height: five foot eleven.

Weight: one hundred and fifty pounds.

Eyes: brown (sometimes too brown)

Hair: miraculously still dark brown, a grey hair here and there.

Distinguishing marks: scars, from feet to head.

Feet: not bad; no corns or bunions. Toes straight.

Left ankle: indented small scar, result of car accident, 1968.

Legs: slight bursting surface veins, not too noticeable.

Buns: not bad, firm, a scar on inner left cheek, result of a boil when I was young.

Penis: Well, it's in damned good shape in spite of several accidents that have attempted its demise. First, a scar, smooth and, I suppose we can say, hand polished for fifty years. When I was six or seven, I stood at the toilet like my dad and big brother. The seat fell, my zizi was split open, and I remember being on the couch in the parlour, my prick in tongue-depressor splints, when a box of water colours arrived from Eaton's, a gift from Aunt Ida and Uncle Jim.

Then in, I guess, 1978 or 1979, a small cyst that had been on my foreskin for a long time swelled to the size of a pea. No pain, but I thought I should have it attended to. The specialist looked, felt, and had me ejaculate (for what purpose other than his amusement, I don't know).

I made an appointment and the thing (the cyst, that is) was removed by a plastic surgeon. I had twenty-seven stitches, and was for a short time a kind of star. Tom Kneebone sent a bouquet of daffodils and bananas wearing band aids. Barbara Hamilton brought me lobster bisque, as chicken soup has nothing to do with foreskins.

In 1980 the pigment from my nipples and my foreskin mysteriously fled. So I have a pinto-pony prick that when erect is more of a piece, colour-wise.

Moving upward, an appendix scar, very neat and flat. I was sixteen when it was removed.

Now, turning rear side, so to speak, a long and finely sewn scar from a laminectomy on my third and fourth lumbar discs, done in 1969. That was a result of the car accident. Hamilton Hall did the operation. I walked after five days, and have rarely felt any discomfort.

We move along and return to front and centre. A rather normal navel, deep enough for salt when eating celery in bed.

Then two large dimple-shaped dents–remnants of the electric shock that brought me back from my eight-hour death in

1981, and above, the narrow, almost elegant scar that says little of the violation and invasion of my heart.

Then nipples – tiny mounds of tingling delight, pink beacons on my natural dusky surface.

Arms, scarred with needles both of past escapes and those administered for survival.

My left wrist is badly scarred from what appears to be a suicide attempt. Not so. When I was eight (I believe) it was my sister's birthday. I went to the cellar to carry up bottles of chocolate milk from the ice box (remember ice boxes, ice trucks?). Well, I fell, and severed my wrist on the broken glass so badly that all the cords and tendons and nerves were slashed. I remember Mother trying to find my drunken father to get me to the Hospital for Sick Children. A neighbour took me. Dr. Mustard operated, and saved my hand. The only reminders are the scar and no feeling in my baby finger; also the inability to close my straightened fingers as the cords are too short.

My hands have always been a mess, as I have bitten my nails, I think, from birth. Shit!

There is a small black mole on the left side of my neck, and another tiny one on the side of my too-large nose.

The lines on my face are from living, and there is not a natural tooth in my head. I was sixteen when the upper teeth were extracted and for years tried without success to preserve the rest. I had little enamel on them, and their demise was foregone.

That's me – an old fart with no pot belly, but no muscular physique either.

Try to put all that shit and the high-wire act of my performances in a portrait. Not easy!

Lots of tales to be told. Please God, lots more joys to be shared.

August 10, 1890
Arles

Cher Gachet,
The painting is finished. I hope you like it. I seem to have caught that pensive and resigned look that I have seen so often – distant wondering and somewhat detached.

The mistral blows again – no letting up – intense and destructive. I try to paint, try to write, but I feel quite empty. A number of my works are scattered about, but no one seems interested. I want friends around, but can rarely stand their presence. Solitude returns, and I long for rest – painless, quiet, dark, and comforting.

The crows seem to go mad as the winds destroy their attempted destruction of the fields. I sense their madness, and run through the wheat fields, arms flung out, crying to the god I once so simply trusted, raging at his lack of understanding, and the sense of denial I feel everywhere.

Be well, dear Gachet. Maybe some day someone will feel in your portrait what I try to express.

A giver, spent from giving. A dreamer resigned to yet another dreamless night.

Your friend
Vincent

February 20, 1987

Dear M.
Your card from New York made me cry a little and prompted the letter to Gachet. My Paris trip was not what I expected and a painful bout of sciatica kept me from seeing any museums or galleries. The expense monies kept me going, and I produced six dinners in all for my friends (most were prepared as I sat on a chair in the kitchen, as I found sitting in one position the least painful).

I am pleased I did not submit to the morphine shots the doctor prescribed. I recall the relief they gave in 1983, but I also recall I returned to needles and cocaine directly after, so it was a logical, though painful, decision to make.

I find the "addictive personality" a queer beast. Yes, I like a Scotch or two, yes, I enjoy wine with dinner, but I could never just sit alone and get pissed. Booze can be in the house for months and I will just ignore it. But my fear of the "white powder mistress" is ever present, and powerful.

I never did "graduate" from the Donwood, even after being "held over by popular demand" for an extra two weeks, as I refused to accept that a chemical-free existence was the only solution. I said, and still say, that I will have wine with a meal if I choose, and an occasional drink if I decide so. I know I can't have an occasional "bong" of cocaine. I can't leave it alone until it's all gone. Most other substances in the world of mood-altering drugs bore me.

My father's life-long pursuit of suicide through alcohol makes it difficult for me to handle drunks. When I arrived here, everyone felt I would just replace one addiction with another. I suppose I have in a strange way, as painting and writing to you are the most addictive things in my life. But booze – never!

I have personally never seen you "in your cups." I have seen your brief and, God knows, essential energy bursts, which let off a minuscule portion of your discontent. Please exorcise some inner demons with personal acts of creativity. I urge you to draw, write, paint more. You are good. You have talent. I admire you!

Today's *Herald Tribune* brings news of the arrest in Germany of a man who has the AIDS virus and has knowingly been spreading it for over two years. He is being charged with some obscure law about poisoning another, and now the West German government is insisting on registration of all known carriers.

Remember my letter over a year ago about personal morality, vengeance, and the inevitable results? Although my role as fucker, not fuckee, was a defence of a sort, my total abandon in regard to injections and needles, not to mention two full blood transfusions, has placed me in a very high-risk category.

Please God, a cure, a sure preventative, a miracle happen soon. Years of attempting education and fostering acceptance for homosexuality are being torn away crudely and viciously by the ignorant and bigoted of a frightened world.

The mail has just arrived with an electric bill. So the world goes on.

February 23, 1987

Dear M.

Today the sun shone gloriously and signs of spring are everywhere to be seen. Almond blossoms are setting up competition for the patches of snow, still lingering.

I walked to the square today and watched the young man who works there occasionally, browsing through the *bandes dessinées* (adult comic books, so popular and highly regarded here). His loose pants could not hide his excitement, and for a moment I was activated, I swelled and strained. Then I bought the *Herald Tribune* and saw Andy Warhol's photo and the report on his death. What have these two incidents got to do with each other?

Well, I've lived through Warhol's several periods of creativity, and I have always thought him the ultimate voyeur. The cool distance from which he approached his chosen subject matter, such as the Campbell soup cans, resulted in brilliant parodies and comments on society and its conventions. Of course they incited anger and hostility. He invested his superstars with a sense of macabre. He created "fun palaces of the flesh," but rarely participated in them. *Blow Job* was an excruciatingly erotic film with no sexual act on the screen. *Sleep* and *The Empire State* were interminably boring. His supermarket marketing was vulgar. Yet his use of the serigraphed photo-image repeated and repeated battered our senses and made statements often as strong as those of the masters of another century.

The Alabama riots, the electric chair, Jackie Kennedy, Mick Jagger, on and on, the sub-cultures and sickness of our society became high art. Black-tie patrons paid homage to Pop. Warhol, Lichenstein, Oldenburg made comics chic and tack taken seriously. The vulgar was crowned.

In all the years I taught art appreciation I found Pop the most difficult school to defend. I used to explain that dislike of Pop images was a logical reaction to being caught in the act of being seduced by supermarket merchandising and mass media madness.

The bulk of dishwashers in the world were women, mothers, tied down (a little less now) with aprons and screaming brats. The husband left for the workplace, she did housework. But she had fantasies, she had day dreams, and so detergents were called Fling and Joy. Mr. Clean became a masturbatory image (not unlike Yul Brynner) and most containers were the shape of male torsos, with broad shoulders and narrow waists.

The Hidden Persuaders was, and is, as we know, a reality (the coke bottle mimics the female form). The guilt on discovering the sense of being used; the realization that most parents don't make home-made soup for the kids, they buy Campbell's, or, worse, give the brats a dollar for a Big Mac and a coke instead of home cooking – when confronted with these truths as visual images, anger is logical.

Pop art compounded the affrontery by its multiple imagery. A single Campbell soup can becomes an icon, a canvas with a hundred cans on shelves becomes *all* tinned merchandise. A single photo of Jackie Kennedy was her, but when repeated it became *all* mothers, widows, and sisters who mourned their loved ones.

The Women's Committee of the AGO must be given tremendous credit for its early recognition of many of the major talents in Pop art, and for putting its money (very little then) where its mouth was.

Brydon Smith was the curator of contemporary art when Warhol's *Elvis* and Oldenburg's *Hamburger* were purchased. They, along with Jim Dine's *Sink*, donated by Carol and Morty Rapp, stand as superb examples of Pop.

I believe the price for *Hamburger* was around twenty-five hundred dollars. Its purchase caused many members to resign from the gallery, and was a mini scandal. The big scandal was, of course, the acceptance, then rejection of Barnett Newman's *Day One*.

Bea Davidson, a woman of the grand manner, an architect and moving force in the gallery, along with others on the Women's Committee, contracted to purchase the picture, a large vertical painting, solid and unyielding orange, with a severe red stripe down one side. It arrived, was hung, and the outcry began. Harold Town, among others, yelled and carried on, and the picture was returned to New York. As Newman was a major figure in the genre of minimalism, and as a superb example of his work had been refused, he stated in writing that the AGO would never own a work of his. They have tried, but to this day (I believe) have failed.

Returning to Warhol and the *Elvis* canvas, it is stunning: the pose, the gun (read phallus), the repetition – from glaring and gaudy cartoon colours to the fading and beautiful haunted silver image of passing time – all combine to make a modern masterpiece.

Of all the Pop artists, two stand out as draughtsmen: Claes Oldenburg, baroque and overblown, and Dine, my favourite. God, can he draw! He is also a fine man. I met him several times as I had two major shows of his etchings and lithos. I remember clearly his painting of a plastic box – a tool box – with scissors, pliers, hammers, and other tools, which were direct, elegant, and somehow erotic. His heart images were very popular, but I, of course, preferred the tools. He told me his grandfather had owned a hardware store when he was a child, and his love of common objects stemmed from those early days.

Jerrold Morris was the Pop pioneer in Toronto. What a fine mind and eye he had! I also knew him to be among the most honest and caring of dealers. His wit was acid-British, and his chuckle deep and rich.

Warhol had his go at Canadian art establishment, or, I should say, they had a go at him. Do you remember the *Brillo* boycott? Jerrold Morris was having a Warhol exhibition; the *Brillo* boxes were held at Customs; Charles Comfort, then director of the National Gallery, said they were not art; and the shit hit the fan.When Jean Sutherland Boggs became director, one of her first purchases was, yes, *Brillo*. What a farce the world of art can be!

Talking about art – are you doing any? When I taught, all my students said they just did not have the time. I said, bullshit! Everyone can make time. Draw the dishes in the sink before you wash them. Draw the books on a table or in a bookcase before you select your reading material. Quickly draw your plants in your office between nuts like me. I feel a sketchbook and very quick images jotted on the pages would do you a lot of good. Don't, for God's sake, take it seriously. One of the problems I see is seriousness and perfection battling against the sensitive, tentative man I know and love.

You know no one is perfect. You also know you can draw. Do it.

March 5, 1987

Dear M.

Update on the sex scene in Lou Paradou: Edna, a female beetle, we presume, has moved in and has Charlie cornered in the john. It must be spring. I have seen them separately off and on for the last few weeks, but it looks like they are about to "do their thing" again.

Old *New Yorkers* never die–they just seem to come my way. In the March 17, 1986, issue, in the book review section, there is an article on Michel Foucault, which talks of power, the seeming maleness of domination, the desire for excess – God! I know the feeling well!

Michael Ignatieff (son of George) is a kind of authority on

Foucault, and he and his wife are coming to Gordes in late April for three or four months. I look forward to talking to him about the ideas Foucault expressed.

I know he died tragically of AIDS. I know he was known in the southwest USA in all the baths as a passive, willing sex slave. What I want to know is why his knowledge and understanding did not prevent his extremely excessive activities.

I suppose, like all of us in one way or another, he was testing his invincibility.

It's difficult for the fucker to totally comprehend the position (so to speak) of the fuckee. But, balance is certainly one answer. Complementary colours grey each other, and I suppose complementary forces dilute and disperse energy.

Everyday, in every way, AIDS grows more and more horrendous. Today in the *Herald Tribune* are *four* articles on the subject.

Did I ever tell you about my last hospitalization before deciding to come here? I was spaced (read needle-ridden and depressed), I walked most of the night, all the way to Emergency at Sunnybrook. A young psychiatrist intern interviewed me, and I was admitted to F2, the floor I had been on before. When I awakened, I was in very heavy quarantine – paper plates, plastic cutlery, nurses with robes, masks, and rubber gloves.

I had no idea what was going on, until I heard yelling in the hall, and Sharon Salloum, the wonderful young doctor who looked after me while under Cowan's care, came raging into the room. The idiot of a young intern had admitted me as an AIDS patient.

Cowan was informed. The shit hit the fan and, of course, I was immediately moved to a normal room in the ward. I laughed at it then, but several people said I had a right to sue, as it was a horrific slur on me personally.

I told that story to many people as a kind of joke. It isn't anymore. It is a nightmare, and I wonder if the records of my admission and the later reversal of opinion are still on record.

Perhaps I should write Don Cowan and make sure it has been erased, cleared, or whatever they do. My complete blood testing and medical last summer assures me of a measure of health.

The problem (and I feel the press is partially to blame) is the paranoia that most gay men and needle addicts must go through these days. The blame, the persecution, the denials of basic human rights are terrifying, and I don't see them getting any better in the near future.

As I wrote almost three years ago, the young, the inexperienced, the innocent, who are just now discovering their homosexuality, are the most tragic victims in this murderous plot. I don't know exactly what can be done to aid their passage through a normal life. (Normal, of course, meaning a full life-span, a sense of self-worth, and the joy of achievement in their chosen goals.)

The challenge to aid, guide, and care for them rests on the shoulders of those in your profession. The laboratories of the world will work on medical cures. Your role is much more difficult and, sadly, much more exhausting. Giving faith to the faithless, giving truth to those who live amongst liars, giving support to those who sense no present or future.

My acceptance and persistant (*pas très, c'est trop*) reliance on self-administered satisfaction comes from a feeling of not being able to be complete with another. Humour can and does cover a lot of pain. Jokes do varnish a lot of inadequacies. But I suppose, dear M, that's part of my survival kit.

I still use cocaine as a fantasy back-up for my backhand pleasures. I imagine the rush, the freedom, the delayed pleasures of its effects. I remember the power I felt (granted, it was false) but the power, the domination of will without any physical abuse.

But I also remember the pain, the tubes, the claustrophobia of a hospital room, and the sadness of faiths broken in those who cared.

I made a choice–to live my private world mostly in fantasy. To attempt in my daily routines to do, to donate (though that sounds corny), to make use of my given time by attempting to explore my being through colour, line, and word.

Fuck off, Pollock – enough!

Dear M.

It is ten, past my bedtime, but this evening all seems to tumble in. The village has gone to sleep. Lou Paradou is dark and quiet, deathly quiet, sensing my heaviness and giving silent support.

The spirit really does communicate. I have often thought of Robin Hunter in past weeks, waiting for a note in response to the letter I sent on the anniversary of my pig valve transplant. He was a special link in the chain of my survival – the first of your profession I respected and loved. His long, lean body was topped by an extraordinary head. He was craggy, yet sensitive, and within his sparkling eyes a sense of wonder gleamed. I never knew him as a doctor, but I cherished him as a friend. It was he who arrived at the loft one day in late 1981, found me unconscious and paralyzed with osteomyelitis, and had me rushed to Sunnybrook. It was he who gave the Toronto General Hospital royal hell, as I was taken there to emergency the day before and refused help or admittance by an intern who saw track marks on my arms.

He also watched my many descents, and was angry, hurt, yet always caring. It was Robin who talked Eddie Kingstone into seeing me. It was the two of them together who decided to ask if you would see me. Three very special men in my life. Eddie was the first shrink I went to regularly (religiously). No one before had been able to give me an intelligent interchange and non-judgemental support. What I now recognize in all three of you is your immense capacity for caring. The old tale of people falling in love with their shrinks holds a lot of water for me. But I also realize the toll it takes on those of your profession who do care for their patients. Although, or perhaps because, I was not a patient, Robin allowed a flow of love and support, but I failed, several times, to live up to his desires and wishes for me. Eddie probably bore the heaviest weight, as I was still heavily drugged while I visited him. I used the washroom in the hall outside his door to "fix" myself before many visits. He knew and, God bless him, tried his best to do what he could.

My initial testing of you was out of anger, rejection, and fear. But it is because of you I am here, I work, and I strive to survive. Robin, Eddie, and M, much loved because of like qualities, and all with a sense of dedication I admire and continue to be thankful for.

My first thought, when going through this type of crisis is to escape. The white bitch mistress of cocaine certainly is a desire. I did have three double Scotches and drank to each of you. I will masturbate to assert life over death. I find it strange that death, complete loss, stimulates the desire to *feel* physically. To know one is still, in some perverse way, celebrating life. I was sexually energized after both my father's and my brother's deaths. Why the physical urge of living and feeling were that strong, I don't know. I just had to exorcise the demons of my loss somehow.

Time to change the subject. What about painting?

Canada has produced very few fine symbolist painters. Gary Slipper is one I have known for over thirty years and, although I have not seen his recent work, I have always admired his obsessive world of figurative fantasy. One of the worst (again using the finest oils on quality canvas) is Toller Cranston, who I think of as a neutered Beardsley. The finest living realist for me is Claude Yvel. You have a small litho of his, *The Bellows*. I spent a few hours with him in Paris, and am more convinced than ever of his greatness.

He is an alchemist, a magician, a being filled with passion, who has mastered the techniques of Vermeer and creates truly amazing *trompe-l'oeil* pictures. Not only does he use the finest canvas (with many coats of hand-prepared gesso), but he grinds and makes his own paints from hundreds of jars of pure pigment, some of which are over a century old.

I discovered him in Paris in the late sixties. He was literally starving, and I bought a small canvas of a shoe box with a pair of women's pumps inside, and he cried.

I arranged a show, flew him over, and he began to gain a reputation.

Mario Amaya had left Toronto (or Toronto left him) and was directing the now defunct New York Museum, a strange structure originally designed by Stone for the Huntington Hartford Collection.

Well, a show of French Realists (arranged by me) was installed, and John Cannaday, the leading art critic for the *New York Times*, gave two successive weekend columns to Claude. The show then travelled to the Corcoran Gallery in Washington. We sold a small picture to Yale University. Alfred Frankenstein, the leading scholar on Harnett and Pieto, the famous nineteenth century American *trompe-l'oeil* artists, saw Claude's second show in my gallery, wrote about it, and since then Claude has been highly successful in the southern United States and throughout Europe.

One day (soon, perhaps?) we shall be in Paris together and can visit Claude in his small, perfect studio. He works usually six months or more on each canvas.

An interesting aside to this story is that from that first show, a Mr. Crang bought three pictures. One, an oil drum in a darkened corner of a garage, is truly masterful. After a few years, Crang contacted me, wanting to dispose of it, as it was not suitable to hang in his home. I arranged for it to be given to the AGO, and to this day have never seen it. You might, one day, out of curiosity, ask if the gallery owns a Claude Yvel, and could you see it. I would be interested in the reply.

P.S. The shoe-box picture was stolen from my gallery on Markham Street.

Dear M.

I am not well tonight. I tremble, and an ache in my arm and chest alarms me.

I feel like a stranger in a foreign land. I have no insurance, and I have no money. I don't know how to deal with my ill-health. If I was in Toronto, I would probably be in an emergency ward at Sunnybrook. Here, I am alone. Peter is working at the Provençal as today was opening day. I wanted to go for lunch, or a drink, but two francs won't buy anything.

Despite all this, I look back on the last three years and feel thankful for the time given me by the powers that be to prove to myself and others that I could, in some sense, measure up. The work I have done will be judged or forgotten; it really doesn't seem to matter. What matters is I did it and, please God, will continue.

Our relationship, an odd couple if there ever was one, is, for me, strangely romantic. I can now somehow believe in the Sonnets of Petrarch (whose ruined château is on the cliffs surrounding the Fontaine de Vaucluse, eighteen kilometres away). The purity of his love for Laure, whom he never met, makes sense.

The defence and support I gain from you is really my invention. True, you care, and God knows I need to know that, but I guess what I am trying to say is that our magical, non-present presence, our non-physical physicality, are measured according to our needs and desires. Fantasy is free for us, and we use it as best we can.

I trust I feed some of the needs and longings that you, like me, are burdened with.

I am constantly in fear of abusing the privilege of our relationship. I should really just write most of this crap and not send it, but somehow I can't do that.

Dear M.

I made it through the night, but I am tired from the tension of my fear: that strange cold I feel when I think of not waking up, that sense of emptiness, that void, the grave.

I still somehow sense a higher power, a Supreme Being, a master with the keys to the wildly dispersed energies that create and destroy here on earth. I know the mortal remains remain, decay, and are a constant recycling process. The native (Canadian) symbol for life is a circle: you came from the earth, you return to the earth, you are one with the earth. I find that not only a logical belief, but a proven fact. The body does decay. But the spirit gives us such joy and pain; the mind heals as well as destroys; the links and threads we have with others – all these are unreliant on the flesh.

It seems as though He gives us many alternate routes, then lets us play in the traffic of life. So, who's the winner, and what's the prize? Is competition purely for survival?

I read the horror stories of Irangate and wonder about the role God seems to misplay in many lives. North, a charismatic Catholic, is for me a psychopathic liar who uses God as a justification for murder, war, and hatred. Oral Roberts is truly crazed, and yet because our society is supposedly free, he is allowed to use, abuse, manipulate, and rob through the greatest instrument of communication in the world, TV.

It does seem hard to believe in a Supreme Power who would allow the atrocities committed in His name to go, in many ways, unchallenged. Was Christ the ultimate masochist? Are suffering and denial the keys to the Kingdom? Who's on first and who's at bat? And is the umpire in the sky watching?

My coat of many colours continues to be fed with patches of bright new acquaintances and is often mended by threads of rediscovered friends. It is a strange robe – part hair-shirt and part the softness of angel's skin, part the black and leather of my loins and part the wispy and satin padding of my heart.

I await the opening of the skies and the radiance of some sort of divine mercy. I hope he, she, it, gets off its ass soon. Meanwhile, the sun still shines, and so do I.

Epilogue

That letter of March 16, 1987, was the last I ever wrote to M. A few days later, my heart was hurting so badly and I was having such difficulty breathing that my doctor advised immediate hospitalization. I decided to come back to Canada, as I could not afford to pay French hospital bills. Once in Toronto, I went straight to the Sunnybrook hospital, where a fine team of specialists – friends I know and trust – ran every test on me they possibly could. They discovered that my heart was failing and also that I was HIV positive.

The treatment I have been receiving since then to control my heart – my mad motor – has made it impossible for me to return to France. But I do feel blessed for those years in Gordes – for that brief but glorious time in Camelot, where I think I finally came to terms with me.

I live now in downtown Toronto. I write, paint, and again teach art, as I have always loved to do. The AGO still has no contemporary Canadian paintings on its walls, so I am still handicapped as a teacher by not being able to show my students the range of styles and talents that makes Canadian art today so exciting.

In my daily life I continue to face the same demons I struggled with in Gordes, but I am also blessed with the same caring and support I received during those years. Preparing these letters for publication has been painful at times, but it has also brought joy and new friendships. The words you have read are me. If they seem rough, it is because I do not enjoy polished, perfect surfaces – life is never without its scars and flaws.

Before I finish, I must tell the end of one story: Alain, I am relieved to say, has now made a complete recovery. We keep in touch by letter.

I live and work. I am who I am. I regret little, and I am thankful for all.